STRATEGIC HOSPITALITY LEADERSHIP

THE ASIAN INITIATIVE

STRATEGIC HOSPITALITY LEADERSHIP

THE ASIAN INITIATIVE

Edited by

Russell Arthur Smith

Judy Siguaw

WILEY

John Wiley & Sons (Asia) Pte. Ltd.

Other Wiley Editorial Offices

John Wiley & Sons, 111 River Street, Hoboken, NJ 07030, USA

John Wiley & Sons, The Atrium, Southern Gate, Chichester, West Sussex, P019 8SQ, United Kingdom

John Wiley & Sons (Canada) Ltd., 5353 Dundas Street West, Suite 400, Toronto, Ontario, M9B 6HB, Canada

John Wiley & Sons Australia Ltd., 42 McDougall Street, Milton, Queensland 4064, Australia

Wiley-VCH, Boschstrasse 12, D-69469 Weinheim, Germany

Library of Congress Cataloging-in-Publication Data

ISBN   978-0-470-82432-0

Typeset in 10.5/13.5 pt Berkeley Oldstyle Medium by MPS Limited, A Macmillan Company
Printed in Singapore by Saik Wah Press Pte Ltd
10 9 8 7 6 5 4 3 2 1

Contents

Foreword

As chairman of the Joint Advisory Board of the Cornell Nanyang Institute of Hospitality Management (CNI), I am pleased that this invaluable resource of reference and insightful compendium on the hospitality industry in Asia is being published. This book, *Strategic Hospitality Leadership: The Asian Initiative*, has been assembled from the vast years of experiences by entrepreneurs and senior executives in the hospitality industry in Asia. The common thread in the book in terms of the contributors comes from the fact that they are the Cornell University's School of Hotel Administration's alumni, the CNI faculty, and members of its Joint Advisory Board. Their varied backgrounds and profound appreciation of the complexities in building enterprises from the ground up, or expanding an on-going business organization, are the types of firsthand knowledge and perspective that would be beneficial, informative, and inspirational to industry veterans and students alike.

In recent times, a critical factor inherent in the business cycles was the unanticipated global economic tsunami that began in the third quarter of 2008 and could continue through to at least the first half of 2010 before economic normalcy will hopefully return. Thus, the underpinning fundamentals of the trade and the skill sets that are needed in addressing these challenges are called into acute focus and usage, especially during such times of crises. The stage that was being readied for steady growth in the hospitality industry in the Asia-Pacific region began in the aftermath of the easing of geopolitical and military tensions. China, formerly an inward-looking, central kingdom of centuries-long dynastic rule, became a new nation in 1949. After going through its own Civil War, confrontations and wars in Korea and Vietnam, and its own Cultural Revolution in the late 1960s, it finally opened its doors to the Western world in 1978. It did this through ping-pong diplomacy, barter trade, international commerce, and a momentous leap into the international tourism fraternity with exponential growth in developing infrastructure, hotels, and other hospitality-related establishments.

After World War II, the conclusion of years of Cold War in Europe, the collapse of the Eastern Bloc of European nations, and the easing of tensions in the Asian-Pacific theater, chilly relations made way for a global community of tourism. By this process, doors were opened through diplomacy and friendship, which ultimately also paved the way for mutual trade, commerce, and investments. Organizations such as the International Air Transport Association (IATA), American Society of Travel Agents (ASTA), Pacific Asia Travel Association (PATA), and others furthered the means for promoting inbound and outbound tourism and travel.

Newly reinvigorated sovereign nations began in earnest master planning with determination and pragmatism through capital-intensive investments in infrastructure and tourist promotions. The progress began to show results in the late 1950s and early 1960s, with the lead taken by international airlines and hotel corporations. These included Inter-Continental, Hilton, Western International (now Westin and part of Starwood), Sheraton (also of Starwood), Hyatt, Marriott, Accor, Four Seasons, Kempinski, Choice, Best Western, and others. Regional hotel brands such as the Peninsula, Mandarin Oriental, Shangri-La, Taj, Jin Jiang, Prince, Dusit Thani, Pan Pacific, and others were also making their geographical inroads in diverse locations on the world map. Each international hotel company over time has brought to bear a vigorous multibranding strategy with the addition of new brands that continue to be implemented globally. These included Ritz-Carlton, St. Regis, Novotel, ibis, Courtyard by Marriott, W, Traders, and others.

As you may be aware, CNI is an educational initiative formed by the Singapore government through the auspices of the Singapore Tourism Board and the Economic Development Board, thus enabling the Nanyang Business School of Nanyang Technological University to be in a joint venture with the School of Hotel Administration of Cornell University. With a full understanding of the heightened need to meet the demand for the recruitment and training of qualified staff and senior managers for the present and the future, Singapore's primary objective is to achieve strategic positioning in hospitality education in Asia-Pacific. The two integrated resorts, which opened in 2010, are the fulfillment of the tourism mission under the Singapore government's pragmatic national planning.

Sovereign nations, multinational hotel and restaurant corporations, commercial enterprises, individual entrepreneurs, and executives all share a vision and passion for taking an active part in assuming financial risks and playing different roles or support staff in any capacity. The growth for the future, though interrupted for the time being by the economic downturn, does portend promise, fun, and excitement. Yet financial return is never assured!

I hope you will enjoy and benefit much from reading this first CNI-produced book on strategic hospitality leadership in Asia.

Michael W.N. Chiu
Chairman, Joint Advisory Board of the
Cornell-Nanyang Institute of
Hospitality Management

July 2010

Preface

Doing business in the tourism and hospitality scene in Asia can be very interesting and potentially rewarding. The dynamic environment is fueled by escalating affluence, greater sophistication, improving infrastructure, better education, and a more welcoming climate for both local and foreign companies.

Indeed, Asia is a very attractive region for business because of its sheer market size. It is a huge continent comprising 3.8 billion people, about 56.3 percent of the world's population, according to World Bank figures. However, in this book when we refer to Asia, we are focusing our discussions on East Asia and Southeast Asia, which has 3.2 billion of the world's population. With such a large population base and promising economies, the potential for growth in the tourism and hospitality business is enormous. The rise in tourism and hospitality expenditures comes not only from Western tourists and businessmen but also from the growing number of affluent Asian tourists and entrepreneurs. Including Australia and New Zealand, the Asia-Pacific tourism industry is booming and is expected to grow by 6.5 percent annually over the next 15 years, according to the United Nations World Tourism Organization. Current trends show that the Asia-Pacific region will continue to have the greatest growth potential for the hospitality industry.

However, doing business in the tourism and hospitality arena in Asia also poses many challenges. These include meeting obstacles such as diverse and multifaceted regulatory environments; variations in the business climate; multiple cultural, religious, and social values; varied political climates; and vast differences in business practices in Asia. These factors can make or break tourism and hospitality ventures in Asia that are trying either to start sowing the seeds or spreading the growth of their enterprises.

Not many books have been written on the hospitality business in Asia. This is where this book, *Strategic Hospitality Leadership: The Asian*

Initiative, can make a useful contribution, as its contents provide the first specialized approach to the business of hospitality in Asia.

The book's key aim is to help current and future leaders address major issues that are being and will continue to be confronted in the hospitality industry in Asia through the insights of top executives who have been successful in this region of the world. Other aims are to increase the success of new entrants into Asia and to provide readers with the collective wisdom of our authors on a range of topics. These strategic topics include brand management, strategic direction, service, marketing, human resource, crisis management, business growth, leadership, portfolio management, best practices, and development.

We would like to thank the authors who are all alumni, board members, and faculty of the Cornell University's School of Hotel Administration (the only Ivy League hotel school) and the Cornell-Nanyang Institute of Hospitality Management (CNI). These authors include chief executives and senior management of hotels and resorts, serviced apartments, restaurants, and food and beverage groups. They have kindly agreed to share their stories as highly successful top executives and entrepreneurs, who have effectively overcome the challenges of doing business in Asia.

We are also grateful for the support of the Joint Advisory Board of CNI, which aims to develop and disseminate best practices in hospitality management. CNI is an alliance between Cornell University's School of Hotel Administration and the Nanyang Technological University's Nanyang Business School. This alliance brings together the world's leading hotel-management school and one of Asia's elite business schools. We would also like to express our appreciation to Tong Suit Chee, a writer and editor who has provided invaluable editorial advice and support in making this book a reality.

Last but not least, we are also grateful to the publisher, John Wiley, and its editorial and publishing teams for their great assistance in publishing this book, and for their kind generosity in allowing the proceeds from sales of this book to go to a CNI scholarship fund.

It is our hope that this book can make a positive impact on the development of the hospitality industry by being a catalyst for better business management and enhanced management practices. We also

hope that you will enjoy the invaluable insights and hard-earned leadership lessons from the various contributors in the hospitality industry
in Asia.

Dr. Russell Arthur Smith
*Interim Dean, Cornell-Nanyang Institute of
Hospitality Management,
Nanyang Technological University*

Dr. Judy Ann Siguaw
*Dean, College of Human Ecology,
East Carolina University*

Editors
July 2010

About the Contributors

Baron R. Ah Moo

Mr. Baron R. Ah Moo is chief executive officer of Indochina Hotels and Resorts, based in Vietnam. A 20-year veteran of the hospitality industry, he has lived and worked in Asia, the United States (US), Mexico, and the Pacific Islands. Before joining the company, he served as senior vice president of operations for the Golden Nugget Hotel and Casino, where he oversaw a US$250 million renovation of the 2000-room property. The property, under his guidance, was awarded its 30th consecutive four-star rating, making it the longest running four-star property in Las Vegas. He has also held executive-management positions and consulted for Marriott International, the Intercontinental Hotel Group, and the Landry's Restaurant Group. He was responsible for the opening and renovation of hospitality projects in Honolulu, San Francisco, the Marianas Islands, and Vietnam. He has also served on the Hotel Advisory Board for the National Business Travel Association, the largest corporate-travel organization in the US, and guest lectured at Cornell University's School of Hotel Administration in Ithaca, New York, US. A native Hawaiian, he holds a Bachelor's degree in International Management from the University of San Francisco, and a Master's degree in Hospitality Marketing and Finance from Cornell University.

Russell Arthur Smith

Dr. Russell Arthur Smith is Interim Dean, Cornell-Nanyang Institute of Hospitality Management at the Nanyang Technological University, Singapore. He is a hospitality and tourism development expert, who has extensive academic and professional experience in Asia, as well as Australia, North America, and the Middle East. He has headed large multidisciplinary teams in preparing major hospitality and tourism development plans. In addition, he has served on many private and public boards and committees throughout Asia Pacific, as well as held appointments in universities in Australia, Malaysia, Singapore, and the US. Dr. Smith's research in academic and industry publications is widely read and cited. He is a prominent speaker and moderator at leading industry meetings throughout Asia. He holds a doctorate from Harvard University and a degree in architecture with first-class honors from the University of Queensland, Australia. He is a certified practicing planner.

Raymond Bickson

Mr. Raymond Bickson's experience in hospitality spans 30 years and four continents. In January 2003, he moved to India and joined the board as executive director and chief operating officer of Taj Luxury Hotels, overseeing the operations of all luxury properties and playing a key role in the global expansion and development of future hotels. He assumed the role of managing director and chief executive officer of the Indian Hotels Company Limited in July 2003. He brings extensive international hotel experience to the Taj Group in operations and management. Previously, he served 15 years as vice president and general manager of The Mark in New York for The Rafael Group Hoteliers Monaco and with the Mandarin Oriental Hotel Group. His career included a 10-year span of management assignments with Regent International Hotels in New York, Chicago, Dallas, Puerto Rico, Melbourne, and Shanghai; as well as training assignments at some of the world's most renowned hotels including the Hotel Plaza Athenee Paris, Le Montreux Palace Switzerland, and the Kahala Hilton Hawaii.

An American national, Mr. Bickson attended the École Hôtelière de Lausanne in Switzerland and the Advanced Management Program at Harvard Business School. He was voted one of the Top 10 Best Hotel Managers by *Leaders* magazine from 1997–2002. A member of the World Travel & Tourism Council and the International Business Leaders Forum, he also is an advisory board member of The Leading Hotels of The World, Cornell Hotel School Center for Hospitality Research, and École Hôtelière de Lausanne in Switzerland. He was the recipient of the Corporate Hotelier of the World Award 2007 by *Hotels* magazine.

William E. Heinecke

Mr. William E. Heinecke is chairman and chief executive officer of the Minor Group, Thailand. He founded the group in 1967 and has since built Minor International Public Company Limited into a multinational enterprise that owns and operates international hotels, resorts, and spas, in addition to diverse restaurant and retail operations. The company today has more than 30 hotels and resorts principally under the brands of Anantara, Four Seasons, and Marriott; and 30 spas under the Mandara and Anantara brands. He created and launched Anantara Hotels, Resorts, & Spas, which operates more than 11 upscale and luxury properties across four major markets in Thailand, Bali, the Maldives, and Abu Dhabi, in addition to holding a 50 percent share of the exclusive Elewana Lodges in Africa.

Currently, he serves on the board of directors of Minor International Public Company Limited, which is Thailand's largest hospitality and leisure operator. The author of *The Entrepreneur: 25 Golden Rules For The Global Business Manager*, Mr. Heinecke also serves as a director of Sermsuk PCL, the publicly listed Pepsi bottler in Thailand and Indorama Ventures PCL, the second largest polyethylene terephthalate (PET) production company in the world.

Michael Issenberg

Mr. Michael Issenberg leads Accor Asia Pacific as chairman and chief operating officer. Accor is Europe's leader in hotels and services with more than 4,000 properties in nearly 100 countries throughout the world. In February 2008, he assumed his current position in Accor Asia Pacific and joined the global executive committee. Based at the Asia Pacific headquarters in Singapore, he is responsible for overseeing the company's overall hospitality development and management activities.

He was previously managing director at Accor Asia Pacific, a position he had occupied since 2003. He played a pivotal role in the establishment and development of Accor Premiere Vacation Club, a point-based time-share business. Mr. Issenberg joined Accor in 1994 from Mirvac Limited as chief executive officer, one of Australia's largest hotel companies, where he spent five years. Previously, he also worked for Westin Hotels & Resorts, Laventhol and Horwath, Horwath Services Pty.

Limited, and Merlin Properties in San Francisco and Sydney. He holds a degree in hotel administration from Cornell University and is a director of the Tourism and Transport Forum in Australia.

Devin Kimble

Mr. Devin Otto Kimble is founder and managing director of the Singapore-based MENU Pte. Ltd. Food & Drinks Group, which owns and operates Brewerkz Restaurants & Microbreweries, Café Iguana, Wine Garage, and MENU Catering. Formerly, he was regional operations manager for Dan Ryan's Chicago Grill, which is headquartered in Hong Kong and has outlets in Singapore and Taipei; and a multi-unit manager and corporate recruiter with Taco Bell in Connecticut, US. A graduate of Yale University, he also holds a Master's degree from Cornell University's School of Hotel Administration. He is a member of the Restaurant Association of Singapore Management Committee, the Board of Governors for the Singapore American School (the world's largest overseas American curriculum school), and the Hwa Chong International School Board of Trustees, and president of the Yale Club of Singapore.

He has been a speaker and panel participant on various business-related topics at the Singapore-based University of Chicago Booth Graduate School of Business, Cornell-Nanyang Institute of Hospitality Management, UNLV Harrah College of Hotel Administration, Singapore American School, and INSEAD where he has also served as chief judge for the annual business-plan competition. Formerly, he served on the American Chamber of Commerce in Singapore's Board of Governors and was its honorary treasurer and an executive committee member. He is a native of California, US, and a Singapore resident since 1995.

Chiaki Tanuma

Mr. Chiaki Tanuma is president and chief executive officer of Green House Group (GHG). It operates 11 hotels, 450 restaurants and takeout shops throughout Japan, and 61 restaurants in Korea and Taiwan. The group also owns Cini-Little Japan (a food-service-facility-design consulting company), and Horwath Asia-Pacific Japan (a hotel consulting company). He is the chairman of the Japan Foodservice Association, a leading association in the Japanese food-service industry. He is also an international director for the National

Restaurant Association in the US, and an executive councillor for the Tokyo Chamber of Commerce and Industry.

Chittimas Ketvoravit

Ms. Chittimas Ketvoravit is managing director of DK Lam Group of Companies (DKL), a private group of companies solely owned by the Ketvoravit family, based in Bangkok, Thailand. DKL's business is primarily in hotels such as Novotel Bangkok and Novotel Suvarnabhumi Airport Hotel; and serviced apartments such as Riverfront Residence. Prior to assuming a leadership role in her family's hospitality-related business, Ms. Ketvoravit was involved in her family's construction and property development companies.

She attended school in Perth, Western Australia from 1982 to 1989, where she completed her senior high school diploma and later obtained a Bachelor of Economics from the University of Western Australia. She received a Master of Management in Hospitality from Cornell University's School of Hotel Administration in 1994. Upon graduation, she returned to Bangkok and joined her family's company in June 1994. In 2002, Ms. Ketvoravit also studied at Chulalongkorn University's Law School in Bangkok on a part-time basis, and graduated with a Master of Arts in Thai Business Law in 2004.

Choe Peng Sum

Mr. Choe Peng Sum has more than 25 years of experience in the hospitality industry. As chief executive officer of Frasers Hospitality Pte. Ltd., he has overall charge of the business performance and global expansion of Frasers' chain of serviced residences worldwide. He stewarded the company from its inception in 1996 with two properties and 414 apartments in Singapore to 45 properties and 8,500 apartments in 33 cities globally. Global expansion covers Europe, the Middle East, North Asia (including China, India, Japan, and Korea), Southeast Asia, and Australia. Mr. Choe started his career in the hospitality industry with Westin International and subsequently moved to Shangri-La International in 1981. He was awarded the Shangri-La overseas studies scholarship, and held top management positions at the Shangri-La Singapore and the Shangri-La Shanghai, China. On his return to Singapore in 1996, he started the hospitality arm of Fraser & Neave Ltd.

He graduated from Cornell University with a Bachelor of Science with distinction (top 10 percent of the university). He was awarded the National Dean's List as well as Phi Kappa Phi for academic excellence.

Jennie Chua

Ms. Jennie Chua is chief corporate officer of CapitaLand Limited, one of Asia's largest real-estate companies. She chairs several organizations such as the Singapore International Chamber of Commerce, Khoo Teck Puat Hospital/Alexandra Health, Community Chest, Singapore Film Commission, and Raffles Hotel among others. She is also a member of the Temasek Advisory Board of Temasek Holdings (Pte.) Ltd., Singapore's Pro-Enterprise Panel, and the Board of Trustees of Nanyang Technological University, Singapore. A graduate of Cornell University's School of Hotel Administration and a Justice of the Peace, she is also Singapore's Non-Resident Ambassador to The Slovak Republic.

Judy Siguaw

Dr. Judy A. Siguaw is Dean of the College of Human Ecology at East Carolina University, US. She was formerly a professor of marketing at Cornell University's School of Hotel Administration. The founding Dean of Cornell-Nanyang Institute of Hospitality Management, she previously held the J. Thomas Clark Chair in Entrepreneurship and Personal Enterprise. She has published more than 50 academic journal articles, is the co-author of several books, and is the author/co-author of more than 30 national and international conference papers. She has been an invited speaker at numerous domestic and international conferences. Dr. Siguaw is the recipient of a prestigious Marketing Science Institute research award, a Chartered Institute of Marketing award, a Jane Fenyo Award from the Academy of Marketing Science, research fellowships, a CIBER travel award from Duke University, a grant from American Express and the American Hotel Foundation, and 11 university research grants. She has also been twice listed in *Who's Who Among America's Teachers*, and was awarded the Chancellor's Excellence in Teaching Award, and was twice named Outstanding Educator by Merrill Presidential Scholars.

1

PURSUING THE RIGHT STRATEGIC DIRECTION

By Baron R. Ah Moo

Introduction

Strategic direction is defined as the course of action that leads to the achievement of the goals of an organization's strategy.

Carter McNamara, in an article "Strategic Planning (in nonprofit or for-profit organizations)" from the book *Field Guide to Nonprofit Strategic Planning Facilitation* (McNamara 2007), points out that strategic planning determines where an organization is going over the next year or more, how it is going to get there, and how it will know if it got there or not. A strategic plan's focus is usually on the entire organization, while a business plan's focus is usually on a particular product, service, or program.

The author said that there are a variety of perspectives, models, and approaches used in strategic planning. The way that a strategic plan is developed depends on the nature of the organization's leadership, culture of the organization, complexity of the organization's environment, size of the organization, and expertise of the planners. For example, there are a variety of strategic planning models, including goals-based, issues-based, organic, scenario, and others.

Goals-based planning is probably the most common and starts with focus on the organization's mission (and vision and/or values), goals to work toward the mission, strategies to achieve the goals, and action planning. Issues-based strategic planning often starts by examining issues facing the organization, strategies to address these issues, and action plans. Organic strategic planning might start by articulating the organization's vision and values, and then, action plans to achieve the vision while adhering to these values. Some plans are scoped to one year, many to three years, and some to five to 10 years into the future.

Quite often, an organization's strategic planners already know much of what will go into a strategic plan. However, development of the strategic plan greatly helps to clarify the organization's plans and ensure that key leaders are all "on the same page." Far more important than the strategic plan document is the strategic planning process itself.

According to Carter McNamara, the purposes and benefits of strategic planning serve a variety of purposes in an organization including to clearly define the organization's purpose and establish realistic goals and objectives consistent with that mission in a defined time frame within the organization's capacity for implementation; communicate those goals and objectives to the organization's constituents; and develop a sense of ownership of the plan. Strategic planning ensures the most effective use is made of the organization's resources by focusing the resources on the key priorities. It also provides a base from which progress can be measured, and establishes a mechanism for informed change when needed.

It also brings together everyone's best and most reasoned efforts, which have value in building a consensus about where an organization is going; providing a clearer focus of an organization, thus producing more efficiency and effectiveness; and bridging and building strong teams within the board and the staff. Strategic planning provides the glue that keeps the board together; produces great satisfaction among planners around a common vision; and increases productivity from increased efficiency and effectiveness. Last but not least, it helps to solve major problems.

This chapter will discuss the development and market potential of tourism accommodation in Vietnam, and use a case study of Indochina Hotels and Resorts (IHR) focusing on how the company develops its strategic direction, and the issues and challenges faced in doing so. It concludes by offering some tips learned from IHR's experience for those who are interested in developing tourism projects in Vietnam.

Development of Tourism Accommodation in Vietnam

According to the World Travel & Tourism Council, Vietnam is the sixth fastest-growing tourism destination in the world, experiencing double-digit growth in international tourist arrivals year-over-year, and growing at 8.5 percent annually. The travel and tourism industry throughout Southeast Asia, of which Vietnam is a part, is growing at 6.5 percent per annum, positioning the region as one of the strongest performing destination markets in the world.

Indeed, tourism is important to Vietnam's economy. The major driver to this has been the *doi moi*, or open-door policy. According to Wantanee Suntikul, Richard Butler, and David Airey in their article "A Periodization of the Development of Vietnam's Tourism Accommodation since the Open Door Policy" (2008), the Vietnamese Congress introduced in 1986 the *doi moi* or "renovation" program of political and economic reforms.

The reforms promoted the role of the private sector in the economy and centralized aspects of governance and planning. State and privately owned industries could trade directly with foreign organizations.

Prior to *doi moi*, the then existing supply of tourist accommodation did not meet international standards. The hotels provided basic accommodation and food service without appropriate leisure and entertainment facilities.

The beginning of the open-door policy brought in a new era for the development of international standard lodgings and facilities for tourists. According to Wantanee Suntikul, Richard Butler, and David Airey (2008), there are five periods, which are outlined below:

Period 1: 1986–Early 1990: Period of State Dominance and the First Joint Ventures

Most tourists to Vietnam, who came from other Communist countries, accepted a basic standard of accommodation and services. The Vietnamese government and its agencies owned and operated most of the hotels.

Period 2: 1990–1994: Rise of Joint Venture Hotels

The Vietnamese government gave up its monopoly, and allowed private and foreign investors to develop hotels for tourists. There was a shortage of international standard hotels and guest rooms, which foreign joint-venture investors sought to address, especially in major Vietnamese cities such as Ho Chi Minh City and Hanoi.

Period 3: 1995–1996: Reaction of State Hotels

The existing hotels had to compete with the new joint-venture hotels. They found that they were unable to meet the demands of tourists from developed countries and had to therefore change their management practices and become much more service-oriented.

Period 4: 1996–1999: Oversupply and Falling Demand

In the mid-1990s, high demand for high-quality hotel rooms resulted in an occupancy rate of 85–90 percent in Hanoi. However, this changed with the government's xenophobic "social evils" campaign, few repeat visitors, visa policy issues, and the Asian economic crisis. Tourist arrivals to Vietnam fell. During this period, many new joint venture hotels opened, leading to an oversupply of guest rooms, thus resulting in a fall in occupancy and room rates.

Period 5: 1999–Present

The changes of the earlier period gave Vietnam greater tourist accessibility, thus encouraging more tourists to visit the country. The tourism market in Vietnam is now much more open and competitive for both foreign and domestic investors and operators of hotels.

As a result, Vietnam's tourism industry has experienced a period of meteoric growth in recent years. The success in tourism can be seen in the jump in tourist arrivals, tourism earnings, and number of jobs created. The number of foreign tourists visiting the country grew from 92,500 in 1988 to 3,583,486 in 2006, according to the Vietnam National Administration of Tourism (VNAT) 2007 statistics. A 2001 estimate stated the nation's earnings from tourism as US$2.6 billion. In 2006, there were 234,000 people employed directly in tourism jobs and 510,000 whose jobs indirectly depended on tourism. In 2008, tourism in Vietnam accounted for 11 percent of the total employment of the country and contributed US$4.5 billion to the gross domestic product (GDP).

According to World Travel & Tourism Council and Oxford Economic Forecasting, Vietnam's tourism sector is expected to experience the sixth-highest growth rate of countries in the world between 2007 and 2016 ("Vietnam's tourism grows" 2006). Aside from this quantifiable growth, tourism in Vietnam also continues to change in character with new tourism niches, new types of tourism attractions and enterprises, and new kinds of tourists appearing since 1986.

Current Issues and Future Outlook
in Vietnam Tourism Industry

According to Wantanee Suntikul, Richard Butler, and David Airey, the joint-venture accommodation sector continues to expand. Despite the growth of foreign direct investments in the accommodation sector, most new hotels developed in Vietnam are state-owned, often as joint ventures with foreign investors. In the majority of cases, especially in cities, the hotels are owned by, and provide a major source of income for city and provincial tourism bodies. Sixty percent of the one- to five-star grade hotels and 65 percent of all hotel rooms in Vietnam belonged to state-owned enterprises in 2001. The owning state bodies ranged from national ministries to district and commune-level agencies. The predominance of state ownership of hotels has been seen as a mechanism of built-in government regulation in the accommodation industry.

However, the diffusion of control over different levels and bodies of government mitigates the effectiveness and homogeneity of policies that was possible within the former centrally controlled market.

A continuation of dual private and public ownership was endorsed in the Revised National Tourism Plan for Vietnam 2001–2010 Draft Report, which also called for a careful thinking-through of privatization, including the establishment of requisite regulatory systems and bodies. However, the same report also mentioned other modes of wholly private, wholly state, or public and private ownership, including the equitization of state enterprises by the sale of shares; the sale or transfer of some entire state-owned enterprises to private interests; the liquidation of nonperforming state-owned enterprises; and the restructuring of remaining government enterprises to enhance their autonomy and accountability (VNAT 2001, pp. 159).

To sum up, the opening of Vietnam's tourism accommodation market to foreign direct investment and domestic private entrepreneurs has brought about competition, consolidation, and differentiation in the accommodation sector that was absent under the previous state monopoly. A more intensively trained workforce and an orientation toward customer-responsiveness are required to serve this more differentiated and discerning market, and Vietnam's accommodation providers are increasingly concerned with meeting international standards.

According to Reno Mueller, senior manager, Hotel Consultancy Services of CB Richard Ellis Vietnam (Hanoi Office) (Mueller 2008), today's tourism industry is not only multifaceted and highly interconnected but also constantly changing in line with the wider economic frame conditions on a global, regional, and national level. Although still in its early stages of development, Vietnam's tourism market is no exception to this, and the lesser the country becomes isolated, the more growth-stimulating factors will originate within the international setting. Many environmental forces impacting this industry makes developing or operating any tourism-related business, like hotel property, increasingly complex and intrinsically more risky.

The grace period given to developing countries is slowly coming to an end for Vietnam. Its economy no longer grows at double-digit figures and wage costs are becoming less competitive. Since Vietnam joined the World Trade Organization (WTO) in January 2007, its commitments such as wider opening of domestic markets, have begun to intensify industry rivalry.

Existing tourism enterprises should see such developments including the current business downturn, as an opportune time to review their business strategy and ascertain their future relevance in light of changed frame conditions. Internationally experienced and business-savvy managers will gladly seize this opportunity to strengthen the position of their companies, a process that is less a matter of size or relative financial resources and more on how sincere they are in providing value for their selected customers.

Having the ability to maneuver risk successfully while simultaneously enhancing the value of a business, which is best achieved in cooperation, requires selecting reliable partners who are capable of providing constructive assistance at all stages of the project cycle. Any such partnership must ensure well-thought-out planning, professional execution of these plans, and ongoing hands-on support in order to turn a project into a flourishing venture, not only for the immediate future but moreover for the entire life span of the investment.

Reno Mueller identified the opportunities in the Vietnamese tourism market as having a steady demand for quality hotel accommodation, a growing number of transient arrivals in most segments, and the inception of a healthy domestic tourism market based on an emergent middle class. Other opportunities are having a considerable proportion of affluent expatriates in the workforce, the cooperation in tourism development within the Indochina region, and a prolonged development of the global tourism industry.

However, the tourism industry is also facing several threats, which include a danger of overbuilding due to a lack of master planning and coordination, lack of sustainable development in the tourism sector, and growing environmental concerns due to rapid urbanization. Other threats are persisting problems with red tape especially at the regional and local levels, intensifying global and regional competition, and long-term knock-on effects of volatility in financial markets.

Vietnam's entry into the WTO also has a significant impact on the tourism industry. Joining the WTO has provided the country with a set of ground rules and a roadmap to improve bilateral trade and a platform by which to negotiate trade agreements. The organization specifically promotes free trade, attempts to remove the barriers of protectionism, and provides a forum by which to settle trade disputes. For the tourism industry, the impact of Vietnam's entry into the WTO requires the Vietnamese government to provide a nonregulatory environment in areas such as airlines, transportation, and travel, and allows for the establishment of legal foreign travel representative offices in the country.

This means that the government must divest its interest in noncore activities such as its stake in Vietnam Airlines, Saigon Tourist (the largest hotel, travel, and tour operator in the country), and other state-owned entities and subsidiaries. Though it has been more than three years since Vietnam's commitment to the WTO, the required changes have been slow in their implementation. The Vietnamese government recognizes the ultracompetitive nature of the tourism industry and is hesitant to fully commit to divesting its interest in noncore activities for fear that its leadership position within the market will be jeopardized. As such, some tourism multinational corporations, who have shown a keen interest in investing or operating in Vietnam, are faced with a difficult regulatory environment to establish their operations and may be discouraged from doing so. However, the VNAT is optimistic. The total number of international visitors in 2008 reached 4,253,740 arrivals, 0.6 percent higher than those in 2007. The travel and tourism industry is expected to directly contribute 3.8 percent to the GDP in 2009 at US$4 billion, rising to US$7.9 billion and contributing 3.5 percent of GDP by 2019.

Employment in this industry is estimated at 4,862,000 jobs in 2009, 10.4 percent of total employment, or 1 in every 9.6 jobs. By 2019, this should total 5,675,000 jobs, 10.4 percent of total employment, or 1 in every 9.6 jobs. Capital investment in this industry is estimated at US$3.4 billion, or 8.3 percent of total investment in 2009. By 2019, this is expected to reach US$6 billion, or 9 percent of the total.

Another positive development is the merger between VNAT and Vietnam's Ministry of Culture, Sports and Tourism (MCST) in 2006. Previous to the merger, the two government bodies had overlapping responsibilities, unclear governance and diverging opinions on the tourism industry. The combination of VNAT and the MCST has provided clarity for the private sector and marked the first time that the two governing tourism bodies were required to participate together in dialogues on improving Vietnam's position in the global market. Progress can now be seen with both government bodies cooperating on a comprehensive sales and marketing plan, including a call for the establishment of a public-private partnership to create a visitors and convention bureau.

Indochina Hotels and Resorts' Business and Strategy

Founded in 2007, IHR is a division of Indochina Land Management, one of the leading owners, developers, and asset managers of real estate in Vietnam, and Indochina Capital, one of the leading financial services and advisory firms in Vietnam. IHR's existing portfolio of eight hotels, three golf courses, and one luxury serviced apartment under management or development is valued at over US$335 million.

In developing its strategic direction, IHR focuses first, on the ownership and operation of premier hospitality properties; and second, on other strategic services such as pursuing potential opportunities that will complement its hospitality real-estate investments. Third, it focuses on its funding and disposition strategy.

Ownership and Operation of Premier Hospitality Properties

IHR's mission is to continually maximize shareholder value through the ownership and operation of premier hospitality properties. Its methodology for increasing investors' returns is to acquire, develop, and finance distinctive lodging assets in all segments of the industry and within key geographic markets throughout the region. It adds value to its portfolio of properties by aligning with internationally recognized brands and top-tier management companies who share the company's dedication to quality, exceptional service, and operational efficiencies.

The company focuses on acquiring and developing cash-generating assets and maximizing revenue growth at its properties through superior asset management. By reinvesting in its assets through renovation, redevelopment, and rebranding, it is staying ahead of its competitive set. Having gained invaluable experience over several market cycles, IHR is ideally positioned to prosper in up cycles and mitigate losses in down cycles through hands-on management of its many assets. It has proven ability to execute this value-add strategy and has consistently generated above-market returns.

IHR is a key component to Indochina Land's Hospitality Residential Plus platform, which combines a hotel/resort element with a residential product. Its diverse portfolio of properties also includes golf courses and serviced apartments. This helps to improve investors' returns through the sales of the residences with the additional income stream generated by the rental program, which IHR manages. The company has a history of acquiring distressed real-estate assets and using its financial and operational expertise to capitalize on their full market potential.

Indochina Land Holdings I and II (real-estate funds launched by Indochina Capital) have invested in IHR's portfolio of projects, which include:

- Dalat—Dalat Palace Golf Club (voted "The Best Golf Course in Asia" by *Asian Golf Monthly*); Novotel Dalat; and Sofitel Dalat Palace

- Central Coast—Nam Hai, China Beach (voted "The World's Best Designed Resort" by *Travel+Leisure* (US); Hyatt Regency Marble Mountain Beach Resort, Danang (projected opening 2011); and The Montgomerie Links Vietnam Estates and Golf Course, China Beach opened in April 2010)

- Phan Thiet—Novotel Ocean Dunes and Golf Resort; and Ocean Dunes Golf Club

- Ho Chi Minh City—Riverside Luxury Serviced Apartments, Ho Chi Minh City

- Con Dao—Six Senses Hideaway at Con Dao

Other Strategic Services

To further its competitive advantage, IHR is pursuing potential opportunities in the marketplace that will complement its hospitality real-estate investments. The company is pursuing several partnerships including the acquisition and development of distressed-asset opportunities. It is also in discussion to form an exclusive joint venture with a leading international hospitality company to debut a chain of three-star properties in the Indochina region.

IHR is also focused on diversifying its portfolio through the redevelopment and rebranding of existing urban-hotel assets. Future pipeline projects will diversify the company's portfolio through the acquisition of sites positioned for city-center hotels located in the Central Business Districts of Hanoi and Ho Chi Minh City.

The preferred investment criterion for IHR is to seek 100 percent ownership, long-term lease or freehold, in unique properties that are leaders in their respective markets. For opportunities that require co-investment, it strives for a majority stakeholder position or controlling interest in the operational direction of the asset(s). The company's geographic focus for its investments is the Indochina region, inclusive of Cambodia, Laos, Thailand, and Vietnam.

IHR also invests and manages joint ventures with reputable strategic investors who contribute land-use rights or equity capital on a per-project basis. Through its reputation, it has also become a preferred development partner with prominent international operators and regional hospitality brands such as GHM, Accor, and Hyatt.

Due to the demand and needs for advisory services in the market, IHR has identified five key services from a strategic direction viewpoint. These are, acquisition, proven renovation performance, operational expertise, asset management, and asset-recovery expertise.

Acquisition—IHR seeks under-performing assets that present potential to improve operations, product quality, sales force, revenue, or reduce overhead and expenses. It looks for assets that are well located, within growing markets and have multiple stable demand generators, whereby through IHR's expertise, the property or project would become or solidify its position as a market leader.

Proven Renovation Performance—IHR utilizes its parent company's in-house resources to accelerate the renovation or repositioning process at a lower cost than third-party project managers or service providers. Renovation costs are considerably lower than those completed by a third party, which immediately enhances the quality and the return for the fund or property owner. It simply "thinks like an owner," fostering better decisions and ensuring the right products are used, which result in the long-term value and sustainability.

Operational Expertise—IHR's core strength is managing hotels and producing above-average gross operating profits through aggressive hands-on management and cost control. At the time of acquisition, the company immediately implements a strategy that focuses on overhead reduction, payroll and expense management, and growth. In addition, IHR focuses on aggressive rate-management strategies to grow and maximize revenue, which results in greater flow-through due to improved operating margins.

Asset Management—IHR Asset Management team understands the priorities and responsibilities of asset management from years of experience owning real-estate assets, which ensure that return objectives, product quality, and service goals are achieved. During the due diligence stage, it will establish a business plan to exploit value-add opportunities such as leasing outlets, reworking operating contracts, evaluating revenue-generating opportunities, and redeveloping existing space and/or developing excess land for compatible uses. Other opportunities are filing tax-assessment appeals, investigating insurance cost reduction through inclusion in IHR's master insurance policy, and refinancing. It is also able to uncover revenue enhancement and cost-containment opportunities during due diligence, or through the annual budgeting process, or as part of an ongoing assessment, which historically results in a significant impact to net operating profits translating directly into value.

Asset-Recovery Expertise—IHR also provides asset-recovery services, turnaround consulting, and investment services. It creates customized solutions to nonperforming real-estate assets in a manner that will maximize returns via effective planning and efficient execution.

Funding and Disposition Strategy

To sustain its current growth pace, IHR is exploring several funding options. First, the company will initially grow organically through the expansion and redevelopment of its existing assets. Second, concurrently, the company is looking to create a joint venture with equity from a strategic partner who shares the company's passion and expertise in hospitality real estate in the Indochina region and can add value to its shareholders and investors. In the second instance, Indochina Land Holdings I and II will inject their assets into the joint venture at an agreed upon valuation, in exchange for an equity position.

The new joint venture will then continue to purchase, operate, or dispose of the appreciable assets until such time a trade sale, institutional sale, or a business trust listing of the portfolio becomes viable. IHR believes a hospitality-business trust focused on Vietnam would be well received by the public markets.

Maximizing IHR's Strengths

IHR's strengths lie in its extensive use of market data and research, experienced senior management, and resourceful staff. The company does this by utilizing extensive research, knowledge and experience in fund management, investment, development and asset management, thus establishing IHR as a leading brand in hospitality real estate in Vietnam.

In developing its strategic direction, IHR's management board has positioned itself to be the leading hospitality asset-management firm in the Southeast Asian region. The company contributes much of its current success to its core senior management team and its ability to attract talented and experienced professionals. Its management team has over 20 years of combined experience in hospitality real-estate investment and development and asset management, and a proven track record of performance in Vietnam. The team also has a strong understanding of Vietnamese business ethics and culture, which is one of IHR's best assets in adding value to its clients.

The company's core resources are made up of individuals who bring different experiences and skill sets, and allow it to develop a fundamentally sound strategy, which provides maximum returns to its stakeholders and severely mitigates risk. Its investment, development, project management, operational, and sales and marketing expertise allow the company to provide comprehensive strategic solutions to investors, who are interested in emerging market opportunities but have very little appetite for its risk.

Challenges and Issues in Managing Strategies

The biggest challenges IHR faces are the lack of resources to keep up with entrepreneurial requirements and uncertainties of the business environment in Vietnam. Often times, the implementation of its strategy involves complex financial products, which are mainstream in most industrialized countries but have no precedent in Vietnam, where IHR is required to invest the majority of its funds according to its charter. In these cases, licensing approvals for investments and land-use rights come to a grinding halt, as it is a safer decision to vote against change than for it. This slow and long process is common in emerging markets but is often not an issue in developed economies. It is important to note that delays and slow processes are not always considered by companies when they are planning the timeline of projects in Vietnam.

IHR's competitive advantage in the market is that it has the reputation and the ability to overcome these obstacles but cannot totally eliminate the risks involved. Enforcement of policy, regulation, and law remains skewed and inconsistent but being a reputable partner in the business community has enabled the company to overcome some of these obstacles. The company's strategy hinges upon its relationships with the local government and community, and its good reputation as a quality business partner has been an asset in building these business relationships.

The company's good relationships with the government and community can be seen in its support of community projects such as the Vietnam Hospitality Management Institute. The proposed site is located adjacent to the Nam Hai, a five-star resort in Quang Nam province and approximately 35 minutes from Danang International Airport. The school will be managed by a well-renowned regional educational institute and be part of a 10.5-hectare development that will include 70 villas and a health and wellness clinic. The hospitality-management programs will be subsidized by public funds made available through local or provincial governmental committees, and by private sector contributions. The private sector contributors will derive a direct benefit from the well-prepared students with their new skill sets. IHR is working with international hotel operators who have shown an initial interest in supporting the school and its curriculum. It believes that the training programs will help to provide jobs and needed skills for the people and enhance incomes in the community.

Vietnam's entry into the WTO and the government's slowness in diverting its interest in noncore activities, and the difficult regulatory environment may be discouraging for the tourism industry. However, these roadblocks, once removed, will enable Vietnam's tourism product to improve and will allow for greater exposure and improved access to IHR's investments. Improvements in tourism infrastructure, such as public transportation, combined with a more favorable environment for hospitality investment, will create a critical mass that will move Vietnam forward as a global travel destination. As the largest private owner of resorts and golf courses in the country, IHR believes that the performance potential of its assets is enormous. Indeed, the company stands to benefit from its market-leader position when roadblocks are removed and improvements to the infrastructure and environment are made.

Another challenge is the current global economic downturn, which started in 2008 and has impacted Vietnam.

IHR agrees with Reno Mueller's view that existing tourism enterprises should see such developments, including the current business downturn, as opportune times to review their business strategy and ascertain their future relevance in light of changed frame conditions. Internationally experienced and business-savvy managers such as IHR will gladly seize this opportunity to strengthen their company's position.

The worldwide economic downturn has forced IHR to not only reposition its operations in Vietnam but has caused the company to review its risk-management systems and strategic direction. The company's focus has radically shifted from actively raising capital and pursuing investment opportunities to value engineering current projects and looking for opportunistic developments.

IHR remains very bullish about Vietnam in the long-term. Despite the current economic challenges, Vietnam is already showing signs of recovery with liquidity improving and commercial lending back to

2007 levels in the market. The profile for investments has changed and the opportunity for returns similar to Vietnamese assets now exist in stable and regulated markets such as Europe, the US, and Australia. The economic downturn has brought the country additional competition for equity and capital, and Vietnam will need to differentiate its product from other opportunities. The company believes that its conservative approach to investment and analysis, combined with good fundamentals and a strong potential for growth, is the right strategic direction to take during this economic downturn.

IHR also feels optimistic about the hospitality scene in Asia. As borders continue to open and personal income continues to grow in the region, Vietnam stands to take advantage of the regional tourism boom.

IHR believes that its strengths in its operational and asset management expertise, full complement of services, and access to the resources of Indochina Capital and its subsidiaries, are well-positioned to help the company takes advantage of the current market conditions. The company creates superior risk-adjusted returns for its investors by utilizing its skills in accessing attractive transactions, executing performance and results-based initiatives, and employing active operational and asset-management policies to maximize cash flow for each hotel or real-estate asset.

As affirmation of IHR's reputation in the industry, it is now chairing the Tourism Working Group for the Vietnam business forum under the auspicious of VNAT and the MCST. This forum represents the private sector in dialogue on improving Vietnam's position in the global market. IHR with its relationships within the ministry is playing a key advisory role as it pertains to rules and regulations regarding tourism investment. These rules and regulations include laws governing resort-residential products, vacation and fractional ownership projects, and the creation of a destination branding and marketing campaign.

Conclusion

In developing strategic direction, businesses have to take into consideration many changing factors, whether political, economic, financial, or social—one has to adapt and respond effectively with plans and actions within a specific time frame.

The test of the effectiveness of IHR's strategic direction will be in the financial results that it achieves. IHR is glad to say that it has achieved better-than-average market returns by leveraging its relationships and experience in the hospitality industry and within Vietnam to provide efficiencies and cost savings in the areas of project development, project management, and debt/financing services.

For those who are keen on developing strategic direction in tourism projects and hotels and resorts in developing countries, IHR offers the following recommendations.

First, in developing strategic direction in tourism projects and hotels and resorts in Vietnam, there are no shortcuts. An effective emerging market strategic model will not only consider standard risk management sensitivities but also plan for contingencies. These contingencies are normally considered common business practice in more developed countries but not in Vietnam. Second, the strategic timeline for development in Asia's newest tiger should be conservative in approach with realistic milestones and deadlines. All too often, IHR has seen strategies fail, not because of poor planning or initiatives, but rather the incongruence of the time frame of when these milestones and objectives can be achieved.

To sum up, developing strategy in an emerging market requires a complex combination of due diligence, risk management, and patience. An understanding of the business environment and ethics of the emerging market is also a key factor in ensuring the success of a business strategy. Those who have the foresight to plan for contingencies and the resources to sustain the cycles of the market will be rewarded.

References

McNamara, Carter. 2007. Strategic planning in nonprofit or for-profit organizations. Field guide to nonprofit strategic planning facilitation. Free Management Library, a service mark of Authenticity Consulting, LLC, 1997–2009. http://managementhelp.org/plan_dec/str_plan/str_plan.htm.

Mueller, Reno. 2008. The Vietnamese Tourism Market—An Insider Perspective. Hanoi: CB Richard Ellis Vietnam. (Issue 2, December).

Suntikul, Wantanee, Richard Butler, and David Airey. 2008. A periodization of the development of Vietnam's tourism accommodation since the open door policy. *Asia Pacific Journal of Tourism Research* 13:1, 67–80.

Vietnam National Administration of Tourism, Revised National Tourism Plan for Vietnam 2001–2010, Draft Report. 2001:159.

World Travel and Tourism Council and Oxford Economic Forecasting. 2006. Vietnam's tourism grows.

2

ACHIEVING SUCCESSFUL DEVELOPMENT PLANNING

By Russell Arthur Smith

Introduction

Planning is a process of shaping optimal future situations in the course of sequential decisions so as to achieve desired future objectives. According to the *Encyclopedia of Tourism* edited by Jafar Jafari (2003), planning occurs at a wide variety of scales, from individuals making plans for their vacations, to destination areas plotting future strategies to achieve community goals, to states charting futures for the tourism industry, and to international organizations preparing their own future activities and assisting countries to look ahead and prepare the way for preferable change. Mostly, it is used in the context of forms of urban and regional planning from local to national levels.

Planning can have many different foci. It can have an economic, social, or more comprehensive orientation, and can primarily be concerned with land uses or infrastructure such as transportation facilities, electricity, water supply, and waste disposal. Planning may focus upon parks and protected areas, or the manpower required by an economic sector. It can be directed specifically at tourism or can be viewed as a part of a broader set of activities.

However, according to Leslie Barker (2009), development planning happens in many different contexts and basically refers to the targeted strategic goals for an organization or community. Normally, a development plan has integrated time-based benchmarks. Ideally, there will be criteria against which it will be determined if the goals are actually met. Development planning is common in cities and other communities. In urban areas, there are many vacant buildings or sites frequently engaged in a development-planning process to help revitalize the area.

Often, there is government support with funding, services provision, and, on occasion, rationalization of land ownership. Development planning commonly includes the community along with the government, the private sector, and a range of development consultants.

Development-planning management therefore refers to the management of the process of development planning. In Asia, some destination or tourism areas, which have undergone significant development planning include highland areas (Penang, Malaysia), urban districts (Singapore), beach resorts (Laguna Phuket, Thailand), and urban hotels (as in Shanghai, China).

In destination development for tourism, it must be mentioned that hospitality, comprising lodging and food services, is a major driver. Hospitality combined with tourism attractions, such as theme parks and MICE (Meetings, Incentives, Conventions, and Exhibitions), airlines, cruise lines, and so on help to create a tourism product or tourist destination area. Therefore, in planning a development such as a destination area, there is a need to look at a full range of tourism facets.

In this chapter, I will be discussing the rationale for development-planning management in the tourism and hospitality sector, cite various models, and discuss some case studies of how these models are being implemented in various destination areas on a macro to micro scale in Southeast Asia, particularly in beach or resort destinations. This draws from and elaborates on my earlier planning theory, particularly my framework of planning levels and model of development strategies (Smith 2000). Some issues in development management such as different viewpoints of various actors and desired outcomes versus actual outcomes will also be discussed. The chapter will conclude with some tips for investors, planners, and managers.

Rationale for Development-Planning Management

The discussion in this section on the rationale for the management of development planning is focused on tourism development. A key concern of tourism development is the economic benefits for individual enterprises, related communities, and the country as a whole. Tourism development does generate wealth and create jobs. There is also considerable potential for community development, conservation of historic and natural sites, and development of the arts related to tourism (Smith 2000).

Unfortunately, tourism development may also lead to undesirable social or environmental or both impacts. Also, economic benefits are not always assured. Clearly, development planning seeks to maximize the positive benefits of tourism development while minimizing any negative impacts in a sustainable way. Managing development planning is, therefore, the systematic process of determining ideal future conditions, which strives to optimize the likely outcomes that may otherwise have been unwanted. The process also provides for managed intervention of tourism development so as to rectify the undesirable and enhance the beneficial.

In theory, the planning process is rational; however in practice, there are distortions because of flawed operational conditions. These practical weaknesses arise from factors such as insufficient data, unforeseen future change in the development context, political interference, ill-defined planning scope, poor coordination, and inadequate planning resources such as funding, expertise, and time. Dysfunctional approval and feedback mechanisms will also weaken the planning process.

Effective development planning management does produce positive outcomes, despite these impediments. Nevertheless, projected and actual outcomes will nearly always be contested because of the diversity of the vested interests and the complexity of the tourism development process. Narrowly defined short-term interests versus wider long-term benefits are often a contentious matter. Properly managed development planning produces sustainable tourism projects that largely meet the planning objectives while benefiting communities and preserving or enhancing resources. Development-planning management delivers sustainable tourism development.

Planning takes place at various levels—international, national, regional, destination area, and project.

a) International planning

This level transcends national boundaries and typically involves the governments of two or more countries such as with international air service development.

Much less common are physical development projects, where proximity of compatible resources is the driving force for development.

A prominent example is Bintan Resorts, a large beach resort of 23,000 hectares located in the north of Bintan Island, Riau, Indonesia. Here, the Singapore and Indonesian governments jointly planned for the resort. Indonesia had prime coastal resources, developable land, and ample low-cost labor, while Singapore contributed development expertise, management experience, and investment security. The large international air hub at Changi, Singapore, was only one hour by ferry from the development site. Finance for the project came from both countries.

b) National planning

National tourism plans have been the driver for development in the tourism sector in many Asian countries. Given the large geographical scale of whole countries, national tourism plans are normally strategic or conceptual. Following evaluation of relevant resources, a national plan is prepared to leverage their strategic advantage in the forecast competitive market of the region. National plans consider natural resources, infrastructure, existing tourism-relevant facilities, labor, and demand in a comprehensive manner for rationalization of resource application. A national plan becomes the focus for a national tourism policy on, for example, tourism taxation, national and international transport, education and training, resource allocation, and the scoping of project types and their locations. The national plan also prioritizes tourism development over time.

An example is the Cambodian National Tourism Development Plan 2001–2005, which was prepared by the national Ministry of Tourism (Asian Development Bank 2000). This plan was designed to guide tourism development and management, and to enable the political and private sectors and bureaucracy to work toward a common vision of tourism development in the country. Tourism in Cambodia has become increasingly important as a tool for economic development and poverty reduction. It was widely recognized that if tourism was to continue to be an important force in Cambodian development, careful tourism planning and management needed to occur or else Cambodia would lose its tourism appeal.

Another example is the Malaysia Comprehensive National Tourism Development Plan (Government of Malaysia 1987), which reviewed existing tourism facilities and other resources suitable for tourism from a national perspective and proposed development in the best interest of the nation. Under this plan, some Malaysian states received little or no support for tourism development because of their limited resources or potential. This was the correct outcome for an objective planning process.

c) Regional planning

Governments at the state or provincial level often initiate regional tourism plans, which may cover the entire area of their jurisdiction or a smaller area of study. Here, the intent is to propose and develop tourism in relation to specific resources or groups of mutually compatible resources. Ideally, these plans acknowledge broad strategies and concepts in the respective national plan. Regional tourism plans are a guide for investors and developers for the tourism projects that will be supported in one way or another by the regional government.

An example is the Boracay Island Comprehensive Land Use Plan (Department of Tourism 2008) where the Philippines government initiated a study to review the existing situation and to identify the developmental and operational challenges that the island faced. This planning report described the development plans for the key aspects, which included the socioeconomy, tourism, infrastructure, environmental management, and institutional development, as well as the implementation of the plan over 10 years (2009–2018). The goal was to recommend a management guide for the development of Boracay Island as one of the Philippines' major tourism destinations, which was in harmony with its environment and made suitable use of the natural resources.

In Malaysia, the Pahang State Government's economic planning unit initiated a tourism plan for the development of the entire 200 kilometers of the state's marine coastline. This plan focused on the future success of coastal tourism in the state. The Pahang State Government took the lead to coordinate the development across local government boundaries (Smith 1997). Also in Malaysia, the Perak State Government coordinated a tourism plan for Pangkor Island, related islands, and the nearby mainland, where the planning study area boundary followed the local government boundaries of the adjacent Districts of Lumut and Perak Tengah (Government of Malaysia 1994). This facilitated post-planning implementation and management of the plan by the two district councils. This study was overseen by the state.

d) Destination area planning

Often referred to as master planning, destination area planning delineates the physical and related development within specific geographical contexts. For example, complete destination areas may be planned as new resort. The Bali Tourism Development Corporation, an Indonesian government agency, with the help of an United Nations agency prepared a master plan for the development of a completely new beach resort at Nusa Dua, where only farming and fishing villages had existed.

In Cambodia, the government gave high priority to coastal development as reflected in the Second Five-Year Socio-Economic Development Plan, which is part of the government's effort to eradicate poverty. The Physical Framework Plan is a multisector approach, which offers a preferred strategy for development to ensure balanced distribution of resources in Sihanoukville, an emerging beach resort. The strategy proposes a master plan, which is to be developed with tourism as the lead sector for future development (Japan International Corporation Agency 2008).

Existing destination areas in cities are frequently planned for rejuvenation with expansion of their tourist function. For example, Singapore sought to build on its past tourism success through rejuvenation of the existing tourism product, addition of new facilities, and implementation of new policies (Singapore Tourism Promotion Board 1996).

Control of land has a dominant role in any destination area plan. In the case when a private-sector developer organization owns the land in the planning area, it will contract and coordinate its own planning team. Should there be government-owned land or several private landowners involved, the regional government is likely to take a lead role. This situation is more common where the land area is large, primarily because only the government has the power and resources for the development of essential infrastructure. Generally, the regional government gives approval of any destination area plan. National government endorsement is sometimes necessary for budgetary reasons, as in the case of major infrastructure development such as airports, water supply dams, or intercity highways.

e) Project planning

This is where there is planning for individual tourism and hospitality projects, such as hotels. It is the final planning stage. It represents the considered output from all of the planning undertaken at the preceding levels. For example, the plan for Nusa Dua included development sites for several hotels, each of which was leased to individual developers. Each of these hotel sites became a separate development project with its own project plan.

Unique urban heritage areas may be planned for conservation with tourism development in mind. Tourism development was the driver with the conservation of the historic Chinatown area in Singapore where a plan was prepared to restore and preserve its old shop houses and urban form (Smith 1988).

Strategies for Development-Planning Management

There are four strategic approaches to tourism development planning and management, which vary with respect to realization of desirable outcomes: *ad hoc*, *limited growth*, *integrated*, and *comprehensive*. These strategies, all of which have merits, differ in purpose, procedure, and end result. The specific developmental and managerial conditions of the developing Asia-Pacific region would benefit most from the comprehensive approach over the other approaches.

a) Ad hoc

For this strategic approach, the *de facto* objective is maximization of short-term business gains as derived from sharply increasing demand and related expansion of supply. Development proceeds project-by-project with little or no attention to wider objectives, long-term consequences, linkages to other sectors, or appropriate allocation and conservation of resources. There is unfettered and largely unregulated development for which overall destination area plans are not prepared or, if they are, not followed. This strategy often works well in the short-term but fails beyond that timeframe (Smith 1991). It is unmanaged development planning.

b) Limited growth

This strategy seeks to conserve natural resources or to limit social impacts on communities. Tourism development may be restricted by way of imposition of a maximum capacity for tourist accommodation or other type of supply. This strategy has been implemented successfully in developed countries such as Australia and the United States. In the developing countries of Asia Pacific, informal development is likely to occur to neutralize the imposed limit as demand for tourism facilities increases. Short-term business gains will generally bypass weak development regulation and result in any development limit being ignored. Initially the limited growth strategy may be effective, however, over time the development process will revert to ad hoc.

c) Integrated

As a way of avoiding the manifold problems of the ad hoc strategy, the integrated strategy, particularly for large-scale resort projects, has gained some prominence. This strategy is applied to large destination areas and results in fully planned tourism areas. At this type of destination, there will be a number of hotels that share infrastructure and recreational facilities, and other facilities such as second homes, meeting centers, marinas, and retail complexes. The hotels tend to face the primary natural resource—beach or excellent view—with the other features of the resort situated behind the hotels. A golf course is a common recreational inclusion.

The large land area in which there are multiple hotels and other tourism features permits a totally planned destination that integrates the desired resort elements so as to better achieve project objectives. It is intended to exclude incompatible activities and land uses. The strategy allows for total control of the destination area. Coordination of resort planning and development creates a consistent and desirable ambience for the area as a whole (Stiles and See-Tho 1991).

d) Comprehensive

The comprehensive strategy maximizes the benefits of the integrated strategy and avoids the shortcomings of the ad hoc and limited growth strategies. This planning approach fully considers tourism and non-tourism functions and does not focus solely on the former.

Designated integrated destination areas are coordinated with other tourism projects. Priority is also given to development and conservation of related, non-tourism functions. Tourism benefits are maximized and negative impacts minimized. The strategy requires identification of suitable sites for integrated development; zoning of the related land for appropriate tourism, community, and other uses; designation of environmental protection areas; policy formulation that addresses tourism development in a comprehensive manner; institutional development; and enactment of regulatory instruments and their enforcement. The comprehensive strategy is the recommended approach for tourism planning and development for the developing regions of AsiaPacific.

Ad hoc Case Study: Pattaya

A good case example of the ad hoc strategy is the beach resort of Pattaya, Thailand, where uncontrolled development with short-term objectives dominated. With a severely degraded environment and reputation, several attempts were made to clean up its negative image as development continued to proceed project-by-project with little attention to long-term consequences until recently.

Pattaya is a resort city located in the province of Chonburi, on the east coast of the Gulf of Thailand, 120 kilometers to the east of Bangkok. From a small and isolated fishing village, Pattaya became a weekend retreat for wealthy Thais living in Bangkok when second homes were built in the late 1940s. With improved road accessibility in the 1960s, Pattaya became a place for recreation for expatriates and American military personnel. Hotels, restaurants, and bars were built and recreational businesses established, marking the city's transition toward being a major resort.

According Aw Wen Ling, Chen Lihui, and Cherh Kai Leng (2009) in their Nanyang Business School research project on Pattaya, problems came with the growth of the tourism trade. Environmental conditions deteriorated. Pollution and congestion became major issues for visitors and the local administration. Crime, prostitution, and other antisocial behavior were rampant. The attraction of the beach resort declined, and there was difficulty gaining further tourist interest. Government, businesses, residents, and tourists alike became concerned regarding the future of the city resort.

In order to revitalize the destination and attract visitors to return, local administrators planned to clean up the beach resort, in both the environmental sense and the sociocultural sense. The destination was repositioned as family-oriented as well as suitable for business travelers, particularly for the MICE (Meetings, Incentives, Conventions, and Exhibitions) sector. Vigorous efforts were made to prevent sewage and solid waste from entering the sea, and thus rid it of pollution, so that water activities could again be conducted safely. Green spaces were revitalized and expanded so as to restore the lost natural ambience of the resort.

Though it was important for Pattaya to attract a quantity of visitors, it was also imperative to attract high-spending tourists who would be able to generate greater total revenue for the destination. Average tourist expenditure per person per day had been fluctuating. It hit a trough in 2005, but steadily increased in 2006 through 2007. Total revenue has also been on the rise. According to the Tourism Authority of Thailand's (TAT) figures, in 2007, Pattaya welcomed 6.68 million local and foreign tourists, who spent a total of 53.2 billion baht (US$1.6 billion approximately), though with the political uncertainty in Thailand in 2008, the number of tourists fell to 5.83 million.

As a result of the environmental clean up and market repositioning efforts, the resort was able to develop further and expand inland. With visitors being attracted, so were the investors. The high number of new international chain hotels and facilities being planned and constructed suggested that there was a significant inflow of foreign investment into Pattaya's tourism sector. In addition, existing tourism businesses were expanding and upgrading their facilities (Eamtako 2008). With the presence of a major convention center, Pattaya Exhibition and Convention Hall, regional MICE business has also seen its numbers increase.

The Nanyang Business School team concluded that overall, the beach resort was invigorated as new investments were made and new visitor types emerged. However, although some considered Pattaya fully rehabilitated (Coplans 2006), others find that more remains to be done.

A new plan seeks to further upgrade Pattaya and transform the destination into a green and clean city (Charoenpo 2009). The plan seeks to ameliorate coastal erosion and traffic congestion, improve public safety, reduce overcrowding, enhance public infrastructure, and remove hazards to residents' health. It is intended to hone the city's competitiveness as a tourism destination. Pattaya's management is acting decisively to heighten the resort's appeal to tourists.

The TAT has hailed the rehabilitation and consequent renaissance of Pattaya as a model for sustainable tourism (Tourism Authority of Thailand 2006). Up to 2001, Pattaya provided a textbook case study of the negative environmental, social, and financial effects of unmanaged development for mass tourism. Significantly, the rehabilitation campaign was instituted and financed by both the private and public sectors, with a plan formulated and a budget set aside for rehabilitation of the resort. The board members of the Pattaya Chapter of the Thai Hotel Association and the Pattaya Business and Tourism Association worked together and had an instrumental role in rallying the active support and participation of private sector businesses. The campaign resulted in the development and subsequent operations of a large-scale wastewater treatment plant, beautification and landscaping of roadways and commercial areas, creation of natural parks, construction of boat piers, and all-important regulation and enforcement of environmental and business operational standards.

The resultant influx of tourists to Pattaya generated more income for members of the community. The project created new jobs dedicated to the maintenance of the environment with numerous other indirect jobs. As a result, the decline that Pattaya once faced had been reversed, leading to an increase in the number of new enterprises that emerged within the destination. These included new hospitals, schools, and other community services to support its growing resident and visitor populations. The rehabilitation campaign served to help stem decline, and has over the past few years, resulted in a growing number of visitors to Pattaya.

Integrated Case Studies: Nusa Dua, Laguna Phuket, and Bintan

Examples of the successful application of the integrated strategy in Asia Pacific include Nusa Dua, Laguna Phuket, and Bintan, which resulted in totally planned tourism destinations. However, some of these resorts faced challenges from adjacent ad hoc village development, informal economies, and protests from the communities.

The first operational integrated tourism development in Southeast Asia was Nusa Dua, Bali. Planning for this 350-hectare coastal destination commenced in 1971 under the direction of the Bali Tourism Development Corporation, which was a government agency (Smith 2000). The first hotel opened in 1983 and now Nusa Dua has 12 high-quality beachside hotels. Shared facilities include an 18-hole golf course, conference center, spa, and a centrally located shopping complex. This destination is clearly a major developmental improvement over other beach resorts that evolved with an ad hoc strategy. The immaculately maintained resort differs markedly from ad hoc destinations. From the resort's inception, there was centralized wastewater treatment that avoided the perennial sea pollution found in other resorts. Litter is rarely seen as solid waste is collected and removed for landfill.

In sharp contrast with this integrated resort, in the adjacent village, there were inadequate streets, crowded housing, clogged open sewers, piles of solid waste, and a polluted groundwater supply. Development of other tourism facilities by the beach, outside of the integrated project boundary, proceeded with an ad hoc strategy. The destination extended to the north as hotels, guesthouses, and other tourist amenities were developed. The physical and environmental degradation of these areas around the integrated resort points to the fact that the larger Nusa Dua area may well resemble other ad hoc destinations except for the immaculate integrated component of the resort.

Another case study of an integrated destination is Laguna Phuket in Thailand, where coordinated planning and development had similarly been applied and resulted in properly planned and developed tourism facilities. According to Henderson and Smith (2009), this integrated resort faced the challenge of managing informal commerce right outside on its beachfront. Laguna Phuket, a well-known Asian seaside destination, includes six hotels, five spas, an 18-hole golf course, a boutique shopping center, 30 food and beverage outlets, and villas. Facing a three-kilometer beach on the west coast of the island of Phuket, the resort occupies 400 hectares. With the first hotel opening in 1987, the destination is operated by Laguna Resorts and Hotels. Mainly international tourists are welcomed in 1,200 four- or five-star guest rooms. Sited on a former tin mine where dredging had created a devastated and polluted landscape, the management has transformed the destination significantly. The integrated resort has won several prominent environmental awards. The resort operators have stressed their continuing dedication to environmental protection (Ettensperger 2001). As with Nusa Dua, Laguna Phuket is beautifully landscaped and has high-quality facilities, which are well-maintained and managed.

Operating on the beach immediately in front of the Laguna Phuket resort were many informal traders. In contrast to the carefully developed and operated resort, these beach traders set up many primitive and poorly maintained stalls, which formed a linear barrier along the beach. Resort guests had to navigate through this barrier to reach the sea. These stalls were constructed of timber, bamboo, and *attap* (palm fronds), which being flammable, posed a serious fire hazard. The vendors had also installed their own makeshift power generator and water supply. The removal and treatment of waste received scant attention, thus contributing to pollution. The concerns by the resort management included food service hygiene and public safety. Management also deemed the stalls on the beach to be unsightly and not in keeping with the high standard of the resort, though some resort guests appreciated the spontaneous color that these vendors brought to the overall area. Collaboration between the Laguna Phuket management and the informal vendors was present, though this was at a low level and tentative at best. Clearly, the destination was at risk from environmental pollution and other hazards, should both formal and informal development continue in its then current form. As a component of a wider plan, initiatives incorporating stricter controls over informal vendor numbers, hours, and places of operation were proposed, though these were viewed by some as commercially disruptive and threatening to local livelihoods. It follows that any reform must be founded on dialogue, which produces cooperation and removes hostile competition between informal and formal businesses. Bridges can be built between the two stakeholders resulting in satisfactory operational contexts for both (Henderson and Smith 2009).

Both informal vendors and developers and managers of formal resorts have roles in shaping the physical and socioeconomic landscapes of destinations. These stakeholders may have diametrically opposed institutional structures, but all are driven by a common business motivation to maximize their respective business results. Both are core players of tourism economies in the destinations of developing countries, though they differ in many ways. Informal businesses tend to be small and often family-run while formal businesses are large. Informal businesses are grounded in the local community, while formal ones are often not. Formal businesses have legal tenure for the land on which they develop and operate and informal businesses do not. Formal businesses drive destination development, which in turn, attracts informal vendors. Despite these differences, both contribute to the local economy and support the local community, albeit in differing ways. The formal industry, which is dominant, often seeks to restrict informal commercial operations. However, the informal sector cannot be ignored, given its contribution to the local socieconomy and overall destination development. Efforts should be made to improve informal-formal relations, possibly through the embracing of the informal by the formal, to eventually erase the actual and perceived divisions, which currently separate them (Smith and Henderson 2008; Henderson and Smith 2009).

A much larger coastal resort that applied the integrated strategy is Bintan Resorts, which is 40 kilometers to the southeast of Singapore. Around a third of visitors are Singaporeans. The remainder is Asian nationals, who reside mainly in nearby Singapore. Visitors have a choice of nine lodging establishments, which range in quality from basic to luxury. Leisure facilities include a golf course, spa, water sports, and beachfront bars (Bintan Resorts 2010).

However, Bintan Resorts has had some serious conflicts with its local community. According to the *Jakarta Post* report, "Singapore minister and Gus Dur discuss Bintan" (the *Jakarta Post* 2000), Indonesian troops were deployed to break up a week-long protest by 200 local residents. During this security operation, some protestors were injured and 70 were arrested. The protestors from the local community had blocked a road leading into the resort. Their protest was in support of their claims for enhanced compensation for the land that they had sold for the development of the resort and a nearby industrial estate. At one point, the protestors had occupied a power plant in the industrial estate, which disrupted power and water supplies to the factories in the estate. It was reported that the management of the industrial estate, SembCorp Industries, regretted that force had to be used to remove the demonstrators, but Bintan as a whole would suffer if the confidence of investors was lost as jobs and businesses on Bintan would be affected.

To build better business-community relations, the Bintan Resort Cakrawala Community Development Program was created with the mission of maintaining stable, harmonious, and healthy relationships with the local community. The local government and volunteer organizations were involved. Programs focused on community development in a variety of ways. Jobs were offered in the resort. Opportunities for income from tourism-related activities were created. Financial support was provided to the younger generation for education, and for the acquiring of skills useful for gaining employment in the resort. The general health and well-being of the community was targeted. Efforts were made to promote a better understanding of the resorts' business via numerous social events and activities.

Issues in Development-Planning Management

In managing development planning, several issues need to be tackled. The first issue is the diverse viewpoints of the different actors. In the Southeast Asia context, these include a range of actors such as national government, local government, developer, operator, guest, and resident who all influence the development and operation of destination areas, such as beach resorts. This often results in many conflicting viewpoints, which often can give rise to complex issues and tensions affecting the development and management of the tourist destinations.

Creation and approval of tourism plans involves politicians, government officers, and private-sector developers, where ultimately a senior government politician, such as a minister, endorses any plan. Developers are investors who strive to maximize the returns on their investments. Given their plan approval role, government politicians have considerable power, yet with a sometimes overriding desire for re-election, they focus on short-term objectives. In contrast, government officers, who head ministries and other government bodies, work to fulfill the missions of their respective organizations and tend to have long-term objectives. It is normal for all three actors to be in continuous conflict as plans are developed and approved. Planning study teams who report directly to either the government officers or the developers will have their objectivity constrained by their client's interests (Smith 2000).

National government drives the overall multisector national economy, in which tourism projects are just one of many competing economic considerations. The local government responsible for the management of a destination area, such as a resort, will have a strong vested interest in the success of that destination. The local government will be actively involved in tourism promotion, transport, and security as well as the normal public health, welfare, and other municipal duties.

Developers are business-oriented. They acquire land and plan for their tourism projects on these sites. Once completed, they often contract operators to manage the business. Developers are profit-driven but are tied to major assets in fixed locations. Operators, who manage the tourism and hospitality businesses on a day-to-day basis, are also profit-driven, but their interest in any specific project extends to the duration of their management contracts with the facility's owners.

Tourists are typically attracted by the leisure potential of the destination, as it is perceived to meet their own needs. They undertake to pay for the apparent value of their expected experience. Residents of resorts have a long-term relationship with the destination, which is generally not dominated by the pursuit of leisure. Resort residents' concerns are those of residents anywhere such as jobs, income, families, and health.

Public involvement in the planning process is somewhat insignificant in Southeast Asia. Similarly, the courts have not played a major role as they have in some developed countries. As noted with the case of Bintan Resorts, individual communities can, on occasion, demonstrate resentment of large-scale tourism development with highly visible protests, blockades, or violence. As seen in the case of Bintan Resorts, there is a need to work in harmony with the community to ensure that investors, management, and the residents work together to achieve mutual benefits. In extreme cases, disruption by communities may mean that tourism development plans are cancelled or subject to review and major changes. Thus, sorting out the different goals, priorities, and agendas of the different actors would be key to the success of development-planning management.

Another issue is the desired versus actual outcomes. Although all actors strive for optimum outcomes, there is often a shortfall. Initial success of a resort will quickly attract more physical development that may outstrip the capacity of local government, which in a less-developed country is most likely to have a limited budget to manage the resort as a whole. Developments may also proceed faster than the capability of national government to fund major infrastructure improvements, such as those for waste removal and treatment. The consequence is a degrading resort ambience that has increasing levels of pollution. This could be seen in Pattaya when environmental and other problems came with the growth of the tourism sector.

Expansion of tourism supply will create more employment that will attract job seekers. Inadequate housing supply and other community services such as health, education, and security further lower the resort quality as squatter settlements expand. Seeking to protect investments and business operations, business leaders will seek to control the political process of the resort, sometimes with a short-term outlook. This can marginalize resident interests.

Conclusion

In conclusion, development-planning management is an important tool that any investors, planners, and managers of destination areas should take seriously. It is key to ensure that developments have some measure of success.

After reviewing the cases on the various planning and development strategies, the recommended approach for tourism development is the comprehensive strategy. An integrated strategy maximizes the benefits and minimizes the pitfalls more effectively than the ad hoc model as seen in Pattaya. The comprehensive strategy addresses tourism development in a comprehensive manner, which will sustain and be advantageous to the developments in the long term.

Investors, planners, and managers of destination areas could take the following tips into consideration. These tips include planning for success, project phasing and roll-out, anticipation of potential environmental degradation and loss of natural ambience, working with communities, and formal and informal commerce.

First, planning should be for success over time. Too often, plans neglect consideration of factors that prove critical for long-term success, thus putting at risk overall project targets.

Second, project phasing and the related timeline for roll-out of the phases are frequently given insufficient attention. Overestimating the rate of demand expansion or following "build it and they will come" thinking results in a disastrous demand-supply imbalance. The consequence is that the revenue cannot service the debt. It is better to let supply be led by demand, thus keeping per capita revenue high.

Third, anticipation of potential environmental degradation and loss of natural ambience as the resort takes on urban characteristics is a key challenge. Research in Southeast Asia has shown that these problems tend to come early in the life of a resort. Strategies that provide for adequate and anticipatory infrastructure expansion will forestall resort degradation.

Last but not least, people who work in resorts have a vested interest in their success because they have a lot at stake. Their well-being and prosperity and that of their families are closely tied to resort fortunes. Having an equitable share in the success of the resort is an important part of the equation. Resort governments, developers, and business operators need to ensure that their communities are educated on the importance of the link between resort success and community prosperity. Demonstration of the flow of benefit to communities must be tangible and have a high public profile. It is only when the community supports the tourism sector that the interests of both will be aligned for success.

Thus, dialogue, productive cooperation, and avoidance of hostile competition between informal and formal tourism business are essential to the success of both the resort and the community. Vendors, who come from the surrounding communities, will therefore be able to see the economic benefits of working alongside the resorts' owners and management, and not be a disruptive force.

To sum up, understanding and implementing the process of development-planning management and applying the comprehensive strategy would certainly help to provide some measure of success in tourism developments.

References

Asian Development Bank. 2000. Cambodia: Building Capacity in Tourism Planning.

Aw Wen Ling, Chen Lihui, and Cherh Kai Leng. 2009. Extending the beach resort model: the case of Pattaya. Unpublished academic paper. Nanyang Technological University.

Barker, Lesley. 2009. Definition of Development Planning. eHow.com.

Bintan Resorts. 2010. http://www.bintan-resorts.com/brcms/.

Charoenpo, A. 2009. Hopes of a more pleasing Pattaya. *Bangkok Post*. April 18.

Coplans, C. 2006. Pattaya refreshed. *Travel Weekly*, Reed Business Information Limited. June 9.

Department of Tourism. 2008. Boracay Island Comprehensive Land Use Plan.

Eamtako, S. 2008. Pattaya aims high. *Travel Trade Gazette*, June 27.

Ettensperger, E. 2001. *Under the Banyan Tree*. Singapore: Pearson.

Government of Malaysia. 1987. Malaysia Comprehensive National Tourism Development.

Government of Malaysia. 1994. Pangkor Tourism Development Study. Government of Malaysia, Ipoh, Perak.

Henderson, Joan C. and Russell A. Smith. 2009. The informal tourism economy at beach resorts: A comparison of Cha-Am and Laguna Phuket in Thailand. *Tourism Recreation Research* 34(1):13–22.

Jafari, Jafar (ed.) 2003. Encyclopedia of tourism. Routledge.

Japan International Corporation Agency. 2008. The study on national integrated strategy of coastal area and master plan for Sihanoukville for sustainable development. Municipality of Sihanoukville, Cambodia.

Johnson, D. 1997. Thailand—returns to all its glory. *Travel Trade Gazette*. June 20:12.

Singapore Tourism Promotion Board. 1996. *Tourism 21: Vision of a Tourism Capital*. STPB.

Smith, Russell Arthur and Joan Henderson. 2008. Integrated beach resorts, informal tourism commerce and the 2004 tsunami. *International Journal of Tourism Research* 10 (3):271–282.

Smith, Russell Arthur. 2000. Tourism planning and development in Southeast Asia and South Asia. In *Tourism in South and Southeast Asia: Issues and Cases*. Hall, Michael and Stephen Page (eds.). Oxford: Butterworth-Heinemann.

Smith, Russell Arthur. 1997. Resort landscapes of the Asia Pacific. *Landscape East* 5:14–16.

Smith, Russell Arthur. 1991. Beach resorts: A model of development evolution. *Landscape and Urban Planning* 21 (3):189–210.

Smith, Russell Arthur. 1998. The role of tourism in urban conservation—The case of Singapore. *Cities* 5 (3):245–259.

Stiles, R.B. and Wilke See-Tho. 1991. Integrated resort development in the Asia Pacific. *Travel and Tourism Analyst* 3:22–37.

The *Jakarta Post*. 2000. Singapore minister and Gus Dur discuss Bintan. January 25.

Tourism Authority of Thailand. Tourism Thailand, 2007. http://www-tourismthailand.org.

Tourism Authority of Thailand. 2006. e-Magazine. August 29.

Tourism Authority of Thailand. 1987. Masterplan for tourism development of Phetchaburi Province and Krachuap Khin Khan Province, Bangkok. Thailand Institute of Scientific and Technological Research.

3

CREATING A WELCOMING SERVICE STRATEGY

By Raymond Bickson

Introduction

"The best way to find yourself is to lose yourself in the service of others."
—Mahatma Gandhi, 20th century pioneer of nonviolent resistance,
spearhead of the Indian independence movement

The heart and soul of India's hospitality style can be summed up in a saying that dates back thousands of years. Like all great wisdom, like all the best strategies, it is simple yet profound.

In Hindi, the saying is *"Atithi devo bhava,"* meaning, "Revere your guest as God." It comes from one of India's oldest Vedic scriptures. But in today's international hospitality environment, when guest histories sometimes serve as a poor substitute for personal touch, when the hotel industry's high employee attrition rate means guests may not see a familiar face the next time they check back in, when amenities try but fail to replace authenticity, the ethos expressed in this phrase is more relevant than ever.

Though Hindus do not have an exclusive on the spiritual element in hospitality, this absolutely and unapologetically spiritual understanding of service in India is the essential core value of Taj Hotels Resorts and Palaces, which is India's oldest and largest hotel company operating under the official name of the Indian Hotels Company Limited. And it will continue to be the core service strategy that will take Taj well into the 21st century.

At its most fundamental, this approach to service may be the most important export India has to offer the global hospitality industry— even more important than spices, teas, *basmati* rice, silks, yoga, and the brilliant wizards of information technology now becoming world-renowned.

While this welcoming spirit is deeply embedded in all Indians' DNA, perhaps in all Asians, it takes much more than natural instinct to deliver the kind of service most guests have come to expect—even from Indians. Though this near deification of the guest is hardwired into Indians, taught and nurtured from their earliest years by their parents and their extended family, and tightly woven in the very fabric of Indian culture, even the finest engine needs a spark to ignite it.

The challenge is heightened when the guests are themselves Indians. Here, even middle-class families are accustomed to having servants, including live-in house cleaners, cooks, and nannies. They are used to being served and are discerning about how they want to be served. When they come to a hotel, where at the end of the day (in fact, 24 hours of every day), service is the most important product they want, they expect and deserve attention that exceeds expectation, especially at the prices the hotels in India hope the guests will pay.

Creating the Taj's Welcoming Spirit

Taj Hotels has developed a number of ways to create the spark that motivates and drives that naturally welcoming spirit of the 22,000 employees at 77 operational Taj Hotels in 14 countries around the world. This spirit of hospitality and generosity permeates the culture of not only the Taj Hotels but also the Tata Group, of which Taj Hotels is the oldest of 96 companies.

Nurturing the Taj's welcoming spirit has become especially important as a service strategy and a marketing thrust in the last few years, as it grew from a brand well-known in India to an internationally recognized name. In India alone, Taj Hotels owns or operates 61 hotels, palaces, resorts, and spa retreats. In the last four years, it has opened six hotels outside of India and plans to open 17 more. The latest to proudly fly the flag of India include such iconic American hotels as the Pierre in New York City, the former Ritz Carlton in Boston, and Campton Place in San Francisco. Yet, even in Taj's home base of India, where it controls some 25 percent of the hotel market share, it has had to refine service operations to remain ahead of the hospitality curve.

The booming Indian economy, well-publicized shortage of hotel rooms, and room rates rivaling those of New York City have attracted intense competition. There are now some 37 brands knocking on Taj's doorstep. Increasingly under pressure, Taj has had to solidify and strongly identify its brand as unique and distinct from all others. These days, longevity and excellence are not enough. The consumer is now a savvy business and leisure traveler, who knows how to separate the wheat from the chaff, how to differentiate the public relations puff from the genuinely substantive, and the virtual from the actual.

That said, Taj seeks to motivate its associates (the preferred term used for its employees) so that they never forget that the primary reason for their job is to assure that every single guest is made to feel like a god. In today's hospitality lingo, the sacred "guest experience" is the Holy Grail and Taj's programs never lose sight of that objective.

India, one of the great cradles of civilization, is a polyglot society and a montage of many influences. It has seen its share of rulers or lords, all of whom left their footprints but none of whom could ultimately suppress the indomitable independent Indian streak. There are 22 official languages in India. One census recorded 1,652 different languages and dialects in India, and in one state alone, Madhya Pradesh, there were 377.

Despite that richly complex history, for a long time India seemed like an idea whose time came . . . and then time passed it by, at least in the eyes of the West.

Then came a period of re-infatuation with all things Eastern starting in the 1960s when young Europeans and Americans rediscovered India's ancient wisdom and traditions, from yoga to meditation to music, food, textiles, and more. These ahead-of-the-curve pilgrims were looking for enlightenment and adventure. What they found were . . . themselves. They were the front-runners of spiritual tourism, which the *New York Times* called "one of the fastest growing segments in the travel industry." (Garfinkle 2006) Dallen Timothy, associate professor at Arizona State University and co-editor of *Tourism, Religion & Spiritual Journeys* (Routledge 2006), said that the niche now embraces weekends at new age spas and wellness centers, yoga and other retreats, metaphysical quests, visits to ancient places such as Stonehenge in England, and journeys in the footsteps of the Buddha in India. He and other tourism experts attributed the increased popularity to the convergence of several factors, including a trend toward vacations that help travelers achieve a higher sense of purpose through volunteering, education, culture, and art. In addition, they cite a rising middle class of expatriate and domestic Asians and Middle Easterners whose religions prescribe traveling to places they hold holy.

In the same article in the *New York Times*, where I, as the managing director of Taj Hotels, have been quoted as saying: "As baby boomers age and gray, they have more time and more disposable income to look within. They used to be the Lonely Planet crowd. Now, still at the cutting edge of the new age, wellness and spiritual frontiers, they continue to travel to feed their souls. They just want to do it without giving up their creature comforts."

So many guests at Taj hotels in India are seeking out spiritual experiences that three years ago, spas catering specifically to this demand were added. As a result, Taj spa program revenues have tripled since then.

Economically, India's spirits have been lifted, riding on the wave of this trend as well as the tourism upswing and the phenomenal business boom in the country.

The World Travel and Tourism Council (WTTC) (2010) expects business and leisure travel both domestically and internationally to produce US$110.7 billion in travel and tourism directly to India's gross domestic product in 2020. Foreign tourist arrivals during 2009 in India were 5.11 million, down 3.3 percent from 5.28 million achieved in 2008. Foreign tourist arrivals had recorded a growth rate of 4 percent in 2008. But the WTTC predicts that travel and tourism demand for India will grow at an average rate of 9.2 percent between 2010 and 2020, making India the second fastest-growing tourist market in the world. Year-on-year growth for India between 2009 and 2010 is estimated at 6.6 percent.

All these influences have converged to help put India in the limelight on the world's center stage. How could Taj take advantage of this historic moment in time, when an abandoned India had become "Brand India," while respecting this country's long and esteemed past and an integrity that transcends time and cultures? This was a significant consideration as Taj developed its service strategies.

The Family: A Service Role Model

Experts such as Lovelock and Wirtz (2004) note that front-line work in the hospitality industry is difficult and stressful because of several job requirements. First, these types of hospitality positions produce person-role conflicts (caused by a discrepancy in job requirements and staff personalities, self-perceptions, and beliefs); organization-client conflicts (generated by a contradiction in guests' demands and company policy); and inter-client conflicts (caused by a disagreement between two guests). Second, front-line workers often suffer from role stress because they are also expected to wear many hats. They may have certain efficiency goals to meet (for example, cleaning so many rooms per hour), but are also expected to stop to meet any guests' requests that may come their way. Finally, the positions of the front-line staff also exacerbate the problem of emotional labor, the difference between the emotions that the staff members feel and the emotions they must portray to the guests.

There is another old Indian saying that guides Taj's service ethos and helps to overcome the daunting elements of the service workers' roles. It is "*Vasudeva Kutumbam,*" which means, "the whole world is one big family." The importance of family in the Indian social structure cannot be overstated. Work and worship rank equally high. But all these begin in the home, within the nucleus of family.

Families that work together are one of India's greatest success stories on the global business landscape. Indeed, four of the top 10 richest men in the world, according to the 2008 *Forbes* list, are from India, and all are family businesses.

Working as a Family

The Tata Group, Taj's parent company, began as a family business and remains in essence a family business. Taj Hotels does not give lip service to the notion of family; Taj associates talk, walk, live, and breathe it. Family is its foundation. And, like any functioning and functional family, Taj takes care of its own. There are a number of ways Taj does this, continually emphasizing that "taking care of our own" motivates "our own" to take care of others just as well—other guests, other colleagues, others in the community, and in the most universal sense, take care of the whole planet.

Thus, in accordance with the philosophy advocated by the service-profit chain (Heskett et al. 1994) in which employee satisfaction is recognized as a strong determinant of customer satisfaction, Taj strives to keep its staff happy. First of all, everyone is an "associate," not an "employee." This is not just splitting linguistic hairs. Though naturally Taj has a chain of command—supervisors, directors, managers, and the rest—it tries as much as possible to treat all associates as equals and with the highest mutual respect. Taj associates are all connected, all part of the same family that operates together toward the same goal—customer satisfaction. Taj does not take this nomenclature lightly, and in rewriting the very way it addresses people within the organization, Taj hopes to change the mindset of the industry in how it views the organization.

Another example is that traditionally, the areas that guests do not see, the area where associates rarely get to interact with guests, is called the "back of the house," giving it and those who work there a seemingly diminutive position in the hospitality hierarchy. Taj, on the other hand, calls this area the "heart of the house," in recognition that the jobs done off stage, as it were, and the people who execute those jobs are the lifeblood of the business.

Recognizing STARS Associates

To emphasize just how important this attitude is within the fabric of the Taj tapestry, 2008 was declared "The Year of the Associate" (YOA). Through this program, Taj is sending the message that if the guest is to be treated like a god, then its associates must be treated as though they too are deities.

The YOA initiative celebrates Taj's greatest asset and secret weapon, which is no secret at all: the members of the Taj family. The YOA program encourages associates' creativity and participation at all levels in proposing new ideas, innovations, and improvements. These elements, in turn, nurture an atmosphere that is congenial and enjoyable to work in.

The program offers associates such opportunities as:

- Taj Idol, a singing competition styled after the popular TV program, "Indian Idol," a contest aimed at finding the country's best amateur performers

- Precious Health, health camps for associates and their families

- Birthday celebrations, complimentary meals for the associate and three others at any of their hotel's eating establishments

- Special occasion weekends, two-day, completely complimentary stays at any Taj hotel for newlyweds and retirees

A primary objective of this program is to encourage associate retention and loyalty to the Taj brand. Keeping staff members happy and loyal has become a major concern in an industry where turnover rates are about 50 percent for non-management positions and 25 percent for management—among the highest of any industry, according to J. Bruce Tracey, Associate Professor of Management at Cornell University's School of Hotel Administration.

Taj underscores its employee initiative with a tagline "Unleashing people power." In conjunction with that theme, Taj has developed a motivational incentive program that encourages associates to aspire to excellence in their performances, awarding and recognizing them before the entire Taj family.

Through a well-organized and well-tracked system, associates accumulate points for delivering what Taj calls "wows" and "delights" to guests. Such points can be earned when associates provide suggestions to their department heads and when associates receive written compliments from guests or colleagues. While Taj takes pride in its fine furnishings, architectural gems, and magnificent landscapes, the whole idea is to showcase its real stars. In fact, Taj calls the programs STARS, which stands for "Special Thanks & Recognition System." Established in 2000, it is the first standardized Taj-wide recognition program, the first employee-recognition programs of its kind in India's hospitality industry, and the first to use a web-based platform.

The Taj Hotels' STARS program won the prestigious Hermes International Hospitality Award for the best innovation in human resource in 2002. This recognition comes from the affirmation of a 22-member jury, comprising representatives from top hospitality chains from across the world, who chose Taj from among 120 applications in the human resource category. Since then, STARS remains a powerful and effective motivational tool. One barometer of its success is Taj's employee retention and loyalty figures. Attrition rates hover at about 12 percent for both management and non-management positions. Significantly, the attrition of high performers is lower as it is not unusual for Taj employees to have stayed with the company for 20, 30, and even more years. Since the implementation of this system, Taj has retained more than 47 percent of employees for more than 10 years, another 18 percent have been retained for more than five years, and 24 percent have stayed between two and five years. In keeping with its diversity goals,

Taj emphasizes a strong focus on attracting and retaining women at all levels. Taj has more than 600 executives who have committed heart and soul to Taj for at least 20 years.

The STARS program is further supported by an annual Academy Awards-like ceremony, initiated in 2004, called The Taj Awards for Business Excellence—the TABEs. If there were any questions on how well this program works, the decibel of noise such as applause, standing ovations, hoots, howls, and whistling that accompany the announcement of each "star" would put any doubt to rest as to the degree to which this program has been embraced by associates.

The following are examples of the kind of over-the-top demonstrations of "wows" that Taj honored at the last TABE awards, stories about acts of selflessness—the very essence of "people power"—by associates, who rose to the occasion and showed grit and determination. These two stories represent the ways extraordinary service can be made to seem ordinary and the ordinary can be made to seem extraordinary.

Firstly, the truly dramatic story of the security team at our Taj Ambassador Hotel in New Delhi. When Brijpal Singh noticed smoke coming from a residence near the hotel, he and the rest of the Taj security team rushed to the scene. When no one answered repeated knocking and shouts, they broke into the flat and found it engulfed in a cloud of smoke. Promptly opening the windows, they then searched the apartment and found the owner unconscious on the floor. They administered first aid to the victim, and at the same time called for the fire department and the hospital, both of which rushed over. Meanwhile, the Taj team ran back to the hotel and returned with fire extinguishers, controlling the raging flames even before the fire fighters arrived. If they had not done so, not just the Taj Ambassador Hotel but the entire neighborhood would have erupted in flames. To Taj's security team, it was all in day's work, just the way they define "security."

Secondly, guests who take the daily delivery of their favorite newspaper as an indispensable given will see the heroism in this "star," who is from the same Ambassador Hotel in New Delhi. When one of Taj's loyal guests walked into the Ambassador Hotel without a reservation on a night when the hotel was operating at 100 percent capacity, (as were sister properties in New Delhi), the Taj duty manager quickly got on the phone to find another accommodation suitable for the guest. After much calling, he found a single room at another hotel and the guest was whisked over there in one of the Taj's house cars. Meanwhile, unbeknown to the guest or the duty manager, an Ambassador Hotel bell attendant saw the familiar face at our front desk and naturally assumed he was checking back in. So, following the guest's Customer Information Service data, he ordered the guest's favorite but hard-to-find daily read, the *Marathi*.

The next day, the bell attendant was disappointed to learn the facts but he went beyond passive disappointment to pro-action. He called the other hotel and suggested it deliver the guest's favorite paper to him. But the other hotel did not subscribe to *Marathi* and was unwilling to follow through. A dimmer star would have let it go at that. Not to be discouraged, as soon as he was off-duty, the bell attendant personally delivered the paper to the man at the other hotel. Speechless, the guest hugged him in the lobby while that hotel team looked on, probably equally speechless. Wow!

They do not teach that at travel, hospitality, and tourism schools around the world, nor would you find it in the hotel trainee manuals. But it is what elevates service from strategy, simply based on who and what the associates are. When giving is in the staff's DNA, all you have to do is energize their natural welcoming and giving spirit.

Serving the Extended Family: Community and the Planet

You could call it the *tao* of Taj Service. The notion of the interconnectedness of all things extends beyond taking care of Taj guests and taking care of its associates. Taj management strongly believes that each of its hotels does not exist in a vacuum. Each is part of the local community, and in the tradition of "*Vasudeva Kutumbam*," giving back to its neighbors is just simply what one should do for one's own big family.

The spirit of generosity—of altruism, of supporting others, of seeing to the needs of others even before one's own—is an attribute Taj does not have to teach most Indians. It is intrinsic to them.

Sharing the bounty of their table has been part of the Tata Group values since its beginnings. The founders of the Tata Group bequeathed most of their personal wealth to the many trusts they created for the greater good of India and its people. Today, the Tata trusts control 65.8 percent of the shares of Tata Sons, the holding company of the group.

The wealth that accrues from this asset supports an assortment of causes, institutions, and individuals in a wide variety of areas.

As a service strategy, Taj continues to model the same behavior of generosity it hopes its associates will adopt. It also hopes its guests respect this level of generosity enough to follow Taj's lead and commit to random acts of giving too.

Among the projects Taj is involved in are:

1. Building Sustainable Livelihoods for Rural Youth

To foster market relevant skills and employment opportunities among unemployed youth from socioeconomically disadvantaged backgrounds, the Taj Residency Aurangabad and the Institute of Hotel Management, also based in Aurangabad, are offering 300 students a year a hotel operational skills training program. The training includes delivering a variety of skill sets relevant to the hospitality sector such as English communication and presentation, cooking, and house-keeping (cleaning, laundry, and ironing). The industry exposure for the trainees shall be affected through a self-learning module developed for their hands-on training.

2. Building Sustainable Livelihoods for Impaired Individuals

At Taj Hotels in Mumbai and elsewhere, hearing-impaired youths are assisted in developing professional competence in culinary skills necessary for commercial food-production operation, thereby increasing their employability in the hospitality industry. In association with the Deeds Catering Institute for the Deaf & Dumb, Taj offers apprenticeships to 20 hearing-impaired students a year. Each student who completes the program and passes a year-end examination becomes certified through the Maharashtra State Vocational Board.

Taj Hotels helps in developing the culinary course, offering exposure to the industry through apprenticeships and stipends to cover the course, and apprenticeship reimbursements. A by-product of the program is that it helps develop hope and self-confidence.

The *tao* of Taj Service goes beyond its hotels, its communities, India, Asia, and the international mosaic of countries. Ultimately, everyone at Taj is in service to the precious but precarious planet, of which all are its citizens, guests, and hosts. As stewards of the earth,

Taj is honored to be its protector, following a philosophy that supports sustainability and leaves as light a footprint as is possible in the hospitality industry.

Taj Hotels has long been at the forefront of developing eco-friendly policies. But times change, weather changes, winds shift, and the planet revolves. Impermanence is probably the only permanence on which one can depend in life.

Which is why Taj, in an effort to stay current with the changing times, and in line with its responsibility as a planetary host, announced a new environmental program mission statement in 2008.

To boost sustainable tourism and integrate environmental management in all business areas, Taj Hotels Resorts and Palaces created EARTH (Environment Awareness & Renewal at Taj Hotels). EARTH has received certification from Green Globe, which is the only worldwide environmental certification program for travel and tourism. Green Globe will provide the EARTH project with independent and comprehensive proof of Taj's environmental commitment. It does this through the monitoring and improvement reports that it will produce for Taj Hotels each year as part of the certification procedure.

EARTH will focus on spearheading several efforts, primarily in the engineering and energy conservation areas. It adds to several initiatives under the existing Eco Taj Policy, which addresses many aspects such as conserving energy and water, purchasing eco-products, and minimizing waste. In London alone, for example, Taj's 51 Buckingham Gate Hotel has reduced energy consumption by more than 22 percent, cut natural gas consumption by more than 32 percent, and lowered water usage and costs by 25 percent since 2005.

In another example, from June to July 2008, Taj took the initiative to convert all heart-of-the-house areas to energy-efficient lighting. That meant replacing all normal incandescent bulbs of 60 watts with energy-efficient CFL bulbs of 11 watts that produce the same light output. By September 2008, Taj was 100 percent energy-efficient in those areas.

To really assure the planet's health, all environment initiatives must start at home. To that end, Taj arranged with a major lighting company to conduct educational road shows and offer energy-efficient lamps at discounted prices for the private homes of its associates. This program met with huge success.

The Architecture of Service: A Strategic Reorganization

Taj has many guest services and programs. Some surprise, delight, and dazzle the guests, and Taj is quite proud and protective of these. And there are some services, which seem obvious, predictable, and expected of a hotel of Taj's caliber—nothing you have not seen or heard or experienced personally at hotels from Tokyo to Dubai.

However, there is a service strategy that folds neatly into Taj's overall philosophy that underscores its main aim—to provide whatever guests need, at whatever level of service they desire. Taj considers offering guests an assortment of services to match what they want as a crucial part of the Taj's strategy. These are guests, whether business, leisure, or group travelers, who are increasingly travel savvy and, at the same time, increasingly budget-conscious.

As such, in September 2008, Taj announced a reorganization of its hotel categories, devised in conjunction with Landor & Associates, the branding and market positioning strategy consultancy firm. Working within globally accepted classification standards established by Smith Travel Research and Deloitte, this new brand architecture distinguishes Taj's portfolio of hotels while still assuring the quality of service to which its guests have become accustomed. Remaining under the umbrella of its official name, the Indian Hotels Company Limited, Taj has organized the brands in a way that will quickly, and eventually intuitively, advise guests as to what type and level of service they can expect when they book a room with Taj so that they will know exactly how big a bang they will get for their buck, rupee, yen, or euro. Here is a short breakdown:

- Luxury: Taj Hotels Resorts and Palaces is the flagship brand for the world's most discerning travelers seeking authentic experiences. Spanning world-renowned landmarks, modern business hotels, idyllic beach resorts, authentic Rajput palaces, and rustic safari lodges, each Taj Hotel reinterprets the tradition of hospitality in a refreshingly modern way to create unique experiences and lifelong memories. With this brand, Taj goes head-to-head with the world's top-tiered five-star hotels.

- Upper Upscale: Vivanta by Taj Hotels & Resorts is a new category, equivalent to four-star hotels. These hotels come from the former Residency family, delivering all the quality of luxury but custom-tailored to target the savvy business traveler.

- Upscale: Gateway Hotels & Resorts is the three-star entry, an upscale and mid-market full-service brand. This pan-India network offers business and leisure travelers a hotel for the modern nomad. At the Gateway Hotel, things are kept simple. Consequently, the hotels are divided into seven simple zones: Stay, Hangout, Meet, Work, Workout, Unwind, and Explore.

- Economy: Ginger is the revolutionary concept in hospitality for the value segment. Intelligently designed facilities, consistency, and affordability are hallmarks of this brand targeted at travelers who value simplicity and self-service.

Taj Hotels strongly feel that, as a service strategy, these four categories streamline the decision-making process for the guest. It also keeps Taj apace with the changing demographics of its guests as well as their evolving multifaceted needs. And it helps Taj as we move into the future, giving Taj more focus and structure at the same time diversifying and augmenting the product line, fulfilling guests needs on the one hand and their fantasies on the other.

Express Checkout: Conclusion

Of course, if God were truly your guest, one assumes He is so all for-giving and compassionate that He would, in His omniscience, overlook the cold tea or the merely lukewarm shower, or the complacent bell-man or the fact that His reservation fell through the cracks. He would see whatever service was provided as coming from the heart and the service provider could do no wrong.

Taj wishes all its guests were *that* godly! But increasingly discern-ing guests know that they have many choices and if they are not sat-isfied with how Taj treats them, they will not return. A hotelier does not need to be omniscient to know the same. That is why after all is said and done, after the 1,000-thread-count bed sheets, marquee chef in your destination restaurant, and original paintings in your lobby, it all comes down to how well the guests are served. It all comes down to the people who serve the guests. That is why Taj has put so much emphasis on its associate training and development.

Taj has created a family culture, capitalizing on the family culture that is so strong in India. This feeling of family ensures that Taj takes care of its employees, who in turn, care of the guests. Furthermore, the sense of family has encouraged staff to remain with Taj—one does not leave family. As a result of the staff's longevity, these associates can provide better service because they know their jobs very well, know the hotel and community very well, and can readily recognize repeat guests and the special needs of these guests.

In Hawaii, the native surfers have a saying that serves well at Taj Hotels: "*Hō a'e 'ike he'enalu i ka hokua o ka 'ale.*" It means, "Show your surfing skills on the back of the wave." In other words, talk is just . . . talk. The proof is in the experience. Guests know they are being embraced by the welcoming spirit the moment they come into its presence—the moment they step from the cab to the curb and are greeted by a warm face that makes them feel as though they have arrived "home," even when that home is 10,000 miles from where they live. The moment their glass is refilled even before they ask someone to do it. The moment their laundry arrives long before they need it. The moment they rest their heads on a bed and sink into the most heavenly, restful, and undisturbed sleep they have ever had.

It is then that the associates at Taj know they have done their job and done it well. Finally, Taj's management extends an open invitation to guests to test its service strategy in action, and be embraced by the Taj welcoming spirit for rest (and the rest) of your life.

References

Garfinkel, Perry. 2006. Easing the inward journey, with modern amenities. New York Times. December 24. http://travel.nytimes .com/2006/12/24/business/yourmoney/24spirit.html?fta=y.

Heskett, James L., Thomas O. Jones, Gary W. Loveman, W. Earl Sasser, Jr., and Leonard A. Schlesinger. 1994. Putting the service-profit chain to work. Harvard Business Review (March–April):164–174.

Lovelock, Christopher and Jochen Wirtz. 2004. Services Marketing: People, Technology, Strategy, Fifth ed. Upper Saddle River, NJ: Pearson/Prentice Hall.

Timothy, Dallen J. and Daniel Olsen. 2006. Tourism, Religion, and Spiritual Journeys. London & New York: Routledge.

World Travel and Tourism Council. 2010. Travel and Tourism Economic Impact 2010. London: World Travel and Tourism Council.

4

WINNING WAYS TO SUCCESSFUL PORTFOLIO MANAGEMENT

By William E. Heinecke

Introduction

Minor International Public Company Limited (MI) is a multinational enterprise that owns and operates international hotels, resorts, and spas, in addition to diverse restaurant and retail operations. It is one of the largest hospitality and leisure companies in the Asia-Pacific region with more than 1,000 restaurants and 30 hotels and resorts worldwide. The hotel division started in 1976 with a small beachfront venture in Pattaya, Thailand. Since then, the company has expanded to include world-renowned brands such as Four Seasons, Marriott, and Anantara. The company, headquartered in Bangkok, operates in Thailand, Vietnam, the Middle East, Sri Lanka, the Maldives, Indonesia, and Africa, and is pushing ahead with projects in India, Morocco, and Cape Verde. In the *Condé Nast Traveler* Readers Choice Awards, November 2008, five of the top 25 resorts in Asia were owned by MI.

In addition to its award-winning hotels and resorts, the company also runs the 30 Mandara and Anantara Spas that have consistently been named as the best in Asia and among the best in the world. Anantara Hotels, Resorts, & Spas operates more than 11 upscale and luxury properties across four major markets: Thailand, Bali, the Maldives, and Abu Dhabi in the United Arab Emirates. Complementing these hospitality operations is a food group that includes many household names such as The Pizza Company, Swensen's, Sizzler, Dairy Queen, Burger King, and The Coffee Club. In 2007, 800 restaurants in Thailand alone served 70 million customers.

MI, which started more than 40 years ago, has always operated a portfolio of different interests rather than adopting a single-focus approach. The very first companies registered were a cleaning firm and an advertising agency—one can hardly get more diverse than that!

Since then, MI has steadily grown through a blend of partnerships with global, best-in-class companies and the development of its own businesses across many different markets and geographies. This strategy has enabled MI to take a clear view on the relative importance of great people and great brands in building a successful portfolio of businesses, reflecting the philosophy that brands do not build people, people build brands. The success that MI brands have enjoyed is a reflection of the great people in the group.

Working together, the people in MI have built brands that are market leaders and have managed this through initiative, focus, and above all, passion. These are the qualities needed for success and which must be instilled in the staff of any broad-based company. MI has always measured itself against the best in the world because every day, its 20,000-plus employees must compete against the best in a competitive global market.

As MI enters its fourth decade, the business model continues to evolve. From its early roots pioneering the introduction of franchises into Thailand to the development of its resorts, spas, and restaurant brands, it continues to innovate the management of its multibrand strategy.

With the completion of the acquisition and subsequent delisting of the Minor Food Group in January 2005, a majority of the company's revenues are not hotel-related. Its aspirations are to expand internationally beyond its roots in Thailand through its branded hotel, spa, and food services. To better reflect its current and future business operations, while also leveraging on the rich heritage and recognition of the Minor Group, it completed a name change in February 2005 to Minor International Public Company Limited and is now listed on the Stock Exchange of Thailand.

This chapter serves as a journey within MI, similar to a train ride. Along the way, the train will be stopping at stations such as leadership, branding, and the importance of people. At each stop, a very personal view as to what has helped the company succeed where others have failed is presented.

Obviously in a single chapter, all aspects of portfolio management cannot be covered. Instead, this chapter will take a sideways view at what matters to MI. It is unlikely that the same perspective will be found in other management books, as this perspective is the MI's approach.

Pursuing a Multibrand Strategy

The definition of a multibrand strategy is striving to gain competitive advantage through the marketing of multiple, similar and competing products under different and unrelated brands. While these brands may compete for the same "share of stomach" or "share of wallet," a multibrand strategy has many advantages. It can reduce the amount of space available to competitors, allow companies to offer different products that fill price and quality gaps, and also cater to brand switchers, namely users who like to experiment with and experience different brands. It enables a more flexible product offering, enabling one to enter different geographies or market segments, or compete at different price points. Finally, it also has the advantage of keeping the managers of the group on their toes by generating some internal competition. It, of course, can have its pitfalls too, and those issues are discussed later.

One of the MI's strengths under a multibrand strategy is being able to leverage more than one of its brands in a single setting. For example, two hotel brands are often located close to each other, or a residential component is integrated within a hotel development. It has also opened its restaurant brands in shopping malls next to MI's hotels. This has obvious benefits. By placing two of the franchise restaurants, for example, Swensen's and Burger King, right next to each other, delivery costs from the warehouse can be reduced. Or MI can open a world-class spa within an Anantara Resort to provide a fantastic and unique guest experience.

In the northern Thailand province of Chiang Rai is an area known as the "Golden Triangle". It is where the borders of Thailand, Laos, and Burma come together, along the banks of the Mekong River. This part of Thailand is infamous for the opium trade and the subsequent opium wars between Britain and China back in the early 19th century. Today, it is a home for many cultural and agricultural projects developed under the initiative of the Royal Family of Thailand to protect the proud history and heritage of this country. It also provides the indigenous setting for Thailand's elephants. Although there are almost no wild elephants any more in Thailand, the northern provinces were the original home of these creatures, and the forests and woods provide their natural habitat.

In the "Golden Triangle," MI owns the Four Seasons Tented Camp, which has been generating praise, awards, and recognition since it opened in 2005. In November 2008, the hotel was voted number one by the *Condé Nast Traveler* Readers Choice Awards, as "Best of the Best" of the top 100 hotels worldwide.

There are 15 "tents" (much too humble a word) that provide luxury accommodation to our guests who come from all over the world. Around the other side of the same hill sits a second luxury resort owned and operated by MI—the Anantara Golden Triangle. It operates in the upper-upscale space rather than the pure luxury of the Four Seasons experience. This hotel is also featured in the *Condé Nast Traveler* Readers Choice Awards, coming 24th in the roundup of best hotels in Asia.

The advantages of having these two MI portfolio properties co-located are immediately obvious. The Anantara provides many guest services shared by the two hotels including laundry and bakery. While the hotels compete to a degree, they cooperate on purchasing, engineering, and other back-of-house issues to the benefit of both. And finally, the Anantara runs the Golden Triangle Elephant Foundation, which is one of the cornerstones of MI's corporate social responsibility program. Today, the foundation looks after 16 adult and 15 baby elephants on 820 rai (320 acres) of land. In addition, MI is feeding, housing, and schooling the 58 traditional *mahouts* (a person who drives an elephant), along with their wives and children. Guests from both properties can interact with these elephants such as bathing, feeding, and going on cross-country treks with them, thus creating an unforgettable experience and providing some amazing stories.

In the Maldives, MI has introduced a model of a luxury, five-star 160-room boutique resort, supporting a smaller, higher-priced, and truly unique experience of around 20 rooms with the Anantara Dhigu, Anantara Veli, and Naladhu properties. In that operation, a single leadership team for even greater efficiencies operates these three resorts, which cater for different high-end audiences. Looking further abroad, MI partners with a hospitality group in Sri Lanka. In that locale, there are three existing properties already earmarked for upgrade and reopening under the Anantara brand. Sri Lanka is one of the great brand names of international tourism—only Bali comes close in my view—and

MI continues to be very positive about the prospects of luxury tourism in Sri Lanka once they solve their internal political conflicts.

This multibrand diversification can also have the added bonus of keeping revenues healthy during periods of crisis or market downturn. During the scare over severe acute respiratory syndrome (SARS) in 2003 and 2004, hotel bookings across Asia plummeted. MI's operations in Bangkok and Pattaya were strongly supported by the restaurants' revenue from the retail malls next door, and its food outlets achieved dynamic growth and performance as the local market continued to spend while the international tourist market temporarily dried up. Consequently, MI was able to switch resources between different entities to reduce the impact on the overall business.

Ultimately, there is value in the flexibility of being able to apply multiple brands to each business ventures. There are several great destinations where MI is present in great depth, for example, Bangkok. The company could not possibly have grown this big with just a single brand in each sector.

Driving the Asset: Deciding what Brand to Place on an Asset

At MI, managing a large and varied portfolio has become something of an art form. The organization is adept at making decisions about which brands to apply to which market opportunities. This is because MI does not allow ego to become part of the decision-making process. In Asia and the Middle East in particular, many hotel developments are ultimately ego projects, overbuilt to such a degree that they have no possible chance of generating a commercially attractive rate of return. They provide venues for that owner to entertain and be recognized.

One has to be careful how branding decisions are made because the wrong brand can easily be placed on an asset, and then the company will suffer over the long term. The problem for some companies is that they may acquire a site that is only worth a four-star hotel, but they cannot resist putting a luxury brand there. When MI looks at sites, management immediately starts working on what the best brand will be for that opportunity from a commercial perspective. There is no room for ego in hotel branding because opportunities will be wasted and a proper return on investment will not be achieved. As much as

MI appreciates its own in-house brands, the organization is always conscious that for any location, there might be more money to be made by working with a partner's brand such as St. Regis or Four Seasons, especially when its brands are already present.

Rebranding also presents many opportunities. Over the years, MI has taken over a number of hotels, upgraded, and then rebranded them under the Anantara Resorts brand. In many cases, this has led to more than doubling of occupancy and average daily rates. The results are the power of branding and the power of great brand management.

In Phuket, MI had a beautiful site where it developed 82 pool villas. These are individual accommodations with their own villa, plunge pool, large outdoor deck, and dining pavilion. The site sits adjacent to the JW Marriott Phuket Hotel, which MI also owns. Originally, MI was going to offer the site to Ritz Carlton to develop a stand-alone Ritz Carlton resort, which is one of Marriott's own family of brands. But the team that runs the JW Marriott brand expressed strong interest in incorporating the villas as part of the high-end room category of their own property. MI reviewed that proposal but the consensus was that the JW Marriott had reached its optimal level at 250 rooms and suites, and to add another 82 keys would be wrong. So MI decided that a much better yield would be obtained by using the site to create a separate resort operation. And so, the Anantara Phuket was born, and opened in October 2008. It is now our Anantara flagship in Southeast Asia. There are no rooms and no suites, just luxury pool villas, each with perfect privacy, indoors and outdoors. There is a peace and tranquillity about the site that is like nowhere else in Asia.

So having originally looked at working with a third-party, MI eventually decided to choose another brand from its own portfolio. This is all part of managing a multibrand portfolio without ego entering the decision-making process. Sometimes, it is better not to expand or overexpand one brand but to add a new one. If the site had been given to JW Marriott, would they have made more money for MI by running 250 hotel rooms and suites and 82 associated pool villas? Or will it make more money by being a stand-alone Anantara? MI believes that it will maximize returns under the latter structure. Time will tell.

In the meantime, MI's brands have been a real public-relations success. Its new hotels receive a lot of coverage in the top travel magazines and publications. Creating properties and brands that garner attention and find their way into leading publications encourages guests to visit the hotels.

Delivering Value and Tracking the Portfolio's Results

People sometimes perceive a disconnection in the fact that MI owns both fast food outlets and Four Seasons hotels. The appropriate response to such criticism is that a Four Seasons guest is just as value-conscious as the man on the street. No brand will survive unless it delivers great value, be it a hotel room or a pizza. Consequently, at MI, investment decisions are often based on pedestrian observation. If people like something in one country or marketplace, other people are also very likely to enjoy the same thing on the other side of the world if it is presented with a twist and in a relevant way.

MI has maintained the most outstanding financial numbers. At the end of the day, all companies are measured for better or worse by financial performance and obviously, success or failure is easy to validate on that basis. The company has a great reputation and wins many awards for being the fastest-growing company in terms of market capitalization and shareholder value. Ultimately, that is why people have invested in MI—to see their investment grow. That is simply a fact that must be accepted when a business decides to become a publicly traded company. That is how the banks look at the organization.

And frankly that is what potential employees look at before they decide to join the company. They want to know how financially solid the company is. Nobody wants to work for a company that has a great brand but is financially weak. To do so means running the risk of having careers disrupted by acquisitions, mergers, and all the challenges of financial weakness, including cost control, consolidation, and withdrawing from target markets. MI's difficulties have always been the challenges of growth such as where to best invest resources, how to prioritize acquisitions, where to place the best people for their own benefit and the company's benefit, and how to maximize asset performance.

In 2008, MI operated approximately 1,000 quick-service restaurants under its own brand, The Pizza Company, and also brands, such as Dairy Queen, Burger King, Sizzler, and Swensen's, where its has taken franchise positions. The quick-service food business is fortunately a very cash-oriented business. Customers pay with money not credit cards, and no one pays 90 days in arrears for their hamburgers. This gives MI a very strong liquidity position, which is recognized and valued by the marketplace, both in MI's share price and also in its ability to raise capital. That capital is then available to expand the operations of all MI's businesses in food, luxury hotels, and property development. It is a mutually supportive model, which has enabled the company to consistently create customer value and deliver strong financial results.

There are many occasions where MI could be in danger of being sentimental in making a business decision, but ultimately management is reminded that they are being judged by their performance. The reality is that only the fittest companies are going to survive. A firm can only live on a reputation for so long and then it is out of business. Companies that overstretch themselves or have relied for too long on past achievements are history. It is as simple as that.

Several years ago, MI introduced a process of tracking all its operational leaders against key performance indicators (KPIs). These KPIs are specific to each leader's overall business, and to their own individual functional responsibilities. KPIs are defined on a balanced scorecard basis, with metrics defined within the areas of financial results, customer satisfaction, internal process improvements, and learning and growth. All metrics are quantifiable and are tracked monthly, quarterly, and annually. They are also linked to the annual incentive process. This ensures that the incentive process is much more objective, and also that people are focusing on the key activities they need to complete in order for the group to deliver against overall strategy. The business is able to clearly identify and communicate how MI is doing against its key targets. Its scorecard enables it to immediately divert focus and resources as required to ensure that it remains on track to deliver against overall strategy.

Importance of Geography in Investment Decisions

Geography is a factor which businesses do not pay sufficient attention to in its own right, both as a strength and opportunity but also as a weakness or threat. Certainly, one of the main reasons to be in different countries is to maximize financial returns. Such a strategy allows the organization to expose its offerings to a wider audience who becomes familiar with them. Ideally they will sample it locally and, in the case of hotels, may even travel internationally to experience it again, recreated and represented in a different way.

Geography is also relevant when it comes to spreading risk. It allows the firm to diversify, working in different markets with different political- and economic-risk profiles. Generally speaking, the ebb and flow of the global economic climate means that there is usually at least one market where business conditions are strong for every market where conditions may be adverse, and in this way overall returns are protected.

However, branching into new geographies also carries serious risks, which are very often underestimated. One needs to learn and get famil- iar with a whole new business culture—in operations, human resource (HR), supplier relations, and marketing. This means sourcing and hiring more people with all those consequent hiring risks, and in parallel, the need to orient and train those people so that the core brand message does not get diluted. Shortly after that, comes an internal pres- sure to set up nonrevenue-generating corporate offices, each with well- paid executives and a pyramid of staff underneath them. A matrix-driven organization starts to emerge. Lines of communication get stretched and the best executives start spending more time on airplanes and less time out in the field directly supporting and driving the business.

Unless very strictly controlled, this situation becomes a breeding ground for corporate politics, the emergence of local priorities that are not aligned with overall strategy, and other negative factors. Suddenly, senior management finds that the time previously spent productively driving business is now spent in managing internal structure. It is best to take great care to minimize the proliferation of satellite corporate offices. MI is happy to have operational units that directly generate revenue around the world, but does not tolerate those profits disap- pearing to support a fat corporate structure at head office, or in regional and national offices.

It is important to MI that each of its resorts has a strong sense of place and is compatible with its surroundings. With the Anantara Resorts brand, it has worked very hard to create an experience for each guest, which is authentic to the location of each resort. Management recognizes that even if guests choose to stay in a hotel that is part of a large chain, they like to feel they are in touch with the community around them. This concept gets lost with many hotel brands. Head offices run these brands in a centralized way in which everything looks the same. But at Anantara in particular, MI takes a different approach. A guest will always know they are in an Anantara. While every resort has its common features, there are indigenous touches that will really catch people's attention. Within its spa business, for example, Anantara has sand compresses at the spas in United Arab Emirates, while in Thailand, there are treatments developed from local produce such as tamarind or rice. Maximum creativity is encouraged within each brand because modern travelers have very sophisticated tastes and want much more than the opportunity to lie every day on a sun-lounger.

Another part of creating an interesting portfolio is not being afraid of going into secondary locations. Obviously, MI has great resorts in excellent primary locations such as Bangkok and Phuket, but its operations in secondary locations create some excitement within the portfolio, and are often the ones that underpin the unique nature of the brand. What one cannot do is get carried away building only small hotels in secondary destinations and go bankrupt while striving for brand uniqueness. MI has been very successful at balancing the marketing message with the commercial reality. Marketing people sometimes come along and say: "This could be such a fabulous hotel." But that is not necessarily what makes a great company or a good business. A better model is in the Maldives where something really special has been created and it makes a great return also!

Selecting Business Partners

This section returns to the importance of people. As a company enters new markets, people become more critical—inside the company and outside. When MI wants to move into a market where it lacks expertise, then it seeks out the people who are the experts. It has used this tactic in Sri Lanka, the Maldives, and also in the new markets it is currently moving into in East Africa and the Middle East. In its food business, MI has partnered with companies in Singapore and Australia. This kind of partnership is very much part of its culture and part of its formula for success.

There should be close involvement with each potential business partnership, whether that is an equity investment, a franchise relationship, or a management agreement. It is important to know the investors and their business partners well. What motivates them personally, how do they judge the success or failure of their businesses, what are the core values of their companies? Understanding these constituents on multiple levels is a key part of leading a company.

All of MI's partnerships share the common trait of being passionate about the business and the people involved. The true test of a business relationship is when the partnership is losing money. In that situation, each partner needs to know that there is respect, open communication, and commitment from the other side. Those partnerships are the ones that can be turned around. The fundamentals are solid, and those partners can look each other in the eye and plan for recovery.

Keep Looking for New Opportunities

MI's approach to portfolio management involves a structured review of the risk and return relationship on each project. In each of its business units, it has small teams of people who are very experienced in deal analysis, and indeed, it considers and assesses a great many deals each year. Each investment opportunity is evaluated based on company goals and the defined appetite for risk. Where cash flows or risks are volatile, a risk premium may be required. Some key risk factors that MI considers separately and collectively are political risk, currency risk, terrorism risk, and the price of commodities.

Generally speaking, building any portfolio of investments means taking into account the following key strategies:

- Define the framework and map out the investment strategy. Include investment criteria, returns required, business locations, commitment of funds, and key executives required to deliver the plan.

- Ensure the strategy can be measured with key milestones. Put in place plans to deliver these. Identify opportunities to acquire assets below market value or with an upside opportunity to unlock value. For example, being able to further develop and add more rooms, real-estate opportunities, and other revenue generating facilities.

- Due diligence is an important factor. Ensure that enough research is completed before committing to an investment. The due diligence process includes market analysis, financial, legal, taxation, and human resource matters.

- Perform sensitivity analysis and ensure that minimum hurdle rates and returns are met.

- Know the exit strategy.

Today, the investment required in hotel developments is so huge that one probably cannot survive by just creating a hotel. Other components have to be added which help spread risk and assist in justifying the hotel investment. Sometimes, the hotel is the cornerstone of the development and the asset mix, and sometimes, it is not. So that is another part of the portfolio challenge, managing the portfolio of different kinds of revenue-generating sources that one has within a hotel.

MI is always open to new opportunities even if it is not immediately obvious how the relationship will play out in the long term. In Vietnam, it was offered a hotel in a town called Haiphong. This hotel is in a location that defied branding. Nobody else wanted it, nobody would provide the management for it, and so the company had to come up with some imaginative solutions in order to take on this project. The hotel is in a harbour, so it was renamed Harbour View, and it has been successful. One of the key advantages of this project is that it has allowed MI a first taste of operating in Vietnam, and over the past 10 years, it has built a team of people who understand the hospitality market in Vietnam and the nuances of labor and government relations required to build in a new market. Admittedly, it was difficult at the start, but what MI learned from the Haiphong Harbour View Hotel has given it the platform from which to launch multiple future resorts in Vietnam.

The truth is that MI would rather be involved in the creation of 100 or 200 exciting hotels than to be part of 3,000 hotels. While those massive hotel groups are respected, they may become machines that pump out hotel after hotel. With its properties, because the company is still small enough for its key people to get personally involved in each venture, the human touch is still very visible. Guests can still see the company culture come through, whether it is in the room design, food, or activities on offer. The big companies with 3,000 hotels cannot possibly expect to offer that genuine personalized touch, which MI can do effectively as a smaller hotel group.

People Leading Our Portfolio of Businesses

Today, the pressures on all professionals are greater than ever. Consumers are getting smarter and more sophisticated, with much more information available to them through the Internet and other media. General managers of resorts have to be a master of much more than just the elements of a traditional resort operation. They have to be aware of spa trends and where that very interesting health and wellness conversation is going to evolve over the next five years. They have to be experts in new food and beverage (F&B) concepts and in running a retail operation in their lobbies. They must understand e-commerce, and how to reach and maximize bookings from that very valuable segment of the guest mix, which books directly through the brand Web site rather than through the traditional wholesale channels. Furthermore, since there are almost no hotel companies that do not have a residential strategy in today's business environment, modern general managers probably run a residence business within their hotels, providing services to a clientele with those distinctly different demands associated with owning their unit, as well as long-stay guests.

Plus, if they work for MI, the general manager has the chief executive officer and also the chief operating officer monitoring business performance and asking how they are maximizing revenues and questioning energy and other utility costs. It is not easy! But on the positive side, the hotel leaders are offered free rein and opportunity to design those unique guest experiences, deliver on brand promises, and lead a committed and motivated team. They are encouraged to set their imagination free and to bring their passion to work while operating in some of the most beautiful and exotic locations in the world. MI only wants the most committed and talented managers in the industry, and the company recognizes that for some hospitality professionals, this goal is instinctively appealing. Fortunately, many of them are already working for MI. While they are held to very high performance standards, the ones who can deliver against expectations are highly respected.

The talent of the best people gives them plenty of great career options, but they are drawn to the opportunities that MI can offer. They have the imagination and creativity to continually keep their property and the brand interesting and differentiated in their marketplace. They have the vision to create original, high-value experiences and events that are memorable, unique, and authentic to their environment. They have a strong network of press, society, or hospitality-industry personalities, who they constantly maintain and develop. And as public speakers, they have a natural ability to hold the attention of an audience. In a one-on-one or group situation, they have the ability to project themselves, creating powerful and influential impressions. In either case, they always speak convincingly about their brand, and are able to articulate the differentiators of the brand in a compelling and exciting way.

Things were much simpler in the past. The hotel managers of around 10 or 20 years ago had to manage their hotel-room inventory and be great hosts. The systems and processes, which today connect them to head office, were in their earliest infancy, so they had a much freer hand from what they might call corporate interference. If you look at F&B operations, while there have always been some great individual outlets around, the quality generally was far lower than it is today. In city hotels in particular, nobody dined in a hotel except for breakfast. Then, there was a resurgence of interest in F&B. MI launched that trend in Bangkok by bringing the recognized brands, Benihana and Trader Vic's into its hotels. Today, it is collaborating with Starwood to identify a signature restaurant to anchor the new St. Regis Bangkok.

Furthermore, the sales function of the hotel was pre-eminent in times past. The science of revenue and yield management that now routinely challenges and validates the business the sales team brings in had barely been established. Today, MI yield manages its outlet tables and spa rooms; the concept is applied within these contexts just as it is to hotel rooms. It is not enough to just accept a restaurant booking—the return on those 1.5 table turns per day must be maximized.

Some people regret the fact that as a result of mobile communication devices, managers in any business today are never out of touch from each other. That is just a fact of life. However, the advantage of this is that managers can stay away for a longer period of time, as there is less impact of being away because managers are reachable. Mobile e-mail is far less intrusive than the phone, as one can reply to it at one's leisure. Without it, achieving success is not imaginable in this complex world of business.

Finally, the human resource challenges of finding, training, and motivating great people to join and stay with one's organization deserve highlighting. Some of the groups in the Middle East are openly stating that they will need to recruit, house, and train 55,000 new associates over the next five to 10 years. Talented HR professionals who can help deliver the strategy of their companies by meeting that supply-and-demand challenge deserve every dirham or dollar they can command in the marketplace.

MI's success, in any part of its business, is fundamentally underpinned by the passion of its people. It is important to then reward them appropriately. With regard to personal compensation, reward in relation to performance has always been at the heart of the MI culture, and is a driving factor in the retention of the best people. The company puts in place a competitive remuneration structure that motivates them to commit their talent and professional energy to the organization. It cherishes those people who take personal responsibility for driving results in their area of the business. But it is also important to publicly celebrate achievements, and give people the recognition they deserve. In this respect, once a year, MI gathers all its business leaders together to acknowledge outstanding performance with "Minor Awards." Each business must have its own specific culture of rewarding and celebrating achievements, big and small.

In parallel, management must establish and then champion an internal business culture, standards, and processes that underpin that success. MI's investors, while happy with their returns, also know that the company develops great people and different products that each creates a buzz in the market. Across MI, while each business has its own internal culture, everyone lives the group's core values of innovation, customer focus, driving for results, and developing people.

Knowing When to Sell an Asset

MI is very reluctant to sell assets, under almost any circumstances. While this could be seen as a potential weakness, it rationalizes that the value of each of its businesses has kept steadily rising. Had it sold any of its divisions, MI would have lost the valuable positions, which it had attained in those businesses. Often, the company has fought very hard to increase its holdings in various assets, moving from minority to majority stakes by actively seeking to buy out our partners. In the case of Marriott, MI acquired 100 percent of the JW Marriott Phuket because it believes in the value of it.

Today, the hotel industry often touts the concept of going asset light. There is no question that the stock markets and analysts, who track this industry, value pure management companies at a much higher multiple than those who own and operate their own bricks and mortar. Maybe MI's multiples are so high because it does not use a lot of bricks or mortar—its construction materials are mainly wood and natural thatching. But the serious point is that there is a significant potential downside to not owning at least a part of the asset that one operates.

First, there is far less ability to enforce one's own brand standards or brand values. Second, one cannot always ensure that the property renovations are carried out according to desired standards. Finally, both the hotel general manager and the corporate office consume a significant amount of time in communicating with and dealing with the third-party owner. This amount of time could be more productively used to drive the revenues and growth of the company.

Looking at MI's food-group model, the organization expects in the long term to move to a situation where franchisees account for 50 percent of the total stores. Today, that figure is closer to 30 percent. As with its hotel group, it will always seek to maintain a significant equity investment in the key properties of the food group.

When considering different ownership models, recall the sobering case study of a well-known European luxury hotel group in which the misjudged policy of "sale and lease back" that they embarked upon in 1999–2000 fundamentally destroyed its ability to stay solvent. Today, the brand remains as part of a wider hotel group, but the company is long gone. As the owner of luxury resorts, with some properties that it operates and some properties that it does not, MI gets greater credibility when talking with other business partners about its suitability and competency to manage partners' assets, and it never intends to move away from that model.

Currently, MI is starting to move away from its original model where it owned everything that it operated. Its plan with Anantara, now that it has 11 operating and profitable properties with a steady pipeline of new properties opening in 2010, is to expand very rapidly through management contracts. MI will always be open to taking an equity stake in the right deal, and fortunately, its financial strength enables it to do so, which means it can compete for prime sites. But each opportunity will be considered on a case-by-case basis.

Decision-Making Role of the Leader

As previously noted, people are the single most important component of the portfolio, followed by the brands that they operate. So the
essence of leadership is really making sure one brings all one's people
along on the journey. This means getting the firm's executives to
be masters of their own businesses but also to see the bigger picture.
They have to understand the company's vision and mission, and be
driving constantly toward that goal. There must be constant communication to build consensus and to ensure passion.

But at the same time, as the leader of the business, one cannot just
be focused on the long-term conditions and risk losing sight of the day-
to-day operations. Some companies and some CEOs go wrong with
leadership because they have an approach that only focuses on their
strategic objectives. However, execution trumps strategy every time.
All strategic intentions must be delivered by detailed tactical steps and
operational discipline but many people do not successfully complete
the journey because they are too busy planning it. They can paint the
picture of the journey and discuss what is going to happen but do not
take that first step. And the first step itself is always the key. It is all
about looking at details and letting nothing slip by. Stay involved, be
seen, walk the business. Build a personal relationship with managers
and associates, and most importantly, customers. Never lose sight of
the customers because they are the people who effectively pay the company's salaries.

One of the ways to stay connected to one's businesses is by utilizing MI's process of quarterly reviews. Immediately at the end of
each quarter once the financial results are confirmed, all the corporate
and operational leaders of that specific business area converge in one
room. There are separate meetings for the food group, fashion group,
and hotel group. In each case, it is a very formal meeting. It takes
much preparation and pulls many senior people away from their day-
to-day work for up to three days at a time. Together, management goes
through the results of the quarter and the plans for the next quarter
in detail. While it takes a lot of time and investment, at the end of
the process, everyone is on the same page. If there are key messages
to be delivered, everyone hears them. If a manager has not hit his
numbers, he is probably going to take a lot of heat at the public forum.

The important thing is that the managers whose brands compete against each other daily—in the food group and hotel group—open up their books and go through their results and their plans in the same room. That is how MI's senior team of executives and its leader stay connected to the details of what is happening in all of its businesses.

Another key to good leadership is being able to recognize that there are certain times when the leader cannot poll everybody's opinion. At other times, the leader must recognize that it is important to achieve consensus. That is, the effective leader has to know when it is time to make a leadership decision alone or when to involve everyone. Recently, for example, MI looked at an investment opportunity to buy a small group of hotels in the Caribbean. The financial projections were very attractive but there were other elements of the deal about which it had concerns. The leader's view was that it would not suit the company to do it but if the rest of the leadership team had wanted to do it and were committed to making it a success, the decision would have been to go ahead with the investment opportunity.

There is no single moment when a leader suddenly finds himself able to trust an executive's opinion. It is something that evolves as the two work together, as they fight battles and hopefully, win them together. And the trust begins when the leader sees that he is consulting that person more and more because the leader finds that the other's judgment is very good. There is not a moment where the leader says, "Now I trust this individual." Rather it is layers of experiences that build up over time.

Great companies should look to stretch and challenge their people to perform at their maximum capability. MI's business is expanding to such a degree that a business leader at any level essentially has to double their personal capability every three years. There is no question that most people, in any business, in any company, are just not capable of doing that. Some people say it is ruthless, but that is what great performing companies are all about. Obviously, MI has had people quit the company because they were unhappy, but it also has passionate people who take ownership for business results, and who each time they are challenged, somehow find a way to keep recreating themselves.

A good leader drives his people very hard. When they reach a level where they cannot go any further, then the leader has to acknowledge that and try to find a way to either amend their scope, or part company with them in a respectful way. Moreover, more people are likely to quit their job because they are not driven than because they have been driven too hard. But when people do leave, then that clears the way for the next generation to rise up and for talented outsiders to come in. MI has never had a problem attracting high-performing, high-potential individuals, even from competitors with a much softer culture, because those people are inherently attracted to its environment.

Conclusion

The preceding discussion should not be viewed as a set of rules but rather guidelines and observations based on what has worked for MI's businesses over the years. As the saying goes, rules are for the obedience of fools and the guidance of wise men. Despite the ups and downs of the global economy, MI sees even greater opportunity for growth today than at any time over the past 40 years. The company will remain focused on delivering great returns to its investors, delivering on its various brand promises to all its different customers, and creating job security and career opportunities for its talented, committed, and passionate employees.

5

STRENGTHENING BRAND MANAGEMENT AND VALUE

By Michael Issenberg

Introduction

Brand management is defined as the application of marketing techniques to a specific product, product line, or brand. It seeks to increase the product's perceived value in the minds of customers and thereby increase brand franchise and brand equity. Marketers see a brand as an implied promise that the level of quality that people have come to expect from a brand will continue with future purchases of the same product or brand.

Research by McKinsey & Company, a global consulting firm in 2000 suggested that strong, well-leveraged brands produce higher returns to shareholders than weaker, narrower brands. Taken together, this means that brands seriously impact shareholder value, which ultimately makes branding a chief executive officer's responsibility.

A good brand name should be well-protected under trademark laws, be easy to pronounce, remember, recognize, and attract attention. It must also be attractive to purchasers and easy to translate into all languages in the markets where the brand will be used and, of course, suggest product benefits or usage. An excellent brand should suggest the image of the company or product and must distinguish the product's positioning relative to the competition.

High brand equity provides several competitive advantages as the company will enjoy reduced marketing costs as a result of the high-level of consumer brand awareness and loyalty. It will have more trade leverage in bargaining with distributors and retailers since customers will expect them to carry the brand. It can also charge a higher price than its competitors because the brand has higher perceived quality and value. The company can more easily launch brand extensions since the brand name carries higher credibility. Last but not least, the brand offers the company some defense against fierce price competition (Kotler, Ang, Leong, and Tan 1999).

John W. O'Neill and Qu Xiao highlighted in their article "The Role of Brand Affiliation in Hotel Market Value" (*O'Neill and Qu* 2006) that a hotel's brand contributes significantly to the property's market value. In their analysis of nearly 1,100 hotel transactions over the past 15 years in the United States (US), they found that brands added value beyond the usual contributors to a property's value, such as net operating income and revenue per available room. The effects of branding were most noticeable in mid-market and upscale hotels. Based on per room sales statistics, certain brands added significantly more value to their franchisees' properties than others. More specifically, they found that hotel brands affect market values of four hotel types, namely, mid-scale without food and beverage (F&B), mid-scale with F&B, upscale, and upper upscale. There was no significant differentiating effect for branded economy and luxury properties in their sample.

According to the these authors, the value of a brand chiefly resides in the minds of customers and is based primarily on customers' brand awareness, their perceptions of its quality, and their brand loyalty. The model of brand-value creation proposed by Keller and Lehmann (2003) indicates that brands first create value for customers by helping to assure them of a uniform level of quality. After customers become loyal to a brand, the brand owner can capitalize on the brand's value through price premiums, decreased price elasticity, increased market share, and more rapid brand expansion. Finally, companies with successful brands benefit in the financial marketplace by improving shareholders' value.

It was reported that 85 percent of business travelers and 76 percent of leisure travelers preferred branded hotels over independent properties (Yesawich 1996). One reason for this finding is that hotel guests rely on brand names to reduce the risks associated with staying at an otherwise unknown property. In that regard, strong brands enable hotel chains to differentiate themselves in the mind-set of customers.

Beginnings and Growth of Accor's Business

Brand management is something that the Accor Group takes seriously, particularly as its hotel arm has numerous brands, which cover the full spectrum of accommodation from luxury to economy. With so many hotel brands, does Accor's brand-management approach dilute the brands or enhance them, and does this translate into achieving its business and profit goals?

This chapter seeks to answer this question by discussing Accor's approach to its business philosophy and brand management. It will also touch on issues and challenges faced and what it is doing in Asia Pacific to differentiate and strengthen its key brands.

Started in 1967 by Paul Dubrule and Gerard Pelisson, the company then known as SIEH, opened its first hotel, Novotel Lille in France, followed by the first ibis hotel in Bordeaux in 1974. Mercure was acquired in 1975 and Sofitel, with its 43 hotels and two seawater spas, five years later. In 1983, Accor was created with the merger of Novotel SIEH and Jacques Borel International, a European leader in managed food services and concession restaurants and world leader of meal vouchers, which was acquired a year before. In 1990, the Motel 6 chain in the US, with its 550 properties, was acquired. By then, Accor, with its global brands, became one of the world's leading hotel groups in terms of properties directly owned or managed, excluding franchises. Since then, the acquisition has continued with Pullman, Etap Hotel, and other businesses and services through the years.

Currently, the Accor Group, which is headquartered in France, is one of the world's largest groups operating in the hotel, tourism, and corporate services sector. It is known as a European leader in hotels and tourism and the global leader in services to corporate clients and public institutions. It now operates in nearly 100 countries with more than 150,000 employees. The Accor Group is structured into two core businesses—Accor Hospitality and Accor Services.

Under Accor Hospitality, the group's hotel operations include more than 15 complementary brands, from luxury to budget, that are recognized and appreciated around the world for their service quality—Sofitel, Pullman, MGallery, Novotel, Mercure, Suitehotel, ibis, all seasons, Etap Hotel, Hotel Formule 1, and Motel 6, as well as Accor Thalassa and other strategically related businesses such as Lenôtre (catering). Present in 90 countries, with more than 4,000 hotels and 500,000 rooms, Accor's brands cover the spectrum of the accommodation market, thus offering travelers a comprehensive selection of hotel styles and locations.

With operations in 40 countries, Accor Services designs, develops, and manages high value-added services for companies and public institutions that make everyday life easier for individual users and organizations. With more than 50 products, Accor Services offers a comprehensive range of prepaid services in the areas of employee and public benefits, rewards and loyalty, and business-expense management. These prepaid services create benefits for all parties—490,000 companies, 1.2 million affiliated service providers, and 32 million users.

Accor's Effective Business Strategy and Brands

Accor's strategic business models are shaped by investment and a technological shift to electronic media in Accor Services and the asset-right property strategy. Since 2006, Accor Hospitality (hotels) has embarked on an ambitious brand-repositioning strategy.

Since the economic downturn, which started in 2008, Accor Hospitality has proved resilient, mainly because of the strength of its economy hotels outside the US, which accounts for 30 percent of revenue. In 2008, the hotels business turned in a good performance, with revenue rising by 5.1 percent. The group's ability to withstand the current downturn was mainly due to the fact that 70 percent of earnings are now generated by a combination of revenues from the economy hotels sector (outside the US) and Accor Services, two businesses that are less sensitive to the ups and downs of the economic cycle.

In Accor Hospitality, its brand portfolio covers the full range of customer needs, extending across all segments, with both standardized and non-standardized hotels. Their positioning and branding are as follows:

Luxury—Sofitel (luxury hotels situated in key business and resort locations, offers the highest level of facilities and services in a personal, refined atmosphere); two new sister-brands known as So by Sofitel (cozy and hip boutique hotels) and Sofitel Legend (a collection of luxury hotels in the world's greatest cities, targeted at high-contribution travelers)

Upscale—Pullman (for business travelers, and meetings and conventions in urban centers and popular resorts, offers round-the-clock services that provide conviviality and connectivity); MGallery (a collection of distinctive boutique hotels with character through their design, history, and/or exceptional setting)

Upper Mid-scale—Novotel (four-star convenient and modern hotels for business and leisure/family travelers); SuiteHotel (targeted at nomadic travelers seeking space in these suites that feature work and rest areas); Grand Mercure Apartments (upscale apartments for independent travelers in major cities, and regional and resort locations)

Mid-scale—Mecure (mid-market hotel, contemporary in style and offers great value for money, with facilities and services that reflect the area's local character and culture); Adagio Aparthotel (chain which offers three-star apartments with a la carte services in major European cities with each residence comprising 80–140 apartments with fully equipped kitchens)

Economy—ibis (hotels in central business districts and major regional and suburban areas, offers affordably priced accommodation in a friendly atmosphere); all seasons (affordable hotels in major business and resort destinations in Australia, New Zealand, and Asia)

Budget—Etap (in Europe only); Hotel Formule 1 (motel-style accommodation at budget rates, which are located in cities and regional areas and close to transport and food services, offers affordability with reliable quality); Motel 6 (in US only)

The standardized brands are Novotel, ibis, and Hotel Formule 1 while Sofitel, Pullman, MGallery, Mecure, and all seasons are non-standardized brands.

In the Asia Pacific, Accor also offers Base Backpacking Hostels (a backpacker hostel chain in Australia and New Zealand); Accor Vacation Club (holiday ownership in Australia, New Zealand, and Asia); Accor Services (offers a wide range of services designed for businesses, public authorities, and professional networks); and Lenotre (catering). It also operates the Sydney Convention & Exhibition Center in Australia and Hyderabad International Convention Center in India (casinos).

Through the design, which ensures the same look and feel of various Accor hotels' façades, signage, and facilities; worldwide advertising; marketing collateral; promotions; and innovative offerings, the group continues to strengthen and build the brand image of its multibranded hotels.

Worldwide, Accor has continued its development in 2008, which saw the opening of 28,000 rooms and the launch of new products such as Pullman in the upscale segment and all seasons in the economy segment. Repositioned in the luxury segment, Sofitel has largely completed its transformation by deploying new standards in design, marketing, distribution, dining, services, and human resource management. The group's traditional brands have all launched ambitious projects to motivate employees and win new customers by optimizing the offer of each brand.

Despite the downturn in the real-estate market, Accor pursued its asset-right strategy. At the end of 2008, 56 percent of the hotel portfolio was comprised of less capital-intensive ownership structures, which means management contracts and franchise agreements, thereby giving the group a more defensive profile. A majority of ownership is in the economy sector, with predominantly management contracts in the luxury segment.

In 2007, Accor saw the introduction of new brands, which are more closely attuned to customer expectations, while 2008 was the year of their deployment. As mentioned earlier, this was the case for Sofitel, now repositioned in the luxury segment; Pullman, a new upscale brand; and all seasons in non-standardized economy hotels. Launched in 2008, the MGallery label further extends the portfolio with a collection of remarkable hotels, each with a highly distinctive personality, for travelers looking for venues with character.

Accor's Asia-Pacific Business Strategy

In Asia Pacific, the Accor Group is one of the largest and fastest growing hotel groups with 385 hotels and 74,329 rooms in countries such as Australia, New Zealand, Fiji, French Polynesia, Cambodia, China, India, Indonesia, Japan, Korea, Laos, Malaysia, the Philippines, Singapore, Thailand, and Vietnam. Approximately 100 hotels are scheduled to be opened in the next two years.

Accor has developed a very focused strategy for development in Asia Pacific. The group is asset-light on its upscale and luxury segments through management contracts, and asset-right for its economy brands with a mix of owned and management properties. The group focuses on economy and mid-scale brands in order to be a market leader, while for upscale brands, it aims to be a major player.

Growth of Economy Brands in Asia Pacific

In Asia Pacific, economy or budget hotels are seeing a boom. Arnaud Deltenre in an article "Asia-Pacific budget in extremis" (Deltenre

2009) highlighted the factors, which have given rise to this boom. A large portion of the region's population has developed an enthusiasm for travel but has limited disposal income for this interest. The recent development of low-cost airlines has been a catalyst in the expansion of domestic and intra-regional tourism. This has helped to contribute to the expansion of tourism in China, India, Thailand, and Vietnam.

While budget hotels welcome many domestic guests, they also receive high volumes of international tourists, who are familiar with and seek international brands. These brands provide a known consistent level of service standard and amenities, which local and independent hotels cannot match. Deltenre believed that the international hotel groups had made a major mistake by focusing on the penetration of Asia-Pacific markets from luxury and upscale segments and have not yet exploited the economy bonanza, with the exception of the Accor Group. This is indeed a compliment for the group in affirming that its business strategy is on the right track.

Accor began spreading its ibis brand through the region, starting with the opening of its first hotel in Jakarta, Indonesia, in 1993. It has also opened up franchising in Australia and New Zealand. Using this business model, Accor is also counting on the new all seasons brand, a non-standardized concept, to go further in these two developed countries as well as in Thailand and Indonesia.

Many global brands have now woken up to the potential of budget brands in China where the number of economy hotels has grown from 189,000 in 2007 to 313,000 in 2008. A Chinese government study in 2008 revealed that there are more than 100 different economy brands in China. Several global hotel groups, including Accor's ibis brand, plus multiple local players such as Jin Jiang, are now actively pursuing this growth in China.

With the economic downturn since 2008, occupancy rates at economy hotels were also impacted by the economic slump and decline in tourism arrivals in Asia Pacific. However, Accor has not changed its view of the large growth potential of China's economy hotel industry in the long term, although it became more prudent in its expansion strategy and financial planning. Testifying to this business strategy, the group opened its 800th ibis hotel in the world in Shanghai, making China one of its most powerful growth countries. The ibis brand is being developed through ownership and management contracts, which is one of the brand's strengths because it brings a higher level of consistency, quality, and a service guarantee compared to local brands.

Another nation with great potential is India, where current hotel properties, which are predominantly independent hotels, cannot rival global brands in terms of quality. After favoring growth in the upscale hotel segment, India's economic segment is rising with the increase of the middle class and businessmen who are thrifty in their business expenses. With its local Indian partner, InterGlobe, the first ibis opened in April 2009 with 12 more being planned. One hundred Formule 1 hotels are also targeted for India.

In Australia and New Zealand, the economy hotels segment has expanded, as its profile is similar to Europe and the US. Accor took advantage of the Olympics in Sydney in 2000 to establish its first Hotel Formule 1, and nine years later, it has a network of 21 Formule 1 and 18 ibis hotels. The group also has a youth hostel niche brand—Base Backpacking Hostels, which is a concept focused only in Australia and New Zealand. Currently, Accor is focusing on two major projects—renovating the Formule 1 network of budget hotels and developing all seasons, its economy concept, with 14 properties in Australia and New Zealand.

In Asia Pacific's emerging countries, Accor is the pioneer for the economy segment as its brands are well accepted for both leisure and business travelers. In South Korea, there are three ibis hotels, while in Thailand, there were four ibis hotels opened in the past two years, and three more are expected to be opened in the next two years. The group sees growth potential in Thailand, Indonesia, and South Korea. In Hong Kong, the high real-estate prices discourage the development of budget hotels but Singapore offers some potential. Accor opened its first ibis hotel in February 2009 and work is underway for a second ibis hotel in Singapore. In Vietnam, high real-estate and building costs are a deterrent, but the group confirmed its first ibis project in Ho Chi Minh City recently.

To increase its brand awareness and market share, both ibis and Formule 1 hotels will increase their online presence and distribution network as a key brand initiative in the future.

Developing Other Accor Brands in Asia Pacific

In Asia Pacific, the Accor Group currently has 388 hotels with 74,824 rooms. Its key brand milestones included the continuing repositioning of Sofitel in the fast-growing luxury-hotel market and the introduction of the MGallery label in the Asia-Pacific region for highly individual upscale hotels. The group is also opening the first Pullman hotels and resorts in Australia, Malaysia, China, Indonesia, New Zealand, India, and Vietnam. Accor's expansion of its network in Asia includes a target of 50 Pullman hotels in the next three years.

The Pullman hotel brand was launched in Asia Pacific in January 2008, and in its first 18 months, Accor developed 12 Pullman hotels throughout the region. The brand has found an excellent business opportunity in the upper mid-scale segment by providing five-star accommodation with affordable pricing. The prospects for achieving the development ambitions for Pullman remain high.

The group will continue to focus on Grand Mercure in the apartments segment and strengthen the brand leadership positions of Novotel and Mercure in the upper mid-scale sector through brand initiatives, innovation, and service. For all seasons hotels throughout the Asia-Pacific region, they will take on the key branding identifying elements of the new global brand and explore greater franchising opportunities.

The Novotel brand was the second of the Accor brands to arrive in Asia, and today enjoys strong brand recognition in key markets where the brand's heritage is strong. These markets include many cities in Australia, Thailand, and Indonesia. This recognition is supported by the fact that these countries also enjoy the largest networks within the region, as brand recognition is a key factor when hotel owners and developers select a brand or international hotel company.

In summary, Accor is opening the following new hotels in Asia Pacific in the near future—seven Sofitel, one So by Sofitel, 13 Pullman, two Grand Mecure, two MGalley, 23 Novotel, 15 Mercure, one all seasons, and 33 ibis. These hotels will add around 20,000 rooms in total—a sure sign of the group's commitment to growing its business and brands in the Asia-Pacific region.

Issues and Challenges in Managing Brands

What are the issues and challenges facing Accor with its multibrands? With Accor's four categories of hotels (luxury and upscale, upper mid-scale and mid-scale, economy, budget), the group needs to ensure is that the stratification of brands and quality are consistent throughout the world. Although hotel standards differ in Asia compared with say, Europe or the US, Accor tries to maintain harmony across its full range of hotels in terms of their concepts, positioning, facilities, and services.

In Asia, one of the issues most global brands face is that Asians have higher expectations in terms of having larger rooms, better amenities, a higher level of service, and higher quality finishes. So when Asians travel to Europe or the US, their expectations may not be met or they are disappointed at the lower standards as per their local experiences.

The group agrees with the view of authors John W. O'Neill and Qu Xiao in their article "The Role of Brand Affiliation in Hotel Market Value" (2006) that the value of a brand lies mainly in customers' minds and is based primarily on customers' brand awareness, their perceptions of its quality, and their brand loyalty.

Accor builds and strengthens its different brands by being innovative, having a commitment to quality, and introducing new brand initiatives tailored to the expectations and experiences of its customers and shareholders.

The group also focuses on brand loyalty, as there are people who want the same experience wherever they travel. They want the same value in their preferred brands wherever they travel and they appreciate this known value in unknown destinations. They can also control their travel budgets with a "no risk" experience. Generally, these travelers are comprised of two types—those who travel to a city for the first time and want the ease of using the same brand hotel, and others who frequently stay in same brand room type as they want the comfort of knowing where to check-in, where to connect their computer, and so on.

As P. C. Yesawich highlighted in his article "So Many Brands, So Little Time," one of the reasons for brand loyalty is that hotel guests rely on brand names to reduce the risks associated with staying at an otherwise unknown property. The group believes Accor brands provide this assurance for their brand-loyal customers. Recently, Accor set up A|Club as its multibranded loyalty program, so as to build a loyal, active membership of hotel users. Since then, the online loyalty program has acquired more than two million users. It is a tiered program, which acknowledges high and occasional Accor hotels users, with varying levels of rewards.

In trying to standardize the group's brands worldwide, there are of course challenges, but it believes it is getting the balance and adaptation right. Accor is very strict with its hardware such as building quality, lobbies, and making restaurant improvements in Asia.

Accor also emphasizes training, and each brand has its own human resource teams, who plan specific training programs in relation to the different brands. It is Accor's ambition for all senior management to work in at least two brands and in two countries, so they can learn to work across-countries and across-brands, which is an asset in a multibrand group such as Accor.

Accor's five key values across its worldwide organization are emphasized to its staff—innovation, the spirit of conquest, performance, respect, and trust unite all its 150,000 employees. The group believes that innovation is its trademark, the spirit of conquest is its growth engine, performance is the key to its continued success, respect is the basis of all its relationships, and trust is the foundation of its management.

In terms of advertising, Accor emphasizes the same look, feel, and taglines for its various brands to ensure consistency worldwide. However, in terms of execution, for advertising and promotions, local management are given some leeway in in terms of media buy and adaptation to suit local cultures and sensitivities.

Conclusion

This chapter has focused on discussing Accor's approach to its business philosophy and brand management, and the issues and challenges the group has faced. It has also given some insights on managing Accor's brands in Asia Pacific.

As mentioned by McKinsey & Company, research has suggested that strong, well-leveraged brands produce higher returns to shareholders than weaker, narrower brands. With so many hotel brands on its plate, the question is—has Accor's brand management approach diluted the bands or enhanced them—and has this translated into achieving its business and profit goals?

Well, the Accor Group's performance in terms of its financial results will gauge whether its brand-management approach has been successful or not. The good news is that its 2008 financial results showed an operating profit totaling €875 million for the year, an increase of 13 percent on 2007. This solid performance extended across both of its businesses and affirms that the group is on the right track. It will continue to move ahead to ensure good financial returns for its shareholders and great satisfaction to its numerous customers, who appreciate and are delighted by its many Accor's brands.

References

Deltenre, Arnaud. 2009. Asia-Pacific budget in extremis. *HTR* 167 (April):62–69.

Keller, Kevin L. and Lehmann, Donald R. 2003. How Do Brands Create Value? *Marketing Management* 12(3): 26–31.

Kotler, Philip, Swee Hoon Ang, Siew Meng Leong, and Chin Tiong Tan. 1999. Marketing Management—An Asian Perspective. Singapore: Prentice-Hall, 465.

O'Neill, John W. and Qu, Xiao. 2006. The role of brand affiliation in hotel market value. *Cornell Hotel and Restaurant Administration Quarterly* 47 (3):210–223.

Yesawich, P. C. 1996. So many brands, so little time. *Lodging Hospitality* 52(9):16.

6

VENTURING INTO AN ASIAN MARKET COMPETITIVELY

By Devin Kimble

Introduction

While many books and articles on marketing, and in particular, marketing for hospitality, have been written, I would like to discuss marketing Western-style food and beverage (F&B) in an Asian context and give the real-life story of the market-driven considerations, reasons, and decisions that went into building MENU Pte. Ltd. Food & Drinks Group (MENU Group), which owns and operates Brewerkz Restaurants & Microbreweries, Café Iguana, WineGarage, and MENU Catering. This group became a successful three-concept, six-restaurant, and two-microbrewery operation in Singapore. The majority of the examples will be drawn from my experience with Brewerkz Restaurants & Microbreweries, which is the flagship brand, but I will mention what has driven our diversification strategy as well.

This chapter is about how we used market considerations every step of the way from developing the initial company strategy, to raising money, then starting and modifying our business model first for survival and then, for diversification and growth. Broadly, this chapter will discuss concept development, start-up, growth, diversification, expansion, and future prospects.

We have not included a lot of examples of market research. Most of the development we did revolved around transporting successful concepts from their home base to a very different part of the world, both geographically and culturally. What we introduced was not a product like toothpaste, which is easy to give to a group of people to try and then acquire their opinions. While aspects of what we were proposing could be researched, such as beer and food, it was pretty obvious that these things were popular in a general way. But this is like saying that action films are popular. While such a statement can be supported by a plethora of blockbusters that have generated enormous revenues worldwide, it is not entirely the genre that makes such movies successful. Rather it is the execution, which is the key.

What we offer is an experience, which is a whole package of products that have to work together, like live theater, because a meal at a restaurant cannot be captured and repeated endlessly and perfectly. Everyday, we have to put on a new "show" just like the folks at the Disney theme parks, who call employees "cast members."

On the other hand, saying that market research is less important for concept development does not mean that we have not surveyed our customers. We actively solicit comments and have studied data from credit cards, for instance, but this information serves really to confirm that we are on the right track, something that also shows up in our sales, but it does not help us develop new ideas.

For the MENU Group, it is not about asking people what they want and then getting it for them. We are ultimately trying to anticipate the needs and desires of the market, using our best guesses about what combination of things will delight our customers. Sometimes, we are right on the money. And sometimes, we have to back-up, re-examine our logic and the steps that led us to make bad assumptions, and then fix what is broken and go back to our customers with the new idea, product, or way of doing things to see if that will strike their fancy and keep the tills ringing.

This chapter in many ways is a story. It is about how and why we made certain decisions based on our market perceptions. Some of these led us to success. Others resulted in failure and had to be rethought. On the whole, we have done more things right than wrong, and hopefully we have learned enough to continue to do so.

Why Venture into Food & Beverage?

Most people eat at least three times a day so there is a large and consistent need for food. It is certainly less expensive to buy ingredients and prepare them in your own kitchen, but the continually increasing popularity of eating away from home, shows that there is a strong and growing demand for the complete experience that food service establishments have to offer. In addition to rising demand, there are several very attractive financial aspects to selling food and beer. One is the relatively low barrier to entry, particularly in terms of the capital required for start-up. The cost of goods is inexpensive compared with most other industries, though certainly not as low as it is for the production of software, but then people need food and cannot survive by eating a computer program.

Additionally, most of the inventory is sold on a 30- to 90-day basis, so an operator is able to collect the cash equivalent of approximately four times the cost of goods every day for a month before paying suppliers, thereby generating a significant amount of working capital. This aspect of the industry also makes it possible for concepts that are troubled by a flawed business model to sometimes be changed to stave off failure and perhaps lead to success.

Low-entry costs and favorable cost-of-goods funding mean that there are a large number of food-service operators and that there is comparatively little consolidation in the food and beverage space. This approach is unlike retail, which requires significant amounts of capital for purchasing inventory and thereby, encourages consolidation. As a result, food service is one of the world's largest industries in terms of both revenues and employees. This means that there are still opportunities for skilled operators to capture market share and then go on to improve their margins through economies of scale.

In particular, the ability to raise capital and the opportunity to attract better quality managers with the additional money, in theory at least, can turn growth and scale into a virtuous cycle. The ability to exploit such opportunities has been done quite well by fast feeders such as McDonald's, mid-scale casual operators like Brinker, and even up-scale eateries such as Lettuce Entertain You in Chicago and BR Guest in New York. In general, however, there is still quite a bit of scope for consolidation within the industry, particularly among higher-check-average restaurants where no one player has any significant market share.

Beyond the financial benefits of operating F&B establishments, there is incredible scope for creativity, feedback is instantaneous, and unlike the art world and theater, which are also obviously creative places to work, there is little chance of going hungry.

Seeing Asia's Attraction

Much has been written about the rapid growth in Asia since the mid-1980s. But for me, it was, and continues to be, literally something I can see. When I first began work in the region in 1992 with stops in Seoul, Hong Kong, and Bangkok before opening a bar called the Rock Hard Cafe in Phnom Penh, the United States (US) seemed to be in the economic doldrums. For me, it certainly was the economy that proved to be the attraction to Asia. The growth was actually tangible. More than anything I was stunned by all of the construction with cranes dotting the skylines in numbers that seemed to be the hundreds. To a large extent, this still tends to be true as India and China continue to drive growth, pulling hundreds of millions of people out of poverty and building a vast middle class, hungry for interesting, new experiences, in spite of a nasty case of economic pneumonia, infecting the world from its epicenter in America (World Bank 2010).

But there is more to my being in Asia than just the growth story. As a blond-haired, blued-eyed, fair-skinned expatriate from California where people like me are ubiquitous, in Asia I am exotic. In the US, Britain, or Australia, I am just another typical Caucasian man. In Asia, I am unique, giving me a point of differentiation physically and culturally, which is virtually impossible for the billions of people in my immediate vicinity to acquire.

Understanding Asian Challenges

While the macroeconomic environment may be propitious and my appearance and background make me clearly different from the vast majority of Asians, leveraging these unique qualities into a successful food and beverage concept is certainly not guaranteed.

Unlike the US or Australia, Asia is and has been densely populated for many generations. For this reason, new concepts generally cannot be introduced at greenfield sites. Nor is there the preponderance of brownfield locations, created as old industries fail, as seen in Europe. Indeed, Asia is still in the process of industrializing, so these types of redevelopment opportunities are not as prevalent. Populations also tend to be young and growing, putting more pressure on scarce land resources and serving to keep real-estate prices high and rising, particularly for retail space.

Obviously, Asia is also not a monoculture. The enormous amount of diversity means that Western concepts must prove themselves unique and worthy not only against local cuisine but also versus the huge array of offerings from the region. For instance, in a city like Singapore, food from Japan or Korea, to a large extent, is just as exotic as that from France, Italy, or America.

To an extent, even the differentiation of one Western-style of cooking from another is problematic because what may be a demarcation in one culture is a line that is unrecognizable in another. In an article I wrote more than a decade ago (Kimble 1996), I discussed how in the US, quick-service restaurants serving hamburgers, pizza, sandwiches, tacos, and fish-and-chips are all viewed as distinct market segments, but in Asia they are just seen as Western food. This is not only an Asian cultural phenomenon. For instance, when I was growing up in California, no one spoke of cuisine from Sichuan, Hunan, Shanghai, or Canton as being different. It was all Chinese food.

Developing Western Concepts in an Eastern Context

Today in California, particularly in Los Angeles or the Bay Area, a differentiated Chinese concept is more than likely the norm, while in less sophisticated areas in the US, the generic Chinese restaurant still predominates. A similar situation also prevails throughout Asia. In gateway cities and resort areas, there is no lack of restaurants focused on cuisine from a specific place or region or even invented from a host of worldwide influences. As in the Western world, the main reason is exposure, which comes mainly from two sources. Regions that flourish on trade come into contact with different cultures and cuisines through their mercantile pursuits. Immigration is the other great introducer of new foods, and cities such as New York, London, Singapore, and Hong Kong are influenced both by their people's travels as well as newcomers who arrive looking to improve their lot in life.

The introduction of foreign concepts seems to follow two paths, which are not necessarily separate. One is the generic, undifferentiated route discussed above. Second is the tendency for the atmospheric creation of foods that have characteristics of a specific type of cooking, but which are not found in the original cuisine. For instance, in America, *chop suey* (an American-Chinese dish consisting of meats, cooked quickly with vegetables in a starch-thickened sauce) is a common dish in Chinese restaurants, but it is unknown in China. Similarly, in Great Britain, much of the food sold in Indian establishments is unlike that found on the sub-continent. This tactic of localizing foreign dishes happens frequently in Asia as well. For instance, in Hong Kong, a popular dish is Singapore noodles, something one does not actually see in Singapore.

Generic and atmospheric cuisine tends to be the norm as a style of food is just entering a market. For many Western concepts starting up in Asia, what this means is that recipe adjustments are made to accommodate local tastes. In the mid-1990s, for example, one mid-scale, Italian-American chain-restaurant operator in Singapore had modified 80 percent of its recipes, while a popular American Tex-Mex chain had Hainanese chicken rice on its menu. But as a market matures and becomes more sophisticated, authenticity is more valued as customers look for more differentiated products, or as more immigrants arrive, they begin to look for the taste of their homeland, which can serve to drive sales of concepts offering a more authentic experience.

So to a large extent where a Western concept is pitched in Asia, it has much to do with demographics. For the MENU Group, we ask the following questions:

- Are there enough people who will appreciate the authenticity of what we are serving?
- Is there a significant number of Western expatriates in the city?
- Have a large enough number of local residents been exposed to Western food through overseas schooling or travel?

The MENU Group's fundamental mission is to operate Western concepts in an Asian context. My intention is to leverage my upbringing and cultural understanding in order to offer our customers an authentic dining experience whether they are looking for the opportunity to eat in a different mode from how they eat at home or perhaps they are expatriates trying to enjoy some familiarity and comfort. Ketchup serves as an example of how we strive to create a correct Western experience. Most other operators use the Heinz brand, which in Asia generally is manufactured in Thailand. We use only Heinz Ketchup made in Pittsburgh, Pennsylvania, US, because I find that the Asian formulation tends to be sweeter and therefore not as authentic. In Asia, knowing one's ketchup, for instance, serves as a competitive advantage. In the Western world, such knowledge would not be so important.

One of the challenges of being authentic and profitable is to find local substitutes if at all possible. For instance, we use local pork, make tortillas with *chapati* (flat Indian bread) presses, and instead of spinach, we use a different green that is similar but do not have to bring in from the West. Service is another area where we make substitutions. Because we operate relatively big restaurants, using a large number of Westerners on our staff would not be cost-effective. It also is not even particularly necessary. We feel that we are able to train our front-house staff to be just as efficient and hospitable as they are in the West and better than in many places. On the flipside, locals are also able to adjust their service style to accommodate the different desires of their fellow Asians. For instance, most Americans do not want beer to be poured out of a jug by a server. Most Chinese, on the other hand, do.

In pursuing authenticity in a Western concept in Asia, it is also important not to lose sight of the fact that there do exist local distinctions. In Singapore, no restaurant can be without chili sauce. And we are frequently asked to cut our large hamburgers into six or eight pieces so that they may be eaten like *dim sum* (savory Chinese dishes served with Chinese tea). We also always employ a *feng shui* (geomancy) consultant when we open a restaurant or seat someone in an office. The point of this is not so much that we believe in the power of geomancy, rather many of our customers and employees do and being respectful of it is certainly good from a human-relations standpoint.

Locating in Singapore

To a great extent, Singapore is "Asia-Lite." The language of business and politics is English as is the legal system. The rule of law is strong and corruption is rare. There is general sexual equality and a well-enforced women's charter. It is safe, clean, has great health care and schools, and fantastic infrastructure, all of which make it a lovely place to raise a family. And the government is actually interested in promoting business. Taxes are low, there is a host of programs to promote innovation and cut red tape, and a single-layer of regulation means that the city, county, state, and national government agencies are all one so there is not a lot of duplication and confusion in terms of regulation.

Diversity is another great benefit. Although the large majority of Singapore's inhabitants are Chinese, they hail from a number of regions, unlike in Hong Kong. A former British Colony, Hong Kong has many similarities to Singapore, but most of its inhabitants come from the region of Guangzhou, which was formerly known as Canton. In Singapore, there are also substantial numbers of ethnic Malay and Indian citizens and other expatriates from Japan, Korea, the US, Australia, Britain, and continental Europe.

This diverse population has offered us the opportunity to get an idea of how our concept may work in the rest of Asia. Certainly, we have proven popular with Western expatriates, who have emigrated in large numbers to escape the high taxes of their homelands and for increasingly important overseas experiences, and may be found in substantial numbers in most of Asia's large cities. Brewerkz and WineGarage, another of the MENU Group concepts, have a noticeable attraction for Japanese and Korean residents as well. To a large extent, it is because many of those who are sent to overseas postings, have worked or gone to school in the West. Furthermore, Japan and Korea have relatively high per capital alcohol consumption, so concepts featuring strong beverage programs as we do, have proven popular with these groups.

We have also learned that our appeal is not universal. Because all of our concepts feature alcohol, none are particularly attractive to the Malay demographic or the Indonesian tourists, who make frequent trips to Singapore, as these groups tend to be Muslim and drinking is forbidden by that religion. However, visits by Malaysians and Indonesians are not uncommon, particularly those who are ethnically Chinese. We also see people who stick to eating in a *halal* (following Muslim principles) manner, while enjoying the environment that we provide.

There have been some positive surprises as well. Cafe Iguana, another MENU Group concept, has actually found quite a bit of popularity with ethnic Indians. This was something that in retrospect, we perhaps should have guessed because the spice profiles of Mexican and many Indian cuisines are quite similar.

Finally, people in Singapore tend to have a Western-level of disposable income and are well traveled because the country is so small. This tends to make the population open to new concepts and able to afford them as well.

Maximizing Brewpub Advantages

There were several reasons that we chose a brewpub as our first operation. Most importantly, brewpubs were a hot concept in the US in the early 1990s when we first decided to start the business, and there was practically no competition in Asia. At the time we were in the planning stage, the number of brewpubs in the US and Canada was growing at a rate of about 30 percent per year with almost 600 brewpubs in the US by 1995. But there were only a handful of them in Asia outside of Japan, where they had taken hold and seen rapid growth as well. Strong expansion for both brewpubs and the then economy in general in the US also meant that American operators were not keen on overseas markets because they had plenty of growth to keep them busy at home. So it appeared to us that we had the opportunity to install a great, new concept in a cosmopolitan city of four million with no direct competitors for the foreseeable future. Granted the popularity of the concept had not been proven in another part of the world, but the natural fit between a cold beer and the warm weather of Asia seemed to be quite compelling, as did the large number of Western expatriates whose non-Asian food choices had been rather limited to upscale hotels and chain restaurants at this point.

A brewpub is also a concept requiring a relatively large amount of capital for start-up. In some ways this benefit seems to be counterintuitive, but what we knew from our experience in investment banking is that practically the same amount of due diligence and negotiation is needed for a small deal as a larger one, so there is a bias for seeking bigger sums rather than smaller amounts from investors. The need for a larger investment also makes it more difficult for other operators to enter the same space. For example, the barriers to opening a *char kway teow* (Singapore fried rice noodles) stall are much lower than those for starting a microbrewery, and consequently, there are a lot more operators of *char kway teow* stalls than brewpubs in Singapore.

In addition to the quantum of the investment, there are other aspects of the restaurant and microbrewery concept that tend to make it relatively more defensible than other F&B operations. Brewpubs are generally larger than most other restaurants mainly because the expense of the brewery is easier to amortize over more rather than fewer seats, and therefore, brewpubs need operators skilled in running a high-volume business. While there are certainly Asian operators in Asia who run high-volume concepts, such as the enormous 2,000-seat Thai restaurants on the outskirts of Bangkok and the 1,000 plus-seat *dim sum* palaces in Hong Kong, there are very few Western restaurants that have more than 200 seats anywhere in Asia.

The exceptions for Western food tend to be casual, US-franchise operators, but there are still only a relatively small number of these, such as Hard Rock Cafe and Chili's Grill & Bar. Perhaps the most successful of the independent, high-volume, Western upscale casual operators in Asia at the time was Dan Ryan's Chicago Grill, with whom I had worked in Hong Kong, Taipei, and Singapore. So the bottom line was and remains that there just are not that many operators in Asia skilled at running a large, Western-style concept.

Microbreweries require specialized staff to make the beer, and because there were not many small brewing operations in Asia, it meant that industry connections in other parts of the world were important in hiring a brew master. Other specialized brewery-related skills include the administrative wherewithal to follow the often-difficult government regimes and additional regulatory expenses related to brewing beer. For instance, Singapore required us to have a customs officer witness that every liter of beer transferred from fermentation to storage pass through a flow meter, which was precisely calibrated and tested by the government on a yearly basis, so we could be charged S$2.70 per liter. And every time that we brewed a new type of beer, it had to be tested several times by the national laboratory and approved by them before it was available for sale. We even have to pay S$43,200 every year just for the license to brew beer, whether or not we actually we produce any.

Facing Brewpub's Challenges and Opportunities

Breweries take up space that could be used for seating. With high rental costs and short-lease tenures in Asia, this puts a lot of pressure on operators to perform financially from the very beginning of operations. In the US, many brewpubs have avoided this issue by opening in marginal areas, where rents are cheaper, and signing long leases. If the brewpub concept, which generally is large enough to be a destination in its own right, is successful, then other retail operators tend to move into the surrounding neighborhood, bringing even more customers and increasing revenues. Because of the long-lease tenures and even the opportunity to obtain financing to purchase the building, there is the opportunity to realize higher profits in the medium to long term in spite of the loss of seating space.

A wonderful example of how this works is the Wynkoop Brewing Company in Denver, Colorado, US. In 1988, it moved into a disused department store in the LoDo area, which was in urban decay, but has since become a vibrant part of the city and a magnet for all sorts of consumers, who are attracted by a wonderful array of shops and restaurants that have been established since the Wynkoop brewery was installed. In Asia, this type of development for an area is a very rare option. Population densities tend to be higher and cities have been settled for long periods of time, and therefore, brownfield sites are very rare and greenfield opportunities nearly unheard of.

To an extent, Brewerkz was able to overcome this size-to-seating issue by selecting a location just outside the Singapore Central Business District. We put the brewpub in an area that was scheduled for improvements, including the deepening of an adjacent river and installation of a promenade as well as building a mass rapid transit station and a modern shopping mall, but which were several years from being realized. We also worked closely with our tank manufactures to shrink the footprint of the brewery. Because we have a very high ceiling, the tanks are taller and the floor area that they occupy is smaller.

An issue in a similar vein is not just that the brewery takes up seating space, but it is in itself rather large. Because of this, the location needs to be bigger than a standard restaurant. On the minus side, this size requirement makes it harder to obtain an appropriate site, which should be somewhere between 750 and 1,000 sq meters. On the plus side, it is also harder for others to find a location as well.

Lack of competition, investment quantum, operation size, and brewery specialization are negatively defensible aspects of running a brewpub. These factors make it difficult for another entrant to attack our market. But there are also advantages to be gained from installing a brewery inside of a restaurant. For one, it is permanent advertising. While there is not much to differentiate one restaurant from another, they all have kitchens and some form of decoration, a brewery really sets a place apart. It is not just a thematic element like the guitars on the walls of Hard Rock Cafe or the plastic flowers and animals at Rainforest Cafe, but a functional part of a diner's experience that reinforces what makes a brewpub different. To really bring this home at Brewerkz, our design team, which also invested in our first outlet and had experience working on projects for Disneyland, Nike Town, MGM Grand, and The Sandlot Brewpub at Coors Field in Denver, highlighted the brewery. They put it in the center of the interior, which is about 1,000 square meters in size.

From the beverage perspective, perhaps the most defensible aspect of a brewpub is that our beer is unique to our concepts. While every bar in town that wants beer as a generic offering can buy it from a distributor, the Brewerkz Restaurant & Microbrewery was the only place where one could get a pint of our beer. Moreover, because we brewed ales, we could offer a wider diversity of beer styles. This is in contrast with the German-style brewpubs that had appeared in a few Asian cities and focused on lager brewing. *Lager* means "to store" in German and for good reason. While a light ale may take 10 days to be ready to serve, even the lightest lager (because of the low fermentation temperature and sulfur-smell associated with lager yeast when the beer has not received sufficient aging), will need about six weeks before it is good condition for serving. In practical terms, this longer fermentation process means that lager breweries tend to limit their selections, particularly in brewpubs where space can be more expensive and seating constrained by storage needs. For this reason, Paulaner, a famous Munich brewpub operator, tends generally to have only two styles on draft, one light and one dark.

Brewerkz, on the other hand, has throughout its existence featured eight styles and today maintains 12 different beers on tap at its original location. This has proven to be quite a successful strategy for Brewerkz. While our three best-selling styles account for about 60 percent of our beer sales, most of the other nine selections also tend to have a relatively good following and our customers are certainly ecumenical, often ordering at least two different beers during a meal.

While the Brewerkz food program is, in terms of offerings, not all that different from other similar restaurants, our quality is much better because we make all of our soups, salads, dressings, breads, and desserts from scratch. An American-style menu is definitely more flexible than that offered at German brewpubs. Where they hew to the line of traditional cuisine, trading on authenticity, Brewerkz has the ability to cater to a wider range of tastes because of the inclusive and eclectic nature of what is defined as American cuisine. The beer program is also a tremendous boon to the food because the higher margins associated with the reduced cost of brewing beer can be used to subsidize the food program, which means larger portions and better quality ingredients. This benefits even those who do not come to us for beer and gives us an advantage over operations that do not have a brewery but still sell a substantial amount of beer.

Establishing Brewerkz Singapore

I cofounded the original company, Brewerkz Singapore Pte. Ltd. in 1996 with Daniel Flores, who, prior to partnering with me, worked for the Singapore office of a major US financial institution. (Daniel retired from Brewerkz in 2000 and is now an investment banker in New York). The venture grew out of a plan for raising investment capital to establish a multiconcept restaurant group with outlets in several major East and Southeast Asian cities over the course of five years. The way that we structured the deal was that we would open a large brewpub in Singapore, perfect the concept over the course of a year and then expand to Hong Kong, Shanghai, Seoul, Tokyo, and other gateway locations in the region until we had enough critical mass to either make a public offering of the company's shares or sell it to a larger restaurant or brewing company. Although we started out with the idea of opening multiple concepts, we felt that each Brewerkz would be large enough that it represented an opportunity to focus on a single concept and outlet in each market.

Before pitching the idea to private equity funds, we assembled a strong team to support the concept. Brewing Technologies, a company that had the rights to sell Newlands Systems Inc. breweries throughout Asia, was our first partner. They had been part of the rapid growth of the Japanese microbrewing industry as a supplier and had been looking for a food-service operator to work with on a brewpub concept. We contacted them through an advertisement that they placed in the *Asian Wall Street Journal*. In exchange for their providing a 10-hectoliter brewery and sourcing a brewer, Brewing Technologies received 25 percent of Brewerkz equity.

Additionally, Brewing Technologies introduced us to a world-class interior-design firm from Pasadena, California, with whom they were familiar through work on the Sandlot Brewpub at Coors Field in Denver, where Newlands Systems Inc. had installed the brewing system. In lieu of fees, the designers also received equity. So by the time we were ready to begin pitching to investors for backing, we had assembled a team with Asian restaurant and brewery operations experience, as well as a design firm that had been involved with an iconic brewpub and had already done work in Asia on other projects. Moreover, we had secured an option on a location at a just completed shopping mall with plenty of outside seating along the Singapore River, which was in the process of being cleaned up and converted from an area of dilapidated warehouses to a lifestyle district.

We took this package to market starting, frankly, by introducing it to the least likely investors so that we could hone our pitch, making it all the better for those firms that we felt would make better financial partners for us. The process was not without its hiccups. One Singaporean and one well-known European venture-capital firm gave us a handshake on the deal. We started to draw up the shareholders' agreement, but the Europeans lost their funds managing director and dropped out of the deal. We were forced to find a replacement, eventually securing funding from a Singapore Stock Exchange-listed food service company and a group of individuals led by an Indonesian financier.

Opening Mistakes

Brewerkz Restaurant & Microbrewery opened in mid-1997 with its own brewery and seating capacity of about 400. It started up just as the

Asian financial crisis began affecting the Thai economy, spreading over the course of our first year in operation to infect most of the emerging countries in the region with a serious dose of Asian contagion. In addition, the weather turned against us and for most of our first six months the noxious haze caused by plantation fires in neighboring Indonesia rendered more than half of our seats unusable because they happened to be located *al fresco*.

While these external factors proved to be extremely challenging, our most serious strategic problem was self-inflicted. The original concept for the food was to produce an all-American menu based on what was available at Rock Bottom Breweries in the US and Dan Ryan's Chicago Grill in Asia. The fare was to be pretty standard menu items, such as chicken wings, salads, pizzas, steaks, and ribs. But Gordon Biersch Brewery Restaurants were proving to be extremely successful at several locations in the Western US with a more sophisticated, upscale menu. And Typhoon, a brewery and restaurant, had opened in midtown Manhattan with a food concept that featured *satay* (seasoned meat on skewers, which are grilled or barbecued over fire) and a sushi bar and was proving to be a big hit.

Beyond that, we hired a chef who had worked closely with Jean-Georges Vongerichten at one of his restaurants featuring an Asian fusion menu, to join us at Brewerkz in Singapore. We saw this as a perfect opportunity not only to get a world-class chef from New York to put us on the map but even better, we thought that his cooking would elevate us to the next level. This would make it even more difficult for another brewpub to enter the market with anywhere near the cutting-edge food program that we could offer, let alone the beer and other inherent advantages that we had as a concept.

The accolades from the Singapore food writers seemed to justify our direction. We were given stellar reviews for our *beggars' purses*, deep-fried sea bass with green papaya salad, and Thai-style green chicken curry. But from day one, our most popular menu item was a hamburger, and despite the glowing reviews, we were struggling. Because of the noise from the Asian financial crisis and the haze, it was rational to believe that our lack of sales was not our fault. And to an extent that was probably true. As we learned in later years, it is nearly impossible to grow sales when the economy is down and there is bad weather, as anyone who operates where it snows or where it gets cold can confirm, also negatively affects sales. But as the economy and the air-quality improved, our sales did not. We were still fighting just to break even.

It was a conversation with a German that led us to change our menu. He was the owner of a brewery-equipment manufacturer, who was in Singapore to dismantle one of his breweries at a brewpub that had failed due to the Asian crisis. (It was a matter not of revenues, but rather the Thai parent company had too many US dollar-denominated loans outstanding and, like so many others at the time, it folded under the weight of its foreign currency lending.) We invited him to Brewerkz and had a good, long conversation about the authenticity of German brewpubs and how important it is for them to be fundamentally like those in Germany.

At this point, a light went on for us. While the urban sophisticates of California or New York City may be hankering for the novelty of Asian food at their brewpub, people in Asia were looking for a Western experience. For those from the West, they wanted something that reminded them of home. For those from Singapore, it was exotic American cuisine. And we were satisfying neither group. So we sent our high-priced New York chef back to the US, took all of the fusion food off the menu, and started making money.

Trying Marketing Ideas

One of the great things about F&B is that it allows an operator to test concepts in real time and get immediate and constant feedback from customers. One of our biggest surprises upon opening was that the India Pale Ale, a relatively high-alcohol, big-bodied, and highly-hopped beer, was our best-selling beer from the outset. As Tiger, a light lager, is Singapore's most popular beer, our original thought was that the preference for Brewerkz beers would start with our lightest offering, the Golden Ale, and next move to a more full-bodied beer such as a Red Ale. This is the progression in the US. But for us, the Red Ale has only ever been marginally popular while our two best sellers are the Golden Ale and India Pale Ale. To a large extent, this shows that the market was certainly ready for something different.

When we opened, it was our belief that the beer would take care of itself, which is why we focused so much effort on the food program.

But food has always accounted for a higher percentage of our sales at Brewerkz than beer. So once we figured out the direction of our menu, it was time to drive beer sales. While our inherent strategic advantage is that we make a wide variety of beers that are not available anywhere else, being a new brand was a definite handicap. The biggest problem was that people could not know how good our beer was unless they had tried it, so we needed to drive trial. To do that, we created the lunch special—order an appetizer and main course and we would give you three pints of beer to accompany the meal. By the end of our first year, Friday lunch was a zoo and all 400 seats were packed. Sunday brunch was also nonstop. Even weekdays were busy. Over time, we began inching the prices up. As a result, while we were not so busy, profitability became much better.

While the three-beer lunch helped introduce our product and make us popular as a lunch destination, it was always a struggle to get people to join us for dinner on Monday. Consequently, we introduced "Monday Madness" and the dollar draft, an unheard of concept in the high-cost beer market of Singapore. The deal was that you could go to the bar and buy up to five 12 oz (360 ml) beers in plastic cups from 5–6 p.m. on Monday. We had lots of complaints that the hour was too early, but by the time we ended the promotion, Monday had become as popular as the other weekday evenings with lines stretching for 200 meters, and our beer volume was the equivalent of keeping three taps fully flowing for an hour. People loved it, but the staff hated the people who loved it. We ended the promotion when we realized that it got to the point where we were no longer attracting customers who would become regulars and pay higher prices because they had come to like our product, but who came only because we were offering cheap beer. This is the real downside of holding onto price promotions for too long—they move from being an enticement to try something new to being an opportunity to obtain a commodity at a low price. In other words, we wanted the promotion to be about trying good Brewerkz beer and not about getting a drink at the lowest possible price.

Using pricing was one way of getting people to try our beer. Another was getting it out into the community for people to try. To create the needed awareness, we sponsored kegs for a large number of organizations from events such as the Singapore Armed Forces, and the

American Association's Fourth of July celebration and its Jazz Festival. We gave beer for banquets and dinner dances, and to business, educational, and service organizations. At the same time, we also offered vouchers that could be redeemed at our restaurants.

The other side of our marketing was to build customer loyalty so that all who did visit us for the first time would return. Excellent execution is a big part of this. Some of the aspects are physical, such as tables that do not wobble, clean restrooms, and being the only stand-alone Hazard Analysis and Critical Control Points certified restaurant chain in Singapore. Even more important is the way that managers treat the staff. The MENU Group is one of Asia's only hospitality providers that offer staff a five-day workweek, no split shifts, and hospitalization insurance. We also provide meals, birthday vouchers, a bonus program, and tips payout at shift's end and strive to fill all of our positions from internal candidates.

The sponsorship of sports has also had a big impact on building loyalty. We have more than a dozen different teams from cycling to ice hockey wearing our jerseys in Singapore. Every team member is given a card, which entitles him or her to a 15 percent discount at all of our outlets. And what we have found is that our revenues are more than double the expenses associated with a team's support.

Earning Street Credibility

One of the difficult aspects of opening a Western concept in an Eastern context is that the audience may not really appreciate what a good job you are doing. While Brewerkz was certainly one of Singapore's most popular Western restaurants, sales did not really take off until we won the World Beer Cup Gold Award for the Best English-style India Pale Ale in 2004. Suddenly, people who had been enjoying our beer became justified in their customary visits, and those who had not gotten around to trying Brewerkz began flooding in. For this reason, we continue to enter our beers into the world's two largest competitions, winning awards on a regular basis.

In addition, Brewerkz beer has been featured in many articles, not just in Singapore publications but also internationally. Charlie Papazian, the founder of the Brewers Association, has visited and written about us on several occasions, and we have been featured in Britain's *Campaign for Real Ale* (CAMRA) magazine as well.

Branching Out

When I was a student at Cornell University's School of Hotel Administration, Professor Chris Muller, who is now at University of Central Florida's Rosen College of Hospitality Management, always said: "Growth is an outcome not a strategy." We had always planned to grow in our original business plan, but it did not occur the way that we thought that it would. For all of the reasons cited above about how a brewpub concept is defensible, it also makes finding an appropriate space in another city difficult and more costly than it would be for a restaurant without a brewery. Another issue is that leveraging scale, particularly in terms of purchasing and management, is more effective when operations are in closer proximity. When we decided to grow in 2000, we took a location in the same development as Brewerkz. Because it was so close, we needed to develop a second concept and decided on a Mexican theme; we called it Café Iguana. Because the space was below 200 sq. meters, we felt that it would be a good laboratory for us. And if a particular idea or type of operation did not work, then it would not be very costly to change. Also, the close proximity to the original Brewerkz location allowed us to manage it easily while at the same time, gaining experience for the organization in running a multi-unit, as well as a multiconcept, operation.

At the outset, we experienced difficulty making money with Cafe Iguana, and it did not really begin to be profitable until we created a half-priced happy hour and changed the menu to be less Mexican and more Tex-Mex, thereby appealing to a wider audience. Since then, Cafe Iguana has become wildly successful and we have recently opened a second outlet.

Our third concept, WineGarage, came about when the 500 sq. meter space directly adjacent to Riverside Point became available in 2005. It would have been a perfect opportunity for us to expand Brewerkz, which was literally bursting at the seams, but the problem was we could not make enough beer for the additional 250 seats. The brewery had been expanded twice for an additional nearly 20,000 liters in storage and fermentation capacity, but we had simply run out of space for any more growth. We had reached our floor-loading limits and more tanks would have meant fewer seats, so we decided to head in a different direction. Based on our experience with getting a concept to spark when we lowered the price of beer and margaritas significantly at Brewerkz and Café Iguana, the idea was to put a wine-based concept in 250 sq. meters of the space and keep the margins razor-thin on the wine. It was originally to be a casual place, and the name was to signal a lack of pretension about the wine. But ultimately, WineGarage did not start making money until we put white clothes and napkins on the tables and the wine into crystal glassware.

Guy Kawasaki, author and former Apple Computer evangelist, talks about how important it is not to hold back on a product until it is perfect because you never know how the end-user will react. The important thing is to be able to respond to criticism and make fixes and changes on the fly and that is exactly what we have done with our concepts.

Next Steps

Perhaps our biggest change since opening is not from moving from a single, large operation in gateway Asian cities to a multiconcept or multi-unit approach offering us a wider portfolio of brands. Where we have really changed is on the brewpub concept. The difficulty of finding appropriate space anywhere in Asia has caused us to rethink the entire business model. In 2007, we set up a second brewery in a Singapore flatted factory that is more than twice the size of our original Riverside Point operation. It has no retail area but what it does give us is the opportunity to expand our beer into smaller locations that do not have breweries, but are easier to find. While we lose the permanent advertising aspect of having an on-site brewery, we are still able to offer our unique range of beers, Brewerkz branding, and food program. This strategy also makes our revenue model less dependent on a single outlet, where a shutdown of the one unit could cripple the company.

Our intention at this point is to try out this hub-and-spoke system, which is generally illegal in the US because of prohibition era laws, and also in the United Kingdom where they are called tied houses. We would like to see if this system might be more practical for rollout in a city such as Hong Kong, where so far we have been unable to find a large enough space for us to site both a brewery and restaurant operation.

Conclusion

Like any successful business, the MENU Group has used strategy to define its goals and focus its efforts, but we have also been opportunistic in pursuit of profits, and we try to be quick to switch direction when our original direction brings us to a dead end.

A few years ago at my university class's 20th reunion, everyone around me seemed to be either a very successful doctor, lawyer, or investment banker. But many of them really looked forward to doing something completely different when they retired. As the conversation came around to me, I gave everyone a bit of a shock by saying that I in fact had absolutely no plans to ever leave my current employment. To a collection of people who viewed their job as a means and not an end, this sounded like heresy. One of them asked me how it was that I could be so happy with what I do for a living. My answer was that as a guy who owns a brewery next to a lazy river on a tropical island in Asia, retiring to do something more fun with my life was not likely as I now have the best job in the world!

References

Kimble, Devin. 1996. Barriers and Opportunities in Singapore. *Cornell Hotel and Restaurant Administration Quarterly* 37 (3):50–54.

World Bank. 2010. Country reports. http://web.worldbank.org/.

7

ACHIEVING GREAT BUSINESS GROWTH

By Chiaki Tanuma

Introduction

Growth strategies are vital if companies are to achieve sustainable growth and produce desired results. Growth not only increases profits but also helps to invigorate organizations and generate new growth. While activities such as downsizing and restructuring may increase productivity, growth has the added effect of bringing profits to a company and its stakeholders. One can say that a sound growth strategy is absolutely essential to ensuring a company's long-term survival. In this chapter, the Japanese food-service industry, and in particular, the Green House Group (GHG), are used to demonstrate how companies can create and maintain strategic growth.

First, an overview of the Japanese food-service industry market and the various problems it currently faces are provided. Next, the GHG and the 60-plus-year growth process it has undergone since its establishment, is presented. GHG serves as a good example of a company that has developed a growth strategy, which has resulted in sustainable growth. Finally, some concluding comments on strategic growth and maintaining a competitive advantage are offered.

Market Trends in the Japanese Food-Service Industry

Prior to the development of a growth strategy, key macro-environmental trends must be researched and analyzed to ascertain the potential impact of these developments on the industry and the individual company. Trends in Japan, similar to those in most industrialized countries, could negatively affect the industry and companies' future prospects if these shifts are not considered and integrated when constructing growth strategies. Consequently, an investigation of economic, demographic, competitive, social responsibility, legislative, and environmental trends was conducted, with the key findings presented here. Many of these trends are common across industrialized nations.

Economic Trends

Within the Japanese food-service market, 1970 is referred to as the first year of dining out, as it was from this year onward that the industrialization of the Japanese food-service industry gathered pace. This is due to, among other things, the chain development of foreign-origin fast-food chains such as McDonald's and Kentucky Fried Chicken, and Japanese family restaurants such as Skylark. The food-service industry market continued to expand from 8.63 trillion yen in 1975 to 29.07 trillion yen in 1997, before shrinking to 24.39 trillion yen in 2005. It recovered slightly in 2006 and 2007 due to a rebound in entertainment spending and an increase in expenditures on eating out. As of early 2008, it stood at 24.7 trillion yen (Crockett 2000; Datamonitor 2008).

Examining the food-service industry in 2007 by business category, the market for restaurants and fast food was 12.48 trillion yen. The market for meals and receptions at hotels and *ryokans* (Japanese inns) was 3.13 trillion yen while 250 billion yen was spent on domestic in-flight meals. The market for institutional food service at offices, hospitals, and retirement facilities in 2007 was around 3.6 trillion yen. This institutional food service category includes contract food services provided by contractors, the market for which was estimated at around 2.8 trillion yen in 2008. The market for the drinking establishments category, which includes coffee houses, bars and the like, was 5.2 trillion yen (Datamonitor 2008).

In addition, the market for *nakashoku*, (takeout and delivery of foodstuffs and ready-prepared meals and box lunches, sold by specialist box-lunch stores, supermarkets, and convenience stores) which also forms a part of the food-service market, is growing annually, increasing from 3.61 trillion yen in 1997 to 6.22 trillion yen in 2007 (Department of Agriculture and Food 2009).

Demographic Trends

Since 2006, Japan has entered an age of population decrease (see Figure 7.1). From a size of approximately 128 million people in 2006, the total population is expected to experience a steady decline to an estimated 124 million by 2020 and 117 million by 2030, reaching just 100 million by 2050. The number of elderly aged 65 years or over stood around 17 percent of the total population. This percentage is expected to grow to 25.2 percent in 2013 (see Figure 7.2). In particular, the need to cater to the senior citizens, who are healthy and self-supporting, provides an opportunity to create an entirely new food-service market. The development of the market catering to the 27 million active seniors aged 50–64 years and the 16.58 million members of the 36- to 46-year-old demographic, who are currently the driving force behind consumption, is also extremely important.

Changes can also be observed in terms of household composition. The number of standard households (married couples with two children), which traditionally have been regarded as the core of marketing, is on the decline, and is expected to comprise just 28.3 percent of total households in 2010. Meanwhile, the numbers of one-parent households and married-couple-only households are on the increase, and are

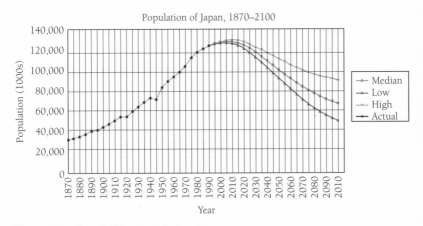

Figure 7.1   Population Trends for Japan
Source: Anthony F. F. Boys, http://www9.ocn.ne.jp/-aslan/pfe/jpeak.htm

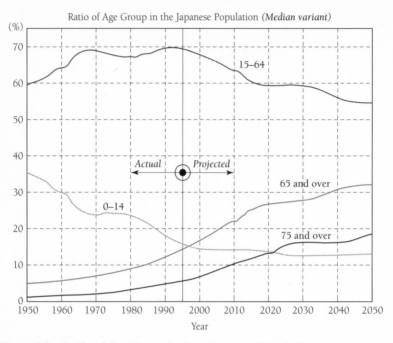

Figure 7.2   Ratio of Age Group in the Japanese Population
Source: Anthony F. F. Boys, http://www9.ocn.ne.jp/-aslan/pfe/jpeak.htm

predicted to compose 30.3 percent and 20.8 percent of total households respectively in 2010. In the future, it will become increasingly important to respond to these changes in household composition, for example, by developing menus and dining environments that can be readily utilized by singles and couples.

In the food-service market, the fierce competition between stores, business categories, and corporations for a slice of a limited pie is continuing. Food-service companies face competition not only from other members of their industry but increasingly from *nakashoku* providers such as convenience stores and supermarkets, while the number of food-service companies entering the *nakashoku* sector is also on the increase. *Nakashoku* providers are expanding their marketing area from the supermarkets' delicatessen sections and department stores' basement food sections to new locations inside and around railway stations, office buildings, and shopping complexes, a development that is having an impact on traditional food-service outlets.

Food-away-from-home expenditures in Japan, as a percentage of total consumer expenditures on food, peaked at 37.8 percent in 1993 and then continued to decline until recovery in 2001, reaching 34.8 percent in 2007. Considering that in the United States (US), food-away-from-home expenditures, as a percentage of total consumer expenditures on food, has remained steady at around 40 percent, the food-service industry's share of this part of the Japanese market can be expected to increase in the future.

Meanwhile, expenditures on food-away-from-home and home-meal replacement, as a percentage of total consumer expenditures on food, have increased annually from 28.4 percent in 1975 to 42.7 percent in 2007. The popularity of these forms of dining is expected to further increase as preparing meals at home becomes less common and dining out and enjoying takeout and delivered meals become more common. This is due to factors such as the greater participation of women in the workforce, the increase in the number of one-parent and senior households, and the shift to a 24-hour lifestyle.

The Japanese leisure market stood at 78.92 trillion yen in 2006. Expenditures on food-away-from-home accounted for 12.34 trillion yen or 15.6 percent of total expenditures in the leisure market, an increase of 1.5 percent compared with the previous year. With leisure-related expenditures by the elderly predicted to escalate from 5.8 trillion yen in 2001 to 7.8 trillion yen in 2011, the amount the elderly spends on food-away-from-home as a part of this leisure activity can also be expected to rise.

Competitive Trends

Total sales for the top 100 food service companies in fiscal 2007 (*Nikkei MJ 2008*) reached 5.0144 trillion yen, up 4.4 percent on the same figure for the previous year. However, even the industry leader, McDonald's Japan, could only achieve sales of around 490 billion yen, or some 2 percent of the entire food-service market, indicating that the market is far from oligopolistic. However, oligopolization is gradually occurring, with the share of sales held by the top 100 companies growing from 13 percent in 1992 to 20.5 percent in 2007.

The composition of the competition may be changing. Looking at the results by industry as a whole, a feature in recent years is that a total of five contract food-service companies, including GHG, have made their way into the top 20 companies in terms of sales, and are putting up a good fight in an increasingly competitive market. At the same time, companies whose core business is family restaurants are finding the going tough, which is reflective of the declining birthrates, an aging population, and a decrease in the average number of people per household.

Social Responsibility Trends

There are a number of social responsibility concerns currently surrounding the Japanese food service industry. These matters are wide-ranging and include concerns such as protecting food resources and ensuring food safety and security, and issues such as the responsibility for healthy diet education, good labor environment and employment issues, and responding to environmental problems.

One of the most pressing problems facing the food-service industry is securing stable food supplies. This challenge is caused by increases in the world population, instability in global food production, and interest in biofuels. Largely as a result of a doubling of the population of developing countries, the world population increased from 3.7 billion in 1970 to 6.5 billion in 2005, while the average income per person rose from US$887 to US$6,896 (World Bank 2008) over the same period. These two factors have had an impact on food demand, with demand for wheat increasing 1.9 times, maize 2.7 times, and soybeans 4.8 times. Instability of global agricultural production, crops, and livestock in Central and South Asia, South America, and Africa have been greatly affected by factors such as the slowdown in the growth rate of grain yields per unit area, increased desertification, and global warming. Finally, the recent increase in the popularity of biofuels has further reduced the amount of food available for human consumption. A result of these problems is the sizeable drop in Japan's food self-sufficiency rate, which has fallen from a calorie-based self-sufficiency rate of 73 percent in 1964 to 39 percent in 2006. This is one of the lowest figures among the major industrialized nations.

In such an environment, food prices have continued to rise since the beginning of 2008, encouraging the economizing tendencies of consumers and even leading to a trend toward restraint in dining out. From now on, consideration will have to be given to ways of absorbing cost increases and implementing measures to ensure customer numbers do not decline even if prices are raised.

Japan has also been hit by a succession of food-related scandals since around 2000, including anxiety over bovine spongiform encephalopathy (BSE) and avian influenza, false labeling of foodstuffs, use of foodstuffs that are beyond their consume-by date, and use of unauthorized additives. The March 2008 food poisoning incident involving Chinese frozen processed foodstuffs in particular, sparked a heightening of consumer concerns over food safety and security and the abandonment of Chinese ingredients and food products.

In future, the food-service industry must not only demand that the government bolster its imported food inspection system but also make an effort to strengthen hygiene management and quality control and provide consumers with appropriate information in the form of country of origin, allergy, and nutritional labeling. From April 2008, as one of a range of measures introduced to combat metabolic syndrome, corporate and other bodies are required to implement designated medical examinations and health guidance. As a result, those companies or health insurance associations that fail to meet standard values are likely to face penalties. As a result of these and other developments, the level of awareness of health-related issues among the general public is becoming even higher, and some members of the food-service industry have even introduced low-calorie menus designed to prevent metabolic syndrome.

Legislative Trends

In conjunction with these efforts, legislation has been introduced to further improve the health of Japanese residents. Healthy diet education is an initiative aimed at equipping people with knowledge so that they understand which foods are required to build a healthy condition, and they are capable of choosing foods that are appropriate for their own bodies. This education is regarded as providing fundamental knowledge for the purposes of living and is one of the cornerstones of knowledge, moral, and physical education in accordance with the 2005 Basic Law on Nutritional Education. This initiative includes not only culinary education but also comprehensive information on attitudes toward food and eating, nutrition science, and traditional food culture.

Another challenge facing the industry is a shortage of labor. A survey of member companies conducted in September 2006 by the Japan Foodservice Association found that they were able to fill only 80 percent of job vacancies, equating to a labor shortage of 20 percent. Efforts have been made to address this problem by raising hourly rates for part-timers and expanding the employment of new graduates. However, competition with other industries to secure personnel is becoming fiercer and little headway is being made in solving the labor shortage. This is regarded not as a temporary phenomenon due to the economic upturn but as a result of the declining birthrate. In the future, measures such as the employment of the elderly, retiring baby boomers, and foreigners, along with the introduction of a daily wage system, will need to be adopted.

Environmental Trends

The 21st century has been designated the century of the environment, and tackling the problem of global warming is a major issue shared by all humankind. Japan is promoting a 6 percent overall reduction in greenhouse gas emissions by 2012, which is the current target under the Kyoto Protocol. The food-service industry is also being asked to actively address this issue across three areas: enhanced environmental conservation activities, development of environmentally friendly products, and development of environmental technologies.

With regard to environmental conservation activities, the food-service industry could lessen its burden on the environment by implementing the three R's (reduce, reuse, and recycle) and, for example, minimizing the use of paper in the workplace. Another issue is the reduction of the amount of energy used in food preparation and production. In addressing these problems, initiatives aimed at introducing energy-saving design and recycling design are in the process of becoming established. Recycling design is based on the development of environmentally friendly products and green procurement, which relies on the use of raw and other materials that place less of a burden on the environment. In the area of the development of environmental technologies, activities aimed at the development of organic farming methods and other environmentally friendly technologies are becoming more widespread.

Green House Group's Management Philosophy and Core Business Activities

In this section, as a premise for discussing growth strategy, I outline GHG's management philosophy and principal business activities. GHG, which in 2010 marked 63 years since its formation, is a conglomerate encompassing mainly contract food services, restaurants, hotel management, and a consulting business.

Management Philosophy

GHG's founder, Bunzo Tanuma, established the company out of a deep desire to "engage in work that brings happiness to people and benefits society." Beginning in 1947, during the period immediately after the war when food shortages were common, he started the business by accepting an offer to provide meals at Keio University's student dormitory. In due course, Japan entered a period of rapid economic growth, and GHG grew, largely due to the backing of former Keio University students who had once benefited from the company's operations and were now entering the workforce. These Keio alumni recommended that their employers invite GHG to run their company cafeterias.

Based on Bunzo Tanuma's founding principle, the corporate motto, "Making others happy leads to our prosperity," is GHG's key management philosophy and the cornerstone of its growth.

As the second generation president and CEO, I brought to this founding spirit a desire to change the world through food. I believed that activities concerning food should not be considered purely from the point of view of pursuing profits. The fact that the Chinese character for "eating" used in China and Japan is written by combining the radicals for "person" and "good" could be interpreted as meaning "make people better and happier." After making a reasonable profit, the degree to which a company can be turned into something that makes people happy and benefits society needs to be at the heart of the food business, which is after all, symbolic of a country's culture. In order for a food company to enjoy support and survive over the long term, this must constitute the basis of its management.

Core Business Activities

GHG operates four core businesses—a business and industry contract food service; a healthcare contract food service (provision of meals for hospital outpatients and inpatients and food-service management within welfare facilities for the elderly); a restaurant and delicatessen operation; and a hotel-management operation. The total annual sales of all these operations combined are around US$1 billion (107 billion yen). GHG also owns Cini-Little Japan, which is a food-service facility-design consulting company, and Horwath Asia-Pacific Japan, which is a hotel consulting company under license agreements.

The contract food-service operation has been GHG's core operation since its foundation, and involves the provision of around 400,000 meals a day due to contracts with some 1,500 sites nationwide. The style in which these meals are provided is wide ranging, including the provision of meals at government and municipal offices, company offices, factories, and schools, as well as the provision of catering box lunches, and airline in-flight meals.

GHG has linked the various business partners with its own food-products distribution center and introduced GAMES (Green House Adaptable Menu Entry System), its unique menu system that operates together with online ingredient ordering. This has enabled the company to put together menus that are rich in variety.

One of GHG's strengths is that its staff of around 1,000 registered dietitians. Their specialist knowledge in food and health is employed to good effect in supporting the daily preparation of healthy meals. Because of recently implemented health legislation and guidelines aimed at reducing the state's share of medical costs from April 2008, improving employees' health has become an important topic for companies and health insurance associations. At GHG, this issue is being addressed by creating programs that support the new healthcare guidelines and by disseminating appropriate nutritional guidance with the assistance of its registered dieticians via the Internet. These initiatives have elicited encouraging responses from a range of companies.

In response to declining demographic trends in Japan, GHG is continuing to put in place strategic arrangements overseas, including entering into an alliance with Albron of the Netherlands and DSR of Switzerland in 2006 and Fazer of Finland in 2008. In all cases, these

European contract food-service companies have management philoso-phies that GHG can identify with. In 2008, GHG also established a joint venture with Beijing Zhen Da Catering Co., Ltd. of China, to run cafete-rias and restaurants for Japanese-owned businesses. Furthermore, GHG's healthcare contract food-service operations provide meals on the basis of its contracts with hospitals, facilities for the elderly and other healthcare-related facilities, which are growth markets. The meals it provides to hospital inpatients are value-added products prepared by registered dietitians, who have undergone specialist training with an eye to ensuring every meal is healthy, easy to consume, and eye-pleasing. GHG also caters to the needs of outpatients by supplying meals to outpatient restaurants, medical staff, and others.

At facilities for the elderly, GHG strives to prepare meals that remind patients of the warmth of their own homes, in addition to tak-ing into account their taste and nutritional aspects. In doing so, the company helps to stimulate people's appetites by coming up with ways of making liquid food, food for people who have difficulty swallowing, and other special meals, which resemble as closely as possible meals for able-bodied people. It also puts much effort into meal presentation, and ensures not only that it provides meals that are enjoyable but also employs food management techniques of the highest quality.

Tonkatsu Shinjuku Saboten, GHG's restaurant and delicatessen operations, commenced the sale of takeout-style delicatessen products in 1987, thus signaling its entry into the *nakashoku* market. The com-pany has subsequently grown into one of the largest operators in this market in terms of sales and outlet numbers. The total number of out-lets, including those overseas, currently stands at around 500. In 2001, the company commenced operations overseas, establishing outlets in South Korea on the basis of a technical tie-up with Our Home of South Korea. In 2004, GHG established outlets in Taiwan in a joint venture with the DaChan Great Wall Group among others. In 2008, the com-pany entered into a joint venture agreement with President Bakery of Thailand, whereby GHG is preparing to open stores in that country. Currently, GHG has more than 40 outlets in South Korea and Taiwan, and is continuing to expand operations in Asia.

At its Shahoden restaurants, GHG has established a cooking method that uses no chemical seasonings, which was once considered difficult in the Chinese cuisine category. The company has also sought to diversify, for example, by entering the casual Chinese dining market. In 2007, GHG opened a branch of the Si Chuan Dou Hua restaurant brand in the Shin-Marunouchi Building, a large-scale office complex in front of Tokyo Station, in a tie-up with a restaurant group associated with United Overseas Bank, one of Singapore's largest banks. In its restaurant operation, the company places a great deal of importance on the quality of ingredients and seasonings, ambience, and providing food that is nourishing to the body, following an approach that is embodied in GHG's principles of focusing on the natural, wellness, and hospitality.

With regard to its hotel-management operation, GHG established a dedicated hotel-management company in 2000, and since then, it has entered into management contracts to run several lodging facilities. The properties range widely from business hotels to city hotels, resort hotels, and hotels as public facilities owned by local governments and education workers' unions. In August 2008, GHG entered into an alliance with Wyndham Hotel Group, the world's largest franchise hotel-chain company, and expanded its operations of Wyndham's brands, Ramada and Days Inn, in Japan. This GHG division provides services that encompass every aspect of hotel operations including food service, and also manages properties while maintaining close contact with the owners to ensure consensus in business direction. Future plans for this division include taking on contracts for the management of large-scale resort hotels in Okinawa and other places, which will eventually raise the total number of properties managed to around 20.

Group's Growth Process

Looking back at the rise and development of the post-war food-service industry permits an examination of the growth process that GHG has adopted and how it has continued to grow against a background of major macro-environmental changes. Over the more than 60 years of its growth process, GHG has, in a timely manner, selected and employed a variety of growth strategies depending on the circumstances. This next section identifies the growth strategies that GHG has selected, discusses how it has transformed turning points into victory, and how it succeeded at several critical turning points over this period. (Refer to Figures 7.3 and 7.4.)

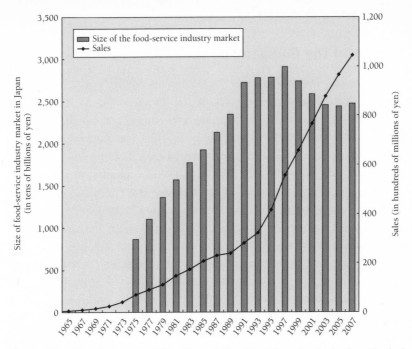

Figure 7.3   Development of the Size of the Food-Service Industry Market in Japan and GHG Sales
Source: Green House Group

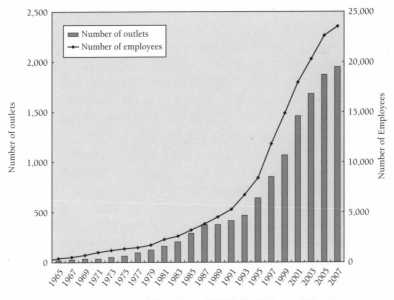

Figure 7.4   Development of Number of GHG Outlets and Employees
Source: Green House Group

Origins of the Company's Foundation

As previously mentioned, the establishment of GHG in 1947 sprang from a deep desire on the part of the founder, Bunzo Tanuma, to "engage in work that brings happiness to people and benefits society." Shortly after, around 1950 and at the start of the Korean War, Japan was swept up in a special procurement boom, and as a result, the country finally entered a stage in which a market economy took hold and consumption was stimulated. Bunzo Tanuma was running a cafeteria at Keio University at the time, but in 1954, as his business began to grow, he established a private limited company and after gathering suggestions from many students, settled on the name Green House.

In 1959, GHG was reorganized into a joint-stock corporation, and in the following year, it made its first foray into the private company employee cafeteria market by signing a contract to run the food service at a factory owned by Matsushita Communications Industrial Co., Ltd. Subsequently, it entered into contracts with one private company after another, including a major automobile manufacturer, Nissan Motor Co., Ltd.; a blast furnace manufacturer, Nippon Steel Corporation; and a food manufacturer. By focusing on the company employee cafeteria market, the company was able to continue reducing costs and accumulating know-how. Against a backdrop of a period of continuing growth, the number of outlets grew to 17 in 1965.

Shortly after its establishment, GHG faced a bitter experience in the temporary closure of its cafeteria at Keio University due to construction work on a new building commemorating the university's 100th anniversary. Based on an awareness of the importance of resolving the instability that is a characteristic of the contracting industry, a business-diversification strategy was devised. In 1966, GHG opened Saboten, a restaurant specializing in deep-fried pork cutlets, and in the following year, it opened the first of its Shahoden Chinese restaurants in Shinjuku. Both restaurants were owned and operated by GHG.

GHG's contract food service, which was centered on private companies, was also gaining greater credit and confidence on the back of strong results. In 1968, a contract was signed for the management of the cafeteria at the Tokyo Metropolitan Police Department headquarters, marking GHG's first foray into the government-cafeteria sector. Its brand equity rose as it expanded further into this market by signing contracts with the Ministry of Finance and the Tokyo Stock Exchange, contributing to even further growth. These contracts provided evidence and recognition of GHG's predominance and advancement in the market. At a time when consumption was extolled as a virtue, the nation's gross national product was second in the world, and rapid economic growth was peaking, the number of outlets grew in excess of 30 in 1969.

The 1970s were characterized by dizzying changes in fortune, from the highs of Expo '70 and "Rebuilding the Japanese Archipelago" advocated by then premier Kakuei Tanaka to the lows of the two oil crises. As previously highlighted, 1970 also marked the first year of dining out. McDonald's Japan opened its first outlet in 1971, marking the arrival of the fast-food era in earnest in Japan. The groundwork for the development of the food-service industry was being laid due to improvements in income levels, a growing sense of belonging to the middle class, and an expansion of the leisure market.

From around the mid-1970s, the competition to open family restaurants became increasingly fierce. Yearly revenue at McDonald's Japan broke through the 10 billion yen barrier, and the sudden growth in the food-service market led to it being recognized as an industry in its own right. In 1974, 7-Eleven opened its first store in Japan, and this period also witnessed the rise of a range of companies specializing in takeout box lunches and takeout sushi. Japan's largest food-service industry body, the Japan Food Service Chain Association (now the Japan Foodservice Association), was also established around this time.

At the time, GHG was going through a process of laying its foundations to consolidate its competitive advantage position, and its attention turned to business reforms within the company. It formulated a green movement aimed at improving the ethics and service mind-set of its employees. Marking its 30th year of business in 1977, GHG hosted a commemorative exhibition, where it introduced original menus, private brand goods, and a food-materials distribution system, all of which were covered extensively in the mass media. Sales reached 10.2 billion yen in 1979 and the number of outlets exceeded 117.

Following the Plaza Accord of 1985, the yen began to appreciate considerably and a low-interest policy continued, resulting in the emergence in the early 1990s of the bubble economy. The food-service market grew from 14.6 trillion yen in 1980 to 25.6 trillion yen in

1990 (Datamonitor 2008). This was due to the opening of new outlets and an increase in food-away-from-home expenditures as a percentage of total consumer expenditures on food, eclipsing the department store industry.

In 1986, the Equal Employment Opportunity Law came into effect, and the number of female employees rose. This resulted in less time being spent on preparing meals at home, encouraging a switch from eating at home to eating out and eating home-meal replacements. Rising numbers of women in the workplace also sparked a gourmet boom as females took center stage in consumption. Menus continued to diversify and the industry continued to develop, leading to the appearance of Japanese food family restaurants and bar chains with an open and healthy image. In the *nakashoku* sector, the competition among convenience stores selling box lunches and home-delivered pizza chains heated up.

GHG also moved to meet the needs of the times by adopting a forward-looking diversification strategy. It launched Tonkatsu Shinjuku Saboten in 1986, a delicatessen specializing in takeout meals, along with a healthcare-facility food service in 1987, based on a technical tie-up with a major US hospital-meal provider and a home-care provider. Its foray into these activities was based on a pre-emptive strike strategy that foresaw the arrival of the age in which patients and residents choose hospitals and other facilities based on the quality of service. This approach bore fruit when in the first year alone, Green House signed contracts with 21 hospitals, including one for a restaurant in Keio University Hospital, which is one of the country's largest private university hospitals.

Geographical Diversification

In the 1990s, the bubble economy burst and land prices plummeted. The collapse in prices spread throughout the entire economy and deflation intensified.

The food-service industry was unable to escape the effects of the ongoing recession. Food-away-from-home expenditures as a percentage of total consumer expenditures on food floundered. There was a noticeable intensification of competition due to a surplus of food service outlets. Fierce competition based on the widespread adoption by various companies of cost leadership strategy resulted. Family restaurants implemented low-price strategies, such as Skylark's opening of its Gusto outlets; fast food chains introduced low-price policies, such as McDonald's half-price hamburgers; and convenience stores also entered into the fray. The market showed signs of maturing, with the food-service market shrinking slightly from 27.2 trillion yen in 1991 to 26.9 trillion yen in 2000, and the size of the food-service industry market as a percentage of total household food and beverage expenditures, increased only slightly from 41.5 percent to 42.1 percent over the same period. These economic results are in contrast to the *nakashoku* market, which grew steadily to reach 5.8 trillion yen in the latter half of the 1990s (Datamonitor 2008).

At the same time, the environment surrounding the opening of new outlets took a favorable turn due to such factors as the collapse in land prices and the onset of globalization. This positive climate prompted some within the Japanese food-service industry to consider expanding into the US and other Asian markets, while Starbucks and other foreign-owned coffee chains sought to make inroads into the Japanese market.

Amid this intense competition, GHG adopted a strategy based on differentiation. In 1990, it became the first company in the contract food-service industry to go public in the over-the-counter market. In anticipation of the age of wellness through food, it prepared the ground for organized activities by its own registered dietitians and strengthened its initiatives aimed at meeting the needs of health-oriented consumers.

Anticipating that the expansion of overseas food-service operations would become brisk in the Asian market, in 1991, it concluded a technical partnership agreement for contract food services with LG Mart Co., Ltd. (now OUR HOME), a group company of one of the four largest industrial conglomerates in South Korea. Today, Our Home has grown into one of South Korea's leading food-service industry companies, with annual sales of 100 billion yen (Our Home 2010). In 1996, GHG moved its head office to Shinjuku in Tokyo. Since that time, it has proceeded to put into place the kind of infrastructure required in an era in which knowledge is paramount by building an Internet-based information network and by strengthening its ability to formulate strategy to meet global competition. As a result, GHG has designed the kind of structure that will enable it to grow in various directions in an increasingly globalized world.

Acceleration in Growth

Even as the world welcomed the onset of the new millennium, there was no let up in the advance of deflation, and consumption continued to experience ups and downs. Starting with the suspension of imports of US beef due to the BSE problem, there was a rash of incidents involving food safety. These included outbreaks of avian influenza, problems with the false labeling of food, and problems with agrochemical residues. These events led to the establishment of the Food Safety Basic Law and Place of Origin Labeling Guidelines, and to the rise of movements advocating a rethinking of Japan's approach to food and the establishment of "slow food."

The scale of the food-service industry market peaked at 29 trillion yen in 1997 before falling steadily to reach 24.4 trillion yen in 2005 (Datamonitor 2008). This tendency went hand in hand with disposable income, which also followed a downward course as the economy continued to stagnate. Problems with food safety dealt a further blow to the food-service industry. The global increases in food prices since 2006 and rising oil prices meant that there was great uncertainty in the earnings environment.

As the food-service industry entered a period of maturity and the market became saturated, increasing one's market share became an important strategy in boosting price competitiveness and maintaining high quality. In response to this, in 1999, GHG embarked on a strategy aimed at developing economies of scale. This strategy involved the development of mergers and acquisitions (M&A) aimed at providing synergistic effects such as the strengthening of bargaining power through the centralized purchasing of food ingredients, use of branding, and efficient management of human resource.

At that time, the various manufacturers, who were pushing ahead with restructuring in an effort to regain their competitiveness, adopted a policy based on a strategy of selection and concentration. Consequently, the manufacturers began outsourcing their employee-cafeteria and food-service outlet operations to outside specialists, as these operations belonged to the welfare section that was outside their core business. GHG established a specialist M&A position and starting with Nissan Motor, bought out the food-service operations of a number of leading manufacturers. These manufacturers included the Oki Electric Industry Group, Mitsubishi Motors, and Kawasaki Heavy Industries, all of which represented a total workforce of several thousand people. The success of GHG's M&A activities and its ability to demonstrate synergistic effects became well-known. It went on to achieve further M&A success not only with manufacturers but also with contract food specialists, regional food-service providers, and companies in the restaurant sector, bringing the total number of M&A to 16. Other companies in the industry embarked on similar M&A campaigns, but the benefits of being the market leader were considerable, and GHG secured a considerable share of the domestic business and industry sector.

In April 2000, as its fourth pillar, GHG established a new hotel management contract operation by setting up a specialized company. This operation involved entering into partnerships with funds using the facilities purchased by these partners, and increasing value through its hotel management. Much of the know-how required for this new operation was shared by the contract food business and restaurant operations, and as they all belong to the same hospitality sector, the synergistic effect was considerable.

Previously, direct management had been the mainstream in the Japanese hotel industry, but in the 1990s after the collapse of the bubble economy, hotels' parent companies and hotels themselves were shaken. Cases emerged in which operations were handed over to specialist companies, and a clear distinction began to be made between ownership, management, and operation. One foreign-owned hotel after another opened for business, and issues such as responsibilities and roles were clearly identified at the time of the signing of contracts. Domestically, the contracting out of the operation of properties became established, with resorts and other facilities owned by local governments and other statutory bodies entrusted to professional management companies. In this sector, GHG's ability to build a solid structure as one of the first Japanese-owned companies specializing in hotel-management contracts has promoted further success.

Toward Greater Achievements

In 2006, with the aim of strengthening its corporate character and increasing its profitability, and with the strategic selection and concentration of corporate activities based on a long-term vision in place, GHG took the step of becoming an unlisted company. The goal was to further streamline and strengthen decision making by integrating the group.

In 2007, which marked the 60th anniversary of its founding, GHG brought the group even closer together by adopting a new corporate logo and establishing the company's four credos. The four credos were established to enable each employee to review their daily behavior and attitude at work. Specifically, they are about desired posture by GHG staff toward customers, employees, society, and the global environment.

First, for customers, we always care about their happiness and work to bring pleasure to their life. Second, for employees, we respect, help, and motivate each other. Third, for society, we contribute to society through our food service and hospitality by delivering the pleasure of cooking and serving as well as eating. Fourth, for the global environment, we will reduce the waste of natural resources and be dedicated to eco-friendly activities.

By March 2008, GHG was the third-largest company in the contract food service industry in Japan, with total group sales of 107 billion yen, a total of 1,950 outlets, and 24,000 employees. It has continued to grow since then. In May 2008, I was appointed the 13th chairman of the Japan Foodservice Association, a food-service industry body that represents some 830 Japanese food-service companies. These companies are looking to GHG to act in its role as an industry leader, and GHG is determined to redouble its efforts to ensure the development of the industry as a whole.

Group's Growth Strategy

In the sense that they determine a company's direction, management philosophy and growth strategy have something in common. Management philosophy and vision provide reasons for a company's existence and its mission. These are the ideals to which the company aspires, and reflect the will of the management and the hopes of the employees. Strategy represents the means and policies by which these ideas are realized.

GHG's management philosophy consists of three promises, which are action guidelines designed to differentiate the group from its rivals at a time when it has become very difficult to grow a company solely through sales volume and the pursuit of profits. The first promise is to pursue safe, reliable, and healthy foodstuffs and create and develop high value-added menus. The second promise is to work at building a health business centering on food, incorporating wellness programs, and creating and offering new products, all with the aim of actively creating healthy minds and bodies. The third promise is to serve GHG customers with hospitality of the highest professional standard.

Meanwhile, GHG's four credos define the organization's responsibility with respect to its customers, employees, society, and the global environment. These credos were established to encourage all GHG employees to share these principles, think about them as individuals, and translate them into action and desired attitudes. The permeation and sharing of these ideas will become the foundation for continued growth.

GHG's goal is to become Asia's number one hospitality enterprise. It used its corporate motto, "Making others happy leads to our prosperity," which expresses its management's philosophy; its three promises, which are guidelines for translating company ideas into action; and its four credos to delineate the company's direction to guide its growth strategies. GHG has conducted external macro-environmental analyses by line of business and self-analysis in the form of internal studies, to define its growth strategies.

According to Professor Michael Porter of Harvard University, the three fundamental strategies for building competitive advantage are: first, differentiation strategy; second, low-cost strategy; and third, focus strategy. In addition to these strategies, GHG also considers fourth, M&A/alliance strategy and fifth, global strategy. Therefore, GHG's strategy is considered from the perspective of these five points.

Differentiation Strategy

Differentiation is carried out on the basis of a wide range of factors including materials and ingredients, depth of service, design, product line-up, and channels. This strategy involves realizing high value by capturing a unique position. In order for this approach to succeed, added-value must be created from the customer's perspective, the customer must recognize high added-value, and imitation by competitors must be difficult. Another condition is that this plan must be sustainable over the long term.

At GHG, implementing the management philosophy's three promises is the most important factor differentiating the company from it competitors in operational terms.

In GHG's business and industry contract food service, the menus on offer at Saboten, Shahoden, and Healthy Food Brand/Kiyo's Kitchen, increase in added-value because of GHG's healthcare programs, which are aimed at reducing the medical bills of corporate health insurance associations and combating lifestyle-related illnesses. These healthy menu options and the enhanced liquid foods GAMES menu system are all examples of differentiation.

Low-cost Strategy

Low-cost strategy involves securing a sustainable price advantage with respect to products and services. This is achieved through such means as the automation of production, low-cost operation, economies of scale, and no-frills products and services.

GHG established a special low-cost operation-development section within the head office by increasing purchasing power, standardizing menus, and concentrating the procurement of ingredients. It also promoted operational improvements, for example, by boosting the efficiency of lines at the various worksites.

Focus Strategy

Focus strategy involves concentrating on certain customer demographics, regional markets, or distribution channels such as delicatessens and mail order, and seeks outcomes such as differentiation and a gradual reduction in costs. GHG employs a focus strategy that seeks to concentrate on different customers for each business and each regional company.

M&A/Alliance Strategy

The aim of M&A and alliances is to acquire established and existing businesses and immediately secure in a short space of time, a certain scale and core competence. According to *MARR* Magazine (Recof Corporation 2007), the scale of the Japanese food-service industry M&A market has increased rapidly in the last few years, from 31 deals in 1999 to 137 in 2006.

At GHG, M&A strategy will be required as a countermeasure to deal with the oligopolization of the business, industry, and healthcare markets. The aims are firstly, regional oligopolization merits and secondly, synergistic effects. Achieved synergies can be seen in the bargaining power that is derived from the centralized purchasing of foodstuffs, use of branding, and efficient utilization of personnel. GHG executes not only on M&A aimed at economies of scale but also at economies of scope, which has led to advances into the *nakashoku* sector.

GHG's basic stance is not to aim for M&A that simply increases scale. It promotes M&A that strengthen the core businesses by adding value to them. Targets include businesses, however small they may be, that possess specialist know-how, are able to boost products and services, contribute to an improvement in management quality, and add to GHG's cultural continuity and creativity.

As keeping purchasing costs down and producing synergistic effects immediately after purchase are the primary considerations, GHG has until now limited itself to friendly acquisitions. This approach has brought about successful results, with GHG completing 16 M&A since 1999.

Global Strategy

Because the Japanese population is decreasing and the mean age is increasing, the food-service industry in this country is being forced to seek overseas markets, particularly in Asia.

Japanese food and ingredients are viewed as healthy and for this reason, are garnering international attention. Consequently, the industry has experienced a recent boom throughout the world, particularly in East Asia, which has a similar food culture to that of Japan. By far, the majority of the recent cases of overseas expansion by food-service companies has been into China, where food-service revenues were 16.3 trillion yen in 2006, outlets numbered 4 million, and the annual growth rate is expected to be 16 percent or greater into the future (Datamonitor, 2008). Following China in terms of popular markets for overseas expansion are Taiwan, South Korea, Singapore, and the US. GHG is pushing ahead with expansion on two fronts by opening Saboten and other outlets, and by becoming involved in contract food services at Chinese outlets of Japanese-owned corporations.

In terms of global strategy, strategic tie-ups play an important role in compensating for key factors, such as distribution, branding, sales organizations, and production capacity that can have a bearing on success in overseas markets. Keeping in mind the uncertainties involved in doing business in other countries, strategic tie-ups are an effective method of averting risk. GHG has successfully thwarted this risk by establishing joint ventures in various sectors in South Korea, Taiwan, China, and Thailand.

Conditions for Maintaining Competitive Advantage

In order to devise a plan for gaining a sustainable competitive advantage and continuing to succeed over the long term, it is vital that one's strategy be appreciated by the market and not be subjected to imitation or neutralization at the hands of one's competitors.

To gain a competitive advantage that is appreciated by the market and to have the ability to influence the market, requires not half-hearted but overwhelming strength. The factors that determine this strength are, firstly, the basic requirements of competitiveness, which include such things as assets, ability, personnel, and corporate culture; and secondly, market selection in the form of where one seeks one's market.

One of the basic requirements of competitiveness for GHG is its high value-added strategy. At GHG, business that gives rise to added-value is viewed not only as something created by products but also accompanied by service that makes customers happy. Value is realized only when the anxiety, distrust, dissatisfaction, and displeasure customers experience in the context of their everyday lives are dispelled and when these customers experience surprise, joy, and fulfillment as the result of more desirable outcomes.

Concrete examples of the fruition of this goal can be found in the growth of the home-meal replacement sector (takeout kiosks, home delivery), operational reform, expansion into new locations (food-court outlets, multipurpose complex outlets, collaborative outlets), and menu development. Menu development refers to the strengthening of security and safety, direct-from-grower distribution, local consumption of locally produced products, and expansion of Japanese menus. Innovations such as the GAMES original menu system and the Asuken health support program, along with health advice from some 1000 registered nutritionists, are also evidence of GHG's success in executing on the value-added strategy.

On the corporate culture front, efforts are being made to empower more employees and raise the standard of the basic requirements of competitiveness. These are done through the permeation of the management philosophy throughout the company and initiatives such as the Plus One Suggestion Campaign aimed at transforming employees' awareness, active responses in the field of corporate social responsibility, and assistance in the development of healthy bodies through food.

With respect to market selection, GHG's business and industry operation and the Tonkatsu Saboten restaurant and delicatessen operation are positioned at the top of their respective sectors in Japan in terms of market share and quality service, and have secured an unshakeable advantage. With respect to the hotel-management operations, the separation of ownership and operation has become increasingly clear of late in Japan and elsewhere, and with the need for specialist management companies increasing, GHG has been quick to make the right choices.

Conclusion

Management philosophy and vision are a universal expression of a company's reason for existence and mission. They represent the ideal a company aims for, and reflect the will of management and the hopes of the employees.

A business-growth strategy is none other than the embodiment of management philosophy. The fact that GHG has been able to maintain growth for more than 60 years is largely because the values with which this philosophy is endowed are universal values widely accepted not only by the managers and employees but also by society as a whole. In particular, with regard to businesses that relate to food, which among other things is a symbol of a country's culture, it is important that these companies forge a utility for people. This tenet must form the basis of management if the company is to enjoy support and survive over the long term.

GHG's corporate motto, "Making others happy leads to our prosperity," emphasizes above all else, its various stakeholders including the customers, employees, local community, international community, and the global environment. The fact that it has been focused on this idealistic goal and has been able to generate and implement successful, congruent growth strategies is directly linked to what the GHG is today, a group that has grown for more than 60 years without once experiencing a decrease in income.

In order for a company to grow in a sustainable way, it must recognize novel and radical changes in the macro-environment, ascertain the precise direction that is advantageous to growth, and decide on the basis of what policies the company will move forward. Decisions must be made about which fields of activity the company's limited resources should be committed through a process of selection and concentration. These decisions' details must be imprinted on the minds of every single employee, and the degree to which this can be achieved determines the success or failure of the strategy implementation, and victory or defeat in competition. Measures are required to ensure that the aims of the strategy are communicated accurately, even down to the level of the part-time employees, who carry out the day-to-day work that is closest to the customers.

Even a company that has achieved one success after another in the past will be unable to continue to survive as the fittest unless it can develop new growth strategies that enable it to respond flexibly to changes in the environment. In the hospitality business world, it is always necessary to have the right strategy to cope with various macro-environmental changes. These changes include deregulation, technological innovations, changes among consumers, trends among rival companies, pressure from overseas governments and corporations, and changes in infrastructure.

The social responsibility environment surrounding the hospitality industry is facing increasingly difficult issues. These include food safety and security problems, food prices, food self-sufficiency rate, labor shortages and other employment-related problems, and environmental problems. Other concerns relate to nutritional education and healthy eating habits.

When a company encounters a major risk, it goes without saying that early response, beginning with media countermeasures, is important. But at the risk aversion and recovery stage, the soundness of factors such as growth strategy and business models is indispensable in maintaining stakeholders' support. GHG is committed to continually reviewing and strengthening its strategy as the occasion demands without limiting itself to past growth strategies. It is also committed to managing the group companies in a way that ensures this strategy is implemented properly while nurturing the personnel who represent the very foundation of the business.

References

Crockett, Sean. 2000.Hungry for a market? Looking for the right export opportunity. Unpublished paper. https://www.agric.gov.ab.ca/vdir/marketnews/alberta/crockett2000-01.html.

Datamonitor. 2008. Foodservice in Japan to 2011. Tokyo: Datamonitor.

Department of Agriculture and Food 2009. Market Outlook Bulletin 4759. Perth Western Australia: Department of Agriculture and Food.

Nikkei MJ. 2008. *Food Service Ranking 2007*. May 13. Japan.

Our Home. 2010. History. http://www.ourhome.co.kr/english/intro/intro300.asp.

Recof Corporation, 2007. MARR Magazine. Tokyo.

World Bank, 2008. Data. http://siteresources.worldbank.org/DATASTATISTICS/Resources/POP.pdf.

8

MANAGING CRISES EFFECTIVELY

By Chittimas Ketvoravit

Introduction

Tourism is the world's largest industry, producing 10.4 percent of the world's gross national product in 2007 and accounting for 231 million jobs or 8.3 percent of world employment (1 in every 12 jobs) (World Travel & Tourism Council [WTTC] 2008). In 2007, tourism contributed over US$7 trillion in economic activity, with industry experts projecting US$13 trillion by 2017 (WTTC 2008). By all measures, tourism is a substantial economic force, but its importance is even more significant in developing countries, especially in the Asia-Pacific region, where tourism is usually one of the primary sources of foreign exchange.

The travel and tourism industry is particularly sensitive to political, economic, or environmental change. Unfortunately for the industry, various sources such as the International Federation of Red Cross (IFRC) and Red Crescent Societies (2006), report that both natural and man-made disasters and crises are becoming more frequent, intense, and geographically dispersed. Indeed, the IFRC (2005) suggests that the world is becoming more divisive and dangerous than ever. Researchers offer conjecture that this seeming increase may be partially due to improved communications, which broadcast disasters around the world or may be the result of heightened complexity and globalization (Hystad and Keller 2008).

The United Nations (UN) (2008) notes that not only are disasters more frequent but their impacts have been increasing. The UN suggests that the cause is unplanned urbanization, environmental degradation, population growth, and poverty, which have made communities more vulnerable. The UN (2008, iii) further notes that "disasters are especially ruinous for developing countries: the smaller the economy and the weaker the infrastructure, the greater the human cost and damage to development prospects."

As the travel and tourism industry continues to expand at a rapid rate, particularly in Asia and the Middle East, there will be more travel, competition, controversies, natural disasters, political unrest, adverse publicity, and deeper economic cycles. It is therefore of absolute importance to prepare for a crisis situation by incorporating crisis management into the organization's strategic planning process. With the help of strategic and tactical concepts, an effective crisis plan can be developed and implemented to resolve the crisis situation.

Thailand is used as a backdrop for this work on crisis management because it has suffered several major natural and political crises in recent years. First, in 2004, Muslim radicals launched an insurgency in the southern provinces of Thailand. This insurgency has continued on to the present and has resulted in the deaths of approximately 2,000 people. As 2004 was coming to a close, the Indian Ocean tsunami struck the west coast of Thailand causing massive loss of life, property damage, and economic destruction. In 2006, a military coup ousted Prime Minister Thaksin Shinawatra and martial law was declared. In the same year, 46 bombs exploded within 30 minutes across southern Thailand. Into 2008, political unrest and security threats in Bangkok and elsewhere in Thailand continued. Moreover, the country was impacted by the 2008 economic crisis, which began in the United States (US) and spread worldwide. Most recently, another major political crisis occurred, resulting in the closure of part of the business center in Bangkok. This was concluded with military intervention in mid-May 2010.

Companies can only survive these natural and man-made crises if they minimize the aftermath through appropriate preparation. A crisis plan permits the organization to continue its day-to-day business of making a profit or providing a service while the crisis is being managed. Many crises can be prevented, and in the case of a political crisis, can be effectively coped with through early preparedness.

What is a Crisis?

There are two types of crises—national disasters and man-made crises. Natural disasters are caused by volcanic eruptions, tidal waves, earthquakes, floods, and typhoons, and can often be predicted. Man-made crises, on the contrary, generally occur randomly and often cannot be foreseen. These types of crises include political troubles, economic downturns, acts of sabotage or terrorism, and employee strikes (Cassedy 1991). Adopting the approach of Hystad and Keller (2008, 152), a crisis is any "major negative event that has the potential to affect a tourism industry." Hence, a crisis is characterized by risk and uncertainty. When a decision to purchase involves risk and uncertainty of the consequences of that risk, the consumer can only react to the amount of risk he or she perceives and only to his or her subjective interpretation of that risk (Cunningham 1967). Therefore, it can be said that the extent of the effect of a crisis on tourism behavior depends on the magnitude of the risk the tourist perceives.

Concept of Perceived Risk

A choice involves risk when the consequences associated with the decision are uncertain and some outcomes are more desirable than others (Alhakami and Slovic 1994; Bauer 1960). The concept of perceived risk falls within the general conceptual framework of consumer decision making, the process by which consumers decide which product or brand to buy (Cunningham 1967). Researchers have shown that the intangibility of services, such as those found in the hospitality industry, heightens perceived risk in decision making (Conchar et al. 2004; Grewal, Gotlieb, and Marmorstein 1994; Grewal et al. 2007).

Bauer (1960) first introduced the concept of perceived risk, organizing the concept around the idea that consumer behavior involves risk when the action of a consumer will produce consequences that he cannot anticipate with certainty, some of which are likely to be unpleasant. In general, consumers are risk-averse, and losses are more of a concern than equivalent gains (Kahneman and Tversky 1984). As a result, Bauer (1960) argues, consumers develop methods of reducing perceived risk, thereby permitting them to make decisions without undue stress when the information is incomplete and it is difficult to anticipate the consequences of a decision.

Risk as it relates to tourism has been separated into two categories—perceived risks that have negative connotations and sensation-seeking behavior, which is essentially positive risk that is actively sought (Dolnicar 2005). Sonmez and Graefe (1998) have empirically demonstrated that a relationship exists between intention to travel to certain destinations and perceived risks and perceived safety.

Role of Marketing Response

It is clear that when customers see risk in a purchase, they may be concerned about either the uncertainty or the potential consequences of that decision. If either or both of these factors are high, then the customer will not purchase. Reducing customer perceived risk can be achieved through the provision of additional information (Cox 1967) and, in the case of services, by ensuring the correct cues are offered in the physical environment (Grewal et al. 2007). Factors which increase perceived risk in a travel purchase include:

- Travel, especially leisure travel, can be complex and its benefits intangible.
- It can be difficult to obtain consistent, credible information about destinations or hotels.
- Wide variation exists between destinations and accommodation choices.
- The price of travel is expensive.
- The purchase of travel is important to the customer.

In sum, a leisure trip is a high-risk purchase. It involves not only a considerable investment of discretionary dollars but also an investment of discretionary time. In general, the greater the degree of perceived risk in a purchase, the greater the propensity to seek information regarding the purchase (Gitleson and Crompton 1983). Obtaining information through external search is one way of reducing perceived risk to more acceptable levels.

Since the most often used strategy of the customer in reducing perceived risk in a travel purchase is to acquire and analyze additional information, the role of the marketing response is to have adequate information available for the customer. To be effective, the information must:

- be accurate, detailed, and extensive
- come from a credible source

- be provided quickly and for as long as necessary
- be in a form the customer can use

One goal of a marketing strategy is to reduce the customer uncertainty and to make it easier for customers to evaluate and reduce negative consequences. Thus, the perceived risk can be reduced to a level that will not hinder purchase and will in fact increase the purchase probabilities.

A political crisis or natural disaster in a popular destination can suspend all tourism-related activities and businesses in that destination because international tourists perceive the location as unsafe. The unsafe image will remain with the destination, and most tourists will avoid the destination until the perceived image improves through the dissemination of new information. For tourists to believe the new information, it must be accurate, timely, and truthful and come from a credible source. This information can be provided via effective marketing communications.

Importance of Information

Prior study has noted that tourists' external search for information occurs prior to and during their travel, especially for independent travel (Nishimura, King, and Waryszak 2007). Hyde (2000) reported that as many as 80 percent of travel decisions are spontaneous decisions made en route, based upon information received during travel. These findings emphasize the importance of making the correct information available to prospective travelers.

To reduce the uncertainty and consequences the customer identifies in purchasing travel, the hospitality company and destination-management organization must provide information to the customer and seek to change or exploit the destination image. While past experience may serve as an internal source of information, the focus here is on external information. The available external tourist information emanates mainly from two sources—formal (commercial environment) and informal (social environment) (Goodall 1989; Mill and Morrison 1985). The first group includes travel agents, brochures, guidebooks, tour guides, travelogs, television, newspapers and magazines, videos, Internet Web sites, and maps (Nishmura, King, and Waryszak 2007).

The latter group comprised word-of-mouth from friends and relatives, social network blogs, or local residents, who rely on their past experiences and current knowledge to offer advice to the travelers (Goodall 1988; Nishmura, King, and Waryszak 2007). Perceptions about a destination's image and risk-level, then, are determined through advertisements and promotions, news accounts, conversations with friends and relatives, travel blogs, Internet sites, travel agents, and past experiences (Dore and Crouch 2003).

Communication Vehicles

During a time of crisis, there are three main communication vehicles that can help manage a country's image—advertising, public relations, and promotions. Advertising is paid placement of an organization's message to the public. Good advertising is memorable, attention-getting, effective, and also quite costly. However, in managing a destination's image during crisis, advertising appears to be of less value due to a lack of perceived credibility and objectivity.

Public relations is predominantly communication with the intention of informing, raising awareness, or educating, or influencing attitudes or behavior (Messina 2007). Public relations seems to be the most useful marketing tool in a time of crisis due to its credibility and reliability, but it is difficult to maintain staying power, that is, keep the message in front of the customer. Promotions, on the other hand, may include price discounting, lucky draws, or special offerings. These promotional efforts can be effective if implemented in the right place at the right time. However, these marketing promotions are of limited value because they do not reduce uncertainty involved in the purchase decision.

Nevertheless, promotional efforts can work when used in conjunction with communication strategies. In 2006, a fiscal crisis in Puerto Rico forced several key government agencies to close for two weeks. The Puerto Rico Tourism Company (PRTC) initiated "an aggressive marketing and promotion plan in the United States, Canada, Latin America, the Caribbean, Europe and locally on the island to showcase Puerto Rico's tourism offering and to counteract the negative perception the fiscal crisis" had generated (PR Newswire 2006). These promotions included a US$200 voucher with CheapCaribbean.com for visitors to spend in Puerto Rico, PRTC visits to travel agents and tour operators in key markets, and a special Puerto Rican culinary event in New York City.

More importantly, PRTC monitored the fiscal crisis and implemented "measures to ensure that tourists felt safe on the island, comfortable keeping their travel plans and were welcomed with open arms upon arrival. Tourist updates were available on PRTC's website, and PRTC communicated with its industry partners to provide accurate information that they in turn could use to communicate to their clients" (PR Newswire 2006). As a result, "occupancy levels remained strong and the number of visitors to the San Juan Metropolitan area was 8 percent higher compared to the same period" in 2005 (PR Newswire 2006).

Marketing Strategies

There are several categories of participants that carry out a marketing strategy—the National Tourist Organization (NTO) of that country or destination, the national airline, individual hotels, and tour operators. The marketing strategies are targeted at two groups of potential customers:

- The customers who have already purchased the trip but have to alter their travel plans due to a political event or natural disaster in the destination. In altering their plans, they may choose to either postpone or cancel the trip.
- The customers who might or might not be aware of the destination and its crisis but have not been motivated to consider traveling to the destination.

The goal of the marketing strategies, after the political turbulence in the destination, is to bring back tourists as rapidly and as effectively as possible. There are three main marketing strategies that can improve the aftermath impacts of political turbulence in a destination.

First, the strategy is to provide accurate, timely, and truthful information to current and potential customers. The NTO must select a medium through which the information will be communicated, be it advertising, public relations, promotions, or a combination of all. This strategy can only be carried out through a group effort, such as the NTO, national air carrier, hotel chains, and tour operators.

The individual hotel is a credible source of information only with customers who know the brand. However, it can give more extensive information to customers than is possible through advertising or public relations. Moreover, the individual hotel can provide penetration of the message into the market through the impact of word-of-mouth referrals. The individual hotel's role is to reduce the risk's consequences by giving customers information to help them evaluate alternative outcomes. For example, a detailed, personalized letter or e-mail from the general manager of a hotel or managing director of a hotel chain to the customer explaining the impact of a disaster on the hotel. It is important that this objective account is not in conflict with information disseminated by the group, that is, the hotel association, NTO, or the Ministry of Tourism. Furthermore, the notice must be specific and factual.

Second, the strategy is to further penetrate the existing markets for additional market share. This strategy must be cost-effective and approach current customers in new ways, be it promotion, distribution, or pricing.

Third, the strategy is to broaden the business mix by pursuing more market segments.

The group, association, or NTO can open up new market segments for a destination. To do so, the promotion to maintain awareness and interest in the destination must be increased. More importantly, introducing or finding other interesting facets of a destination may be necessary in order to broaden the appeal among potential customers.

Developing a Crisis Marketing Plan

The popular press is replete with stories insinuating that no travel destination is safe from some type of crisis situation that can disrupt or cause irreparable harm to business (*Entertainment & Travel* 2008). During recent years, the world has witnessed dozens of crises occurring in popular tourist destinations, including political instability in Kenya, Malaysia, Pakistan, the Philippines, and Thailand; natural disasters including earthquakes, tsunamis, fires, cyclones, and hurricanes; pandemic diseases such as severe acute respiratory syndrome (SARS) and bird flu; bombings in the tourist areas of Bali, Egypt, India, Indonesia, Israel, the United Kingdom, and Turkey; airline-route cancellations because of high fuel costs; and a global credit crisis. Unfortunately, many countries and cities have still failed to implement a crisis-management plan to help cope with crises, often adopting a wait-and-see view (Hystad and Keller 2008).

A well-developed crisis-management plan provides a destination with a framework from which to make proactive decisions. Crises must be managed quickly and efficiently to minimize the negative impacts on tourism businesses, and having a plan in place helps to return business to normalcy as quickly as possible (Yu, Stafford, and Armoo 2005). As tourism becomes increasingly important to the world economy, it is imperative that travel and tourism organizations around the globe include crisis plans in their strategic business schemes.

While tourism success within a destination can be readily achieved, the same qualities that create that success can also facilitate its demise. The spirit of adventure and the desire to visit novel locations have helped spur the industry's development on an international level. Yet, locations across the world now have a moderate to high probability of a crisis (Rousaki and Alcott 2006). Therefore, safety and the perception of safety become dominant factors for the continuation and growth of particular destinations and modes of travel. Given the travel industry's dependence on transportation, exchange rate, political situation, discretionary income, and weather, the industry is particularly sensitive to unexpected change, even when the crisis is not directly related to the industry.

Because leisure travel is not a necessity and business travel can often be postponed, the travel industry's vulnerability to capricious and volatile events is immense. For example, recent political strife in Thailand, although largely peaceful, has had a modest but negative impact on tourism (*McClatchy-Tribune Business News* 2008). Indeed, after minor violence broke out between police and protesters there, Australia, Britain, New Zealand, and the US warned their citizens to exercise caution when traveling to Thailand, while South Korea and Singapore encouraged their nationals to postpone holiday plans and nonessential travel (*Bangkok Post* 2008; Breitbart.com 2008). Prakit Chinamourphong, president of the Thai Hotel Association stated: "The current political stand-off will absolutely have an adverse effect on our tourism industry but the extent of the damage will depend on how long the turmoil lasts" (Breitbart.com 2008).

A crisis situation, no matter how temporary, can create circumstances with an aftermath far worse than it warrants. Tourism is often unable to rebound as quickly as other businesses since much of a destination's attraction is derived from its image. Because of the increased importance of the tourism industry and its interrelationship with travel segments, the importance of preparing for a crisis situation is vital (Yu, Stafford, and Armoo 2005).

A Crisis-Management Plan

Crisis management is the process of "planning for, responding to and recovering from a crisis. . . . [It] implies being prepared before the crisis strikes, effectively executing the crisis-management plan during the crisis, and quickly [recovering]" (Yu, Stafford, and Armoo 2005, 94). A crisis-management plan provides guidelines that can assist a destination in avoiding or lessening the negative impact of a crisis situation on business. When a crisis occurs in a destination, it is usually a problem of the destination's negative image as perceived by international tourists that has to be corrected.

The problem of image and perception can only be corrected through marketing tactics and tools such as advertising or public relations. Marketing plays a vital role in every crisis-management plan since its action plan employs marketing strategies, tactics, and tools to help restore the destination's image and to revive tourists' confidence in traveling to the destination. Marketing strategies are the most important tools used to increase the probabilities of a travel purchase to a destination following a crisis. A crisis-marketing plan is therefore an integral part of a crisis-management plan.

As previously noted, when customers perceive risk in a travel purchase, they will try to reduce that risk by seeking more information and analyzing it more extensively. Therefore, it is important that customers receive accurate, detailed, and encompassing news regarding the destination's crisis as quickly and as long as necessary from a credible source. Customers purchase probabilities can also be increased through various marketing promotions, such as the launching of special travel packages at discounted prices.

Pre-crisis

Before the formulation of the crisis-management plan, a crisis-management team must be formed. In the case of an NTO, the team should be composed of representatives from different segments of the industry such as the airport authority, tour operator association, and regional hotel association. In the private sector, the crisis team leader is often the chief executive officer of the organization. In the public sector, the leader is usually the director or president of the NTO. Harmony and close cooperation across the industry will ensure that the plan developed will be followed and will succeed.

To prepare a formalized crisis-management plan, tourism businesses, such as the NTO, should first develop individual plans that include a media and marketing strategy. This strategy will consist of goals and objectives of the marketing plan; a communication plan for tourists, other tourism businesses, emergency organizations, and the media; and actions plans for several crises scenarios (Hystad and Keller 2008), including rescue and relief efforts. These action plans should be shared with all tourism businesses and emergency organizations. A single, credible source should serve as an official spokesperson. This person should have the power to coordinate information for responding to the media and public.

Once finalized, the crisis-management plan should be communicated and readily available to everyone in the industry. All employees should know and practice their roles. In addition, the NTO should seek to monitor the region for warning signs of any impending disaster (Yu, Stafford, and Armoo 2005).

During a Crisis

Once disaster has struck, the situation should be carefully analyzed. Rescue and relief efforts should commence immediately if needed (Yu, Stafford, and Armoo 2005). Communication with emergency organizations, tourists, and all tourism businesses should be initiated to ensure that tourists and properties are safe (Hystad and Keller 2008). Updates on the situation should be regular and frequent and posted on a key Web site. Procedures should be in place to assist tourists in providing reassurances to family members and to provide compassion and care to the families and friends of any victims.

A 24-hour communication-response center should be set up to provide the media, tourists, and the tourism industry with accurate, factual information (Hystad and Keller 2008; Marconi 1992).

A media campaign should be initiated that is sensitive to the nature of the crisis, although Hystad and Keller (2005) warn that starting such a campaign too early into the disaster can be harmful to tourism. When possible, direct communication with travel agents and tour wholesalers should commence to prevent cancellations. Communications should utilize the fastest means available such as e-mail, telephone, facsimile, television, radio, and video (Marconi 1992; Yu, Stafford, and Armoo 2005). The operational and financial structure of the organization should be adjusted to account for some decreases in revenues (Yu, Stafford, and Armoo 2005). Finally, tourism businesses should be coached to rapidly deploy sales and marketing teams to disaster relief teams, the military, clean-up specialists, and so on (Yu, Stafford, and Armoo 2005).

Post-crisis

Once the disaster has abated, recovery marketing should begin (Hystad and Keller 2008), directed toward the markets that are ready to return (Yu, Stafford, and Armoo 2005). The media campaign should continue and be refined. If accurate, the media and public should be made aware that the disaster area is limited in scope. Existing and potential customers should be pursued through special promotions, distribution, or pricing, and utilizing selected media. Communication with tourism businesses and tourists should be continued. Tourism-focused events such as festivals should continue as planned. The goal of post-crisis efforts should be to establish the perception of normalcy as rapidly as possible. Finally, the results of the crisis-management plan should be measured.

By taking action promptly, the negative impacts on business caused by the crisis can be decreased. Communication, cooperation, and collaboration within the broad tourism industry will be key to managing the crisis and moving rapidly on the road to recovery.

Case Study: Political Crisis in Thailand

From 2006–2008, Thailand underwent a period of serious political instability. In this section, this tumultuous period is reviewed and the crisis-management strategies utilized are explored.

Background

Although the Thai economy grew rapidly in the 1980s and 1990s, the currency crisis of 1997–1998 left millions of Thais unemployed and impoverished. Prime Minister Thaksin Shinawatra entered power in February 2001 with the goal of improving the economy. His administration pursued both enhanced domestic economic activity and an increase in foreign investment. His efforts had some success but gross domestic product (GDP) growth was uneven (see table 8.1). Unfortunately, a series of events in late 2004 and 2005, including the Indian Ocean earthquake cum tsunami, rising oil prices and trade deficits, severe droughts and floods, the Southern Thailand insurgency, and anti-Thaksin demonstrations caused an economic growth slump.

The economy rebounded somewhat in early 2006 but the military coup d'état on September 19, 2006, ousting Thaksin and undermining the 1997 Thailand constitution, curbed growth (see Timeline on following page). From September 2006 to late 2007, governmental power rested solely with a military council, known as the Council for National Security. The political turmoil, as well as other unfortunate events, was reflected in a steadily downward trending GDP, which decreased from 7.1 percent in 2003 to 6.3 percent in 2004 to 4.8 percent in 2007 (Economist Intelligence Unit 2008).

Political Crisis

Following an election in December 2007, Samak Sundarvej assumed the role of prime minister in January 2008, and economists projected

Table 8.1 Thailand Main Economic Indicators

	2003	2004	2005	2006	2007
Real GDP growth (%)	7.1	6.3	4.5	5.1	4.8
Consumer price inflation (av; %)	1.8	2.8	4.5	4.6	2.2
Current-account balance (US$ bn)	4.8	2.8	−7.9	2.2	15.1
Exchange rate (av; Bt:US$)	41.5	40.2	40.2	37.9	34.5
Population (m)	64.0	65.1	65.1	65.3	65.7
External debt (year-end; US$ bn)	51.8	51.3	51.6	55.2	58.5

Source: Economist Intelligence Unit, Country Data 2008

strong economic growth for Thailand. These predictions were modified downward, however, when political demonstrations, including airport takeovers, against Samak began in earnest the following August. The protesters viewed Samak as Thaksin's puppet. On September 2, 2008, Prime Minister Samak Sundaravej declared a state of emergency in Bangkok. The emergency decree lasted 12 days.

Timeline in Thailand's Political Crisis 2006-2008

- September 2006: Military stages bloodless coup to oust Prime Minister Thaksin Shinawatra following months of antigovernment protests by the People's Alliance for Democracy.

- May 2007: Thaksin's party is banned; he and 110 party executives are barred from politics for five years for election-law violations. Thaksin stays abroad, effectively in exile.

- July 2007: Hundreds of Thaksin supporters join the little-known People's Power Party, which becomes a proxy for his disbanded party.

- December 2007: The People's Power Party wins elections and goes on to lead a six-party coalition that chooses Samak Sundaravej as prime minister.

- February 2008: Thaksin returns from exile to a hero's welcome.

- May 2008: The alliance, a loose group of monarchists, union activists, and business leaders, launches protests against Samak. It accuses his government of corruption and being a proxy for Thaksin. It demands Samak resign.

- 11 August 2008: Thaksin flees to England after attending the Beijing Olympics. Facing several corruption cases, Thaksin complains he could not get a fair trial.

- 26 August 2008: The alliance raids a government-controlled television station and launches protests outside several government ministries. Tens of thousands of protesters take over the prime minister's compound.

- 27 August 2008: Police issue arrest warrants for nine of the alliance's leaders on charges of insurrection, conspiracy, illegal assembly, and refusing orders to disperse. A court order is also issued demanding the crowd that has ranged from 2,000 to 30,000 disperse.

- 29 August 2008: Thai police fire tear gas at thousands of antigovernment protesters besieging their headquarters, while demonstrators outside the capital shut down three airports and halt rail service.

- 31 August 2008: Samak refuses to resign during a heated parliamentary session called to deal with the political crisis.

- 2 September 2008: Government supporters clash with the alliance followers in the early morning, leaving one dead and dozens injured. Samak responds by imposing a state of emergency. The decree suspends certain civil liberties and bans all public gatherings of more than five people, among other measures.

- 2 September 2008: Thai Army Commander General Anupong Paochinda tells reporters [that] the military's goal was to avoid violence. He also rules out a coup, saying, "We will try to use democratic means to solve the problems."

Source: The Associated Press, *International Herald Tribune*, September 2, 2008.

While industry and manufacturing contribute approximately 44 percent of Thailand's GDP and agriculture contributes 11.4 percent, tourism is also an important source of revenue for Thailand, accounting for 6 percent of GDP, a contribution greater than that of any other Asian country (Economist Intelligence Unit 2008). Indeed, in certain parts of Thailand, such as Phuket, tourism represents more than 40 percent of the gross provincial product. It now remains to be seen what the impact of Thailand's latest round of political crises will have on tourism.

Despite all the political instability, terrorist acts, and natural disasters, Thailand tourism has been remarkably resilient and tourist arrivals have attained new records in recent years (*The Brunei Times* 2008). International arrivals reached 11.7 million in 2004, before dropping back to 11.6 million in 2005 in the aftermath of the Indian Ocean tsunami. These arrivals then rebounded to 13.8 million in 2006 and 14.5 million in 2007 (Economist Intelligence Unit 2008). However, under Samak's state of emergency powers, all public gatherings of five or more people were banned in metropolitan Bangkok. If enforced, all corporate meetings, conferences, conventions, and association meetings would have to be cancelled, severely harming tourism businesses in Bangkok. Further, countries began issuing travel advisory alerts to their citizens warning of travel to Thailand and the threat of violence from political protesters.

Industry Point of View

Andrew J. Wood, general manager of Pata Member Chaophya Park Hotel & Resorts, dispatched this update to his contact list at 0945 on 2 September

Thailand—Emergency Decree
   Quick Snapshot:

- Three groups have already cancelled this morning mainly from the government sector but also a local MICE function and we are receiving cancellations from FIT Corporate Japanese.

- The question of whether five or more pax can meet under the emergency degree will wipe out conference market. Bad news if it is enforced.

- Action to be taken: Cancel all casual staff and all overtime. Occupancy is down to 55 percent and dropping it could reach 40 percent if things do not improve. Normally we would anticipate 75 percent in September, which is the start of the rainy season and one of our quieter months. Bedroom floors are to be closed to conserve energy.

- Strikes that effect water, electricity and transportation, are going to lead to some restrictions for tourists but at present all airports are now operating normally.

- 99 percent of Thailand remains largely unaffected . . . the "hot spot" is in and around Government House, an area to be avoided.

- The effect of the military on the streets will give a message that things are actually worst than they are.

- We expect September business to be effected in all three major revenue areas: rooms, restaurants, and conference and banqueting. The loss could be as high as 4 million baht for our Bangkok property alone.

- Skal Bangkok meeting next Tuesday is likely to be cancelled.

- HRH Prince Andrew's visit to Bangkok organized by the British Chamber of Commerce and evening function at the Grand Hyatt on Wednesday 3 September 2008 has been cancelled.

- Driving into work this morning, everything was normal, traffic was normal and people appeared to just be getting on with things as yesterday. There were no signs of any military and the police were directing traffic as usual.

Source: Asia Travel Association (2008), "News," September 3, http://www.pata.org/patasite/index.php?id=1303.

Tourism Authority of Thailand's Crisis-Management Strategy

Issuing Fact Sheet and Press Releases

Just hours after Samak declared a state of emergency in Bangkok, problems for the tourism industry began surfacing (see the feature above for an industry account). The Tourism Authority of Thailand (TAT) responded by issuing a fact sheet (displayed below). This fact sheet was posted on three Web sites—Amazing Thailand, TAT News, and Pacific Asia Travel Association (PATA). The fact sheet highlighted how limited the affected area was and reassured travelers that nearly all transportation services were still operational and travel to other parts of Thailand was still possible. It did specifically pinpoint areas that tourists should avoid and provided reassurance that TAT was assisting stranded tourists.

Tourism Authority of Thailand Fact Sheet *as of* *2 September 2008, 1330 hours*

1. On 2 September 2008, Prime Minister Samak Sundaravej declared a state of emergency in Bangkok. If asked, please kindly refer to the official announcement from the Ministry of Foreign Affairs Web site (www .mfa.go.th) and Thai embassies.

2. Four international airports: Phuket, Hat Yai, Krabi, and Surat Thani have now resumed normal operations (call center: 0 2132 1888). Tourists planning to travel to Thailand are therefore advised to check the latest situation regarding their travel plans with their travel agents or contact:

   • Tourist Information at the airport: 0 2134 0041-2
   • Association of Thai Travel Agents (ATTA): 0 2237 6046-8
   • TAT Call Center: 1672

   —Tourism Authority of Thailand, Chumphon Office

   Tel: 0 7423 1055, 0 7423 8518, 0 7424 3747

   Fax: 0 7424 5986

   E-mail address: tatsgkhl@tat.or.th

   Web site: www.tourismthailand.org/hatyai

   – Tourism Authority of Thailand, Phuket Office

   Tel: 0 7621 1036, 0 7621 7138, 0 7621 2213

   Fax: 0 7621 3582

   (Continued)

E-mail address: tatphket@tat.or.th

Web site: www.tourismthailand.org/phuket

– Tourism Authority of Thailand, Krabi Office

Tel: 0 7562 2163

Fax: 0 7562 2164

E-mail address: tatkrabi@tat.or.th

Web site: www.tourismthailand.org/krabi

– Tourism Authority of Thailand, Trang Office

Tel: 0 7521 5867-8

Fax: 0 7521 5868

E-mail address:tattrang@tat.or.th

Web site: www.tourismthailand.org/trang

– Tourism Authority of Thailand, Surat Thani Office

Tel: 0 7728 8818-9

Fax: 0 7728 2828

E-mail address: tatsurat@tat.or.th

Web site: www.tourismthailand.org/suratthani

3. Rail services in some provincial areas of the north and northeastern regions of Thailand have resumed. (Call Center: 1690)

4. TAT has been in cooperation with the local authorities concerned in Phuket, Hat Yai, Krabi, Songkhla, and Surat Thani in order to facilitate tourists and [sic]expatriates stranded in those provinces.

5. Mass transportation such as the BTS skytrain, subway, and bus services are in normal operation.

6. Official bureaus, shopping centers and restaurants are open as usual except schools in the Bangkok area that have been announced to close for three days.

7. Tourists and expatriates in Bangkok should avoid the following areas: Chamai Maruchet Bridge, Government House, Sanam Luang (Royal Ground), and Ratchadamnoen Road.

8. Travel is possible to all other parts of the country.

9. To keep updated, please check online at www.mfa.go.th as well as other media sources.

TAT news.
The initial fact sheet was appended with:
THAI Suspends Operation to Had Yai

Posted 2 September at 1620: Thai Airways International has announced the suspension of flights due to the closure of Had Yai Airport. Other THAI flights and airports in Thailand are operating normally.

The airline is unable to operate its flights and services on the following routes:

Bangkok – Had Yai: TG1233 and TG1235
Had Yai – Bangkok: TG1234 and TG1236

Source: Pacific Asia Travel Association (2008), "News," September 3, http://www.pata.org/patasite/index.php?id=1303

TAT also posted a press release from the Ministry of Foreign Affairs (see below) on its Web site, which positioned the state of emergency as a measure to protect innocent people. The message also emphasized that the political problems were limited to only a few districts in Bangkok and that the citizens in the rest of the city were going about their typical routines with no disruption. Finally, the press release underscored that the emergency powers in place were the same as those other countries would put into effect in a similar situation and that the measures were just temporary.

Message from the Thai Ministry of Foreign Affairs

Prime Minister Samak Sundaravej declared a state of emergency in Bangkok on 2 September 2008. This was done in response to acts committed by certain groups which could lead to public disorder, affecting government administration and the general populace, as well as posing a threat to the state. Such acts have also undermined the democratic process and the rights and freedoms of innocent people.

To urgently remedy the situation, the Prime Minister therefore had to invoke the Emergency Decree on Government Administration in States of Emergency B.E. 2548 (2005), with the Commander-in-Chief of the Royal Thai Army appointed the Competent Official responsible to remedy the situation. While certain rights and liberties of individuals have been curtailed, this has been done only to the extent required and as provided for in such situations by the Constitution.

As noted above, the state of emergency has been declared only in Bangkok. Within Bangkok itself, only a few districts have been affected by

(Continued)

the incidents. The clash that took place between anti- and pro-government demonstrators occurred in the government district during the early morning of 2 September 2008, has since subsided with the police and military taking control of the situation. In other districts of Bangkok and the rest of the Kingdom, people continue to carry out their livelihood as usual with the country's economic and financial system functioning normally.

Thailand's emergency decree is not unlike those that exist in other countries. It is consistent with democratic principles and international human rights standards. Measures to be undertaken under the decree will also be carefully calibrated to correspond to the severity of the situation.

The state of emergency is a temporary measure. The Government will continue to exercise utmost restraint and will work with all those concerned to resolve the current political situation within the framework of the Thai Constitution and the rule of law.

Source: Thailand's Ministry of Foreign Affairs http://www.mfa.go.th/web/2654 .php?id=20614

Promotions

TAT also continued to heavily promote travel to Thailand in Asian markets, especially Malaysia, Japan, Korea, China, and India, and the Middle East via advertisements and participation in travel marts. The emerging countries of China, India, and the Middle East represented new market segments that TAT wanted to target. TAT felt that tourists were more likely to select shorter-haul flights for their holidays given escalating oil prices. Plus, the size of the emerging markets was very appealing, as China was forecast to become Thailand's top source market for tourism by 2011 (TAT, 2008).

Assistance from Industry

TAT also had assistance from other sources, which tried to downplay the 2008 political crisis and its impact in Thailand. PATA issued and posted the press release shown below on its Web site and included this press release as the top link on its electronically distributed newsletter. The press release expressly noted that the purpose of the news was to provide visitors with information to prevent unnecessary cancellations and to reassure tourists that the threat to their safety was minimal.

This press release was picked up by travel Web sites, particularly those in the United Kingdom, but tourists searching for information were also shown pictures of confrontations, which were likely to generate apprehension.

Thailand Ready to Welcome Visitors, Despite Domestic Politics

By Pata Communications

BANGKOK, THAILAND, September 3, 2008—The political standoff in Thailand is starting to impact tourism, despite almost all tourism facilities and services operating normally and protests currently limited to a small area of Bangkok.

The state of emergency announced by Thai Prime Minister Samak Sundaravej on Tuesday followed clashes among protesters in Bangkok and temporary disruption at some regional airports, including Phuket.

The decree does not involve a curfew or any other measures restricting the movement of people around Bangkok or the Kingdom.

The Thai Ministry of Foreign Affairs says the decree is a "temporary measure" applicable only in Bangkok and that "the Government will continue to exercise utmost restraint."

The current protests are limited to the immediate area around Government House in Bangkok. Visitors to Bangkok should avoid this area.

The Pacific Asia Travel Association (PATA) and Thailand-based PATA members can confirm the Ministry of Foreign Affairs' statement that "in other districts of Bangkok and the rest of the Kingdom, people continue to carry out their livelihood as usual with the country's economic and financial system functioning normally."

PATA has gathered industry views to accurately describe what prospective travelers can expect in Thailand to help them make informed decisions and to limit unnecessary cancellations.

The tourism facts as of September 3 are as follows:

- Bangkok International Airport is operating normally. Services have resumed as normal at Phuket airport. There continue to be some concerns about Hat Yai airport. All other regional airports are operating normally.

- Major surface routes between Bangkok and other parts of Thailand are unaffected, although there may be disruptions to rail services to some provinces.

- Bangkok's city taxi and rail services are unaffected.

(Continued)

- All hotels and resorts in Bangkok and throughout Thailand are open for business as usual.

- All tourist attractions, shopping centers, markets, restaurants and clubs are operating normally in Bangkok and throughout the Kingdom.

"Many of Thailand's prospective visitors are understandably reluctant to travel when they hear about a state of emergency being declared and see images of violent clashes in media reports," said PATA President and CEO Peter de Jong.

"The reality, however, is that life is continuing as normal in Bangkok and Thailand and that, as of today (September 3), there is minimal threat to the safety of visitors to the Kingdom."

Mr. de Jong said PATA would continue to monitor the situation and advise of any changes.

Inevitably, the travel and tourism industry is being affected by the situation.

PATA member Asian Trails has received cancellations, and has implemented contingencies for clients affected by the temporary disruption of domestic rail and air services.

Asian Trails' boss Luzi Matzig said: "We hope that by end of this week things will return to normal in which case damage will be limited to maybe 10 percent of September arrivals, 5 percent of October arrivals."

"September is traditionally the low season for international travel to Thailand, therefore, in terms of volume, the impact may well be minimal if things return to normal soon," noted PATA Director, Strategic Intelligence Center, John Koldowski.

PATA member Indochina Services Travel Group's bookings and client itineraries have yet to be affected by events.

"As long as the demonstrations remain non-violent and localized to a small area, we feel the impact will be minimal, even if it is not resolved for a few weeks," said CEO Gregory Duffell.

Both Mr. Duffell and Mr. Matzig agree that the biggest challenge for the Thai travel and tourism industry will be restoring the reputation of the destination in the wake of media coverage and travel advisories.

Web site Updates

After Samak stepped down and the state of emergency ended on September 14, the TAT issued a statement (see below) again emphasizing the limited area of the protests and the normalcy of Bangkok. TAT also noted that its updates were posted on popular Web sites such as YouTube.com.

Situation Update: 17 September 2008 Thai Parliament Elects Thailand's New Prime Minister

1. The Thai parliament this morning elected His Excellency Somchai Wongsawat, deputy leader of the People Power Party, as its choice as Thailand's 26th Prime Minister. The vote was 298 in favor of Somchai Wongsawat and 163 in favor of Democrat Party leader and leader of the opposition, Abhisit Vejjajiva, with five abstentions.

2. The list of proposed new cabinet members will be submitted to His Majesty King Bhumibol Adulyadej for royal endorsement, and the new Prime Minister and his cabinet will be granted a royal audience.

3. The Emergency Decree was lifted on Sunday morning (September 14, 2008) thereby ending the state of emergency in Bangkok.

4. The People's Alliance for Democracy (PAD) anti-government rally is restricted to the designated protest site and the immediate areas. Tourists and expatriates in Bangkok are advised to avoid traveling to areas near the demonstration site namely—Government House and Ratchadamnoen Nok Road (Makkawan Bridge).

5. For visitors planning trips to various sites around Rattanakosin Island (Koh Rattanakosin), shuttle boats and river taxis that serve the various public piers along the Chao Phraya River provide fast and convenient transportation to several of these sites.

6. All other areas in Bangkok remain unaffected by the rally. There has been no significant disruption to life and business in the capital beyond added traffic congestion in a few areas. The vast majority of the city including all the major tourist spots, shopping centers and riverside attractions, as well as all roads and public and private transport systems are functioning normally. Bangkok's city taxi and rail services are unaffected. All hotels and resorts in Bangkok and throughout Thailand are open for business as usual.

7. Suvarnabhumi Airport (Bangkok's international airport) and all regional airports around Thailand are operating normally. Rail services in provincial areas of the north and northeastern regions are operating normally. Service has also resumed on most of the rail services to destinations in the south. (Call Center: 1690). Major surface routes between Bangkok and other parts of Thailand are unaffected. Travel to key destinations around Thailand, such as Pattaya, Chiang Mai, Phuket, Northeastern Thailand (Isan) and other parts of the country remains unaffected.

Thailand Tourism Update Web Links

Main TAT web site:

http://www.tourismthailand.org/thailandtourismupdate/

(Continued)

YouTube.com

http://www.youtube.com/thailand

DailyMotion.com

http://www.dailymotion.com/amazingthailand

Sharkle.com

http://www.sharkle.com/member/amazingthailand

For further information, please call the Tourism Authority of Thailand Hotline. Simply dial 1672 from anywhere in Thailand. For overseas enquiries, please contact the Tourism Authority of Thailand office nearest to you.

Familiarization Trips and Roadshows

To restore tourism arrivals to their normal levels, the TAT enacted an immediate recovery plan in conjunction with Thai tourism businesses. On its TATNews Web site, TAT reported undertaking the following activities:

- TAT has been conducting random interviews with individual tourists at various popular tourism sites around Bangkok, such as the Temple of the Emerald Buddha, Khao San Road, Chatuchak Market, Suan Lum Night Bazaar, Siam Square, and CentralWorld at Ratchaprasong intersection. Foreign tourists were asked how they felt about their stay in Thailand over the past week and early this week. All of the individuals responded positively and indicated that the situation has not in any way affected his/her visit to Thailand.

  Videos of these interviews from September 6 onwards have been posted on community web sites such as YouTube.com, DailyMotion.com and Sharkle.com, as well as on the TAT's main Web site and under "Situation Updates" on the Home Page of the TAT News Room Web site www.TATnews.org

  TAT has also participated in several online travel forums such as Tripadvisor.com, Lonelyplanet.com, and VirtualTourist.com

  Web link to the Thailand Tourism Update page on Tourism Thailand.org

  http://www.tourismthailand.org/thailandtourismupdate/

- Thailand Invitation Mega Familiarization Trip—As part of Thailand's tourism recovery plans, TAT will be hosting a "Thailand Invitation" mega-familiarization trip (fam trip) for over 800 media representatives and travel operators from around the world. During their stay in Thailand during October 8–12, fam trip participants will be presented with several opportunities to experience products from the various categories presented under the *Seven Amazing Wonders of Thailand* theme, with a special focus on Northern and Northeastern Thailand (Isan).

  The travel itinerary will feature a total of 16 routes covering Northern Thailand and another 14 routes covering Northeastern Thailand.

  The Thailand Invitation fam trip itinerary for each participant will feature specially selected tourism products and services that are likely to be of most relevance and greatest interest to individual consumers and travelers in their home country. Fam trip participants will also be attending the Chiang Mai and North Tourism Forum on October 10. Upon their return home, media coverage generated by the fam trip participants will include special destination features, articles, film documentaries for the various media channels including broadcast (television and radio), print media and electronic/digital media (Web sites and mobile devices).

- TAT will also be organizing a total of eight international "Amazing Thailand" roadshows from September to November 2008.

  - Amazing Thailand Roadshow to China: September 10–12 covering the cities of Xian, Xiamen and Schenzen

  - Amazing Thailand Sales Seminar in Vietnam: November-December covering the cities of Hanoi, Haiphong and Danang

  - Pre-World Travel Mart 2008 Road Show to Stockholm and Copenhagen, Sweden, November 4–6.

- TAT and Thai tourism industry representatives will also be participating in 13 international travel trade shows.

Thailand Presence at International Travel Trade Shows	Date
ASIA (3)	
PATA Travel Mart 2008 in Hyderabad, India	16–19 September
JATA World Tourism Congress and Travel Fair in Tokyo, Japan	18–21 September
China International Travel Mart in Shanghai, China	20–23 November
EUROPE & THE MIDDLE EAST (8)	
Top Resa Paris International Travel Market in Paris, France	16–19 September
MATIW -Leisure 2008 in Moscow, Russia	23–28 September
INWETEX-CIS Travel Market in St. Petersburg, Russia	1–3 October
Ukraine International Travel Market in Kiev, Ukraine	7–9 October
TTG Incontri in Remini, Italy	24–26 October
Global Health Care Travel Exhibition & Congress in Dubai, United Arab Emirates	2–4 November
World Travel Mart (WTM) in London, UK	10–13 November
International Luxury Travel Mart in Cannes, France	8–11 December
UNITED STATES (2)	
DEMA Show 2008 (dive expo)in Las Vegas, USA	22–25 October
Luxury Travel Expo 2008 in Las Vegas, USA	2–4 December

- TAT will be hosting the 2008 Thailand Tourism Awards and the 6th Friends of Thailand Awards on World Tourism Day on September 27.

- TAT is also jointly hosting the 2008 Bangkok International Film Festival organized by The Federation of National Film Associations of Thailand, September 23–30, 2008. Web site: www.bangkok film.org

The following actors and celebrities will be attending the red carpet and gala screening as Thailand's distinguished guests: Hong Kong film director, producer, cinematographer, and actor Andrew Lau (*Internal Affairs*); Singaporean film director Eric Khoo (*Be With Me* and *August*); Hong Kong actors Li Ming (*Seven Swords* and *Fallen Angels*) and Robin Shou (*Mortal Kombat*, which was filmed in Thailand); Korean actor Lee Dong Wook (*My Girl*); British actor Michael York OBE (*Austin Powers*); Hollywood actress Arielle Kebbel (*American Pie, Be Cool* and *John Tucker Must Die*); Scottish film producer, editor and director Iain Smith OBE (*The Fifth Element* and *Cold Mountain*); and Dutch film producer and founder of Fortissimo Film Sales Wouter Barendrecht (*Short Bus* and *Party Monster*).

Developing a Crisis-Management Plan for an Individual Property

Despite TAT's efforts, tourism arrivals were estimated to have dropped 30 percent during the period of the emergency decree and did not readily resume (Lim 2008). To protect themselves, individual companies and properties could have taken additional steps beyond those of TAT. First, hospitality companies should have personally contacted all booked guests and events and provided reassurance that travel to Thailand would be safe. For large events, hospitality organizations should have made a face-to-face visit to the organizer to offer concrete solutions regarding safeguarding the event and its participants.

Company Web sites should have carried reassurances and pictures illustrating the normalcy of life for company guests. Additionally, hospitality organizations should have developed specific emergency plans for each guest, including contacting appropriate consulates, just in case problems did arise.

Conclusion

In today's environment, there is no doubt that every organization will face a crisis of some sort. However, the aftermath impacts of a political crisis on a destination can be managed, and in some cases, turned into opportunities through strategic and marketing concepts and tools.

References

Alhakami, A. S. and P. Slovic. 1994. A psychological study of the inverse relationship between perceived risk and perceived benefit. *Risk Analysis* 14 (6):1085–1096.

Bangkok Post. 2008. State of emergency: Business impact on several fronts. September3.http://www.bangkokpost.com/030908_Business/03Sep2008_biz29.php.

Bangkok Post. 2008. Tourism sector fears protest effect. August 26.

Bauer, R. A. 1960. Consumer behaviour as risk taking. In *Dynamic Marketing for a Changing World* ed. Hancock, R. S., 389–98. Chicago: American Marketing Association.

Breitbart.com. 2008. New woes for Thai tourism as protests hut Phuket airport. August 30. http://www.breitbart.com/article .php?id=080831023603.ysj1iarz&show_article=1.

The Brunei Times. 2008. New woes for Thai tourism. September 1. http:// www.bt.com.bn/en/asia_news/2008/09/01/new_woes_for_thai_tourism.

Cassedy, K. 1991. *Crisis Management Planning in the Travel and Tourism Industry: A Study of Three Destination Cases.* Bangkok: The Pacific Asia Travel Association.

Conchar, M. P., G. M. Zinkhan, C. Peters, and S. Olavarrieta. 2004. An integrated framework for the conceptualization of consumers' perceived-risk processing. *Journal of the Academy of Marketing Science* 56:55–68.

Cox, D. F. 1967. Risk handling in consumer behavior—An intensive study of two cases. In *Risk Taking and Information Handling in Consumer Behavior*, ed. D.F. Cox Boston: Harvard University.

Cunningham, S. M. 1967. The major dimensions of perceived risk. In *Risk Taking and Information Handling in Consumer Behavior*, ed. D. F. Cox, 82–108. Boston: Harvard University.

Dolnicar, S. 2005. Understanding barriers to leisure travel: Tourist fears as a marketing basis. *Journal of Vacation Marketing* 11 (3):197–208.

Dore, L. and G. I. Crouch. 2003. Promoting destinations: An exploratory study of publicity programmes used by national tourism organizations. *Journal of Vacation Marketing* 9 (2):137–151.

Economist Intelligence Unit. 2008. Highlights: The economy. June 3. http://portal.eiu.com.ezlibproxy1.ntu.edu.sg/index.asp?layout=display IssueArticle&issue_id=763441861&article_id=813441866.

Entertainment & Travel. 2008. Puerto Rico tourism company; Government of Puerto Rico pledges commitment to safeguard air access to Caribbean. July 7:94.

Gitelson, R. J. and J. L. Crompton. 1983. The planning horizons and sources of information used by pleasure vacationers. *Journal of Travel Research* (Winter): 2–7.

Goodall, B. 1988. How tourists choose their holidays: An analytical framework. In *Marketing in the Tourism Industry—The Promotion of Destination Regions*, eds. B. Goodall and G. Ashworkth, 1–10. London: Croom Helm.

Grewal, D., J. Gotlieb, and H. Marmorstein. 1994. The moderating effects of message framing and source credibility on the price-perceived risk relationship. *Journal of Consumer Research* 21:145–153.

Grewal, D., G R. Iyer, J. Gotlieb, and M. Levy. 2007. Developing a deeper understanding of post-purchase perceived risk and behavioral intentions in a service setting. *Journal of the Academy of Marketing Science* 35:250–258. Harwood, J. 2008. Antigua tourism board in marketing plan crisis talks. *Marketing Week.* August 7: 3.

Hyde, K. F. 2000. A hedonic perspective on independent vacation planning, decision-making and behavior. In *Consumer Psychology of Tourism, Hospitality and Leisure,* eds. A.G. Woodside, G.I. Crouch, J.A. Mazanec, M. Oppermann, and M.Y. Sakai , 177–191. Wallingford: CABI Publishing.

Hystad, P. W. and P. C Keller. 2008. Towards a destination tourism disaster management framework: Long-term lessons from a forest fire disaster. *Tourism Management* 29 (1):151–162.

International Federation of Red Cross and Red Crescent Societies. 2006. World disaster report 2005. Geneva.

International Federation of Red Cross and Red Crescent Societies. 2005. Mid-term Review: Strategy 2010. Geneva.

Kahneman, D. and A. Tversky. 1984. Choices, values and frames. *American Psychologist* 39:341–350.

Lim, Jessica. 2008. Fewer S'pore tourists head for Thailand. *The Straits Times.* September 19. Part B:1

Messina, A. 2007. Public relations, the public interest and persuasion: Ann ethical approach. *Journal of Communication Management* 11 (1):29–52.

Mill, R.C. and A.M. Morrison. 1985. *The Tourism System: An Introductory Text.* Englewood Cliffs, NJ: Prentice-Hall.

Nishimura, S., B. King, R. Waryszak. 2007. The use of travel guidebooks by packaged and non-package Japanese travelers: A comparative study. *Journal of Vacation Marketing* 13 (4):291–310.

PR Newswire. 2006. Enhanced tourism initiatives keep Puerto Rico's vibrant image strong; – Tourism unaffected after two-week closure of several government agencies. May 15.

Rousaki, B. and P. Alcott. 2006. Exploring the crisis readiness perceptions of hotel managers in the UK. *Tourism and Hospitality Research* 7 (1):27–38.

Sonmez, S. F. and A. R. Graefe. 1998. Determining future travel behavior from past travel experience and perceptions of risk and safety. *Journal of Travel Research* 37(2):171–177.

Tourism Authority of Thailand. 2008. TAT gears up tourism promotion activities in three emerging markets throughout the year. http://www.tatnews.org/tat_release/detail.asp?id=3895.

United Nations International Strategy for Disaster Reduction. 2008. Toward national resilience: Good practices for national platforms for disaster risk reduction. Geneva. http://www.unisdr.org/eng/about_isdr/isdr-publications/16-Towards-National-Resilience/Towards-National-Resilience.pdf.

World Travel & Tourism Council. 2008. Progress and priorities 2007/2008. http://www.wttc.org/bin/pdf/temp/finpp_2007.html.

Yu, L., G. Stafford, and A. K. Armoo. 2005. A study of crisis management strategies of hotel managers in the Washington, D.C. metro area. *Journal of Travel & Tourism Marketing* 19 (2/3):91–105.

9

ESTABLISHING STRATEGIC HUMAN RESOURCE

By Choe Peng Sum

Introduction

Creating and managing a human resource (HR) strategy is the process of setting up a detailed blueprint for building a workforce that can carry out an organization's strategic goals. Staying abreast of current issues calls for HR professionals with a thorough knowledge of their company's business, fiscal responsibility for department expenditures, and the sensitivity to recognize and recruit individuals who can help the company thrive.

With just a quick peek into the current climate we are in, many shall agree with me that responsiveness is inevitable for the hospitality leader.

- Companies today—competitive, information-dependent, cost-sensitive, are facing the tough challenge of hiring and retaining good staff
- Employees today—employable, free-ranging, technology-dependent, are looking for more than just a job, and seeking Maslow's (1954) "self-actualization" over their career years
- Customers today—discerning, high expectations, brand-conscious, are looking for a complete and holistic experience

In order for a company to thrive in this current time, its setup must satisfy more than just the customers or else any external marketing result will be short lived. Creating a steadfast workforce that is able to meet with the organization's strategic goals becomes an integrated function of what we call internal marketing.

As such, HR is no longer a stand-alone function, and its efforts must now be redirected into providing the right job to the right people rather than getting the right people for the right job. HR is becoming, interestingly in itself, a *marketing* effort before our staff can turn into our best marketers.

Marketing effort comes from the inside out. It is a persuasive art, and we ourselves must first be convinced of the value of our own products. Hence, it is a fundamental initiative for current businesses to embark on internal marketing. Employees are really our first customers, so instead of selling to the customers, should we not first be selling to our employees?

With regard to the 4Ps (product, price, place, and promotion) in hospitality marketing, the success in any company's strategic goals will suffer a shortfall should *people* not be part of the marketing mix. Our people make or break our business. After all, they are the ones who are a large part of the total hospitality-experience, covering the majority of touch points, and distinguishing moments from "moments of truth." (This is a hospitality-industry expression referring to the point at which a specific customer expectation is either met or not.)

In moving with the times, the human-capital factor can ill afford to be ignored any further as *service* marketing is becoming part and parcel of the hospitality product. In comparison to traditional product marketing, the 4P-marketing mix has now to reach out to its fifth P, *people*, in order for hospitality marketing to be complete or holistic.

Internal Marketing and Its Place

As it gets clearer that our human capital is intrinsically linked with the level of customer satisfaction and thus, the bottom line of the company, we must take a closer look at what internal marketing means and how it should be playing its role. Internal marketing is an ongoing process of preparing our employees at all management levels to be customer-conscious and to handle every customer interaction with complete knowledge and awareness of the company's brand promise. It is about getting every staff member to buy into our brand message and to speak of this same brand story *all the time*. It is a long-term exercise rather than short-term.

A good internal marketing strategy is able to pay off handsomely for the organization as having the employees "be the brand" is not only a more holistic approach to hospitality marketing, it is also rather cost-effective. Organizations can implement internal marketing much less expensively than they can external marketing.

In the long run, an organization is able to capitalize on its internal marketing communication where there is an alignment of the organization's purpose with employee behavior, senior management leadership style, continual staff motivation, and fulfillment. In turn, employees will naturally be happier, more productive, and less likely to leave the company, which means staff-turnover rate can see a marked improvement, in an industry where job-hopping is a perpetual problem.

Internal marketing focuses on using the same voice that communicates with the brand customers to the brand employees. People are what make a company unique. By ensuring that employees are cared for and cultivated to represent the company's brand, they will go the extra mile in providing the most unique brand message.

The integrated function of internal marketing to employ and retain good staff stands to provide a real competitive edge for our company, Frasers Hospitality. When we have the best designer, top sales manager, or first-rate sommelier in our company, we have the majority of the customers buying into the brand because of these people. Internal marketing cultivates a people product that cannot be replicated.

Kick-start Your Internal Marketing Practice

With internal marketing considered to be a prerequisite for successful external marketing (Gronroos 1990), it is a pretty tall order for HR to play its role in search of, and in the making of, the internal customers, who will eventually make or break the business. If employees are well trained and highly motivated, they will live our brand and do a better job of serving our customers. Customers will come back for more if they have had positive experiences, and successful retention of a customer is, after all, the goal of marketing efforts. Hence, employees need to be brought onboard with a well-executed, internal marketing program.

So what can HR departments do to market to these internal customers?

In a nutshell, HR divisions need to sell:

1. *Product*—by packaging the *job* to attract the best possible prospective employees, who will serve our external customers;
2. *Price*—by understanding the *opportunity* cost (perceived benefits in terms of salary package, working conditions, and staff welfare) that will retain good employees in the organization;
3. *Place*—by creating the ideal working and learning *environment* that is conducive to staff growth and development; and
4. *Promotion*—by establishing reward policies and a consistent message (information) that will serve as *motivation* for excellent staff performance in alignment with the organization's vision and contributing to its financial goals.

While HR may be the first line of formal contact with our employees, it does not exclude the rest of the company from taking part in this internal marketing exercise. On the contrary, it greatly concerns each and every person in the organization so internal marketing is a concerted effort. An effective and measurable internal marketing strategy is indeed paramount to the ultimate success of any business.

Some of the best-performing companies use a strategic approach known as the McKinsey 7S model, a value-based management model that helps to holistically and effectively organize a company.

The McKinsey 7S Model

1 S—Shared vision and core values
2 S—Strategy on organization level
3 S—Structure of organization
4 S—Systems and measures on organization competence
5 S—Style of individual/team competence
6 S—Skills of individual/team competence
7 S—Staff Alignment

The 7S framework of McKinsey is a *value-based management* model that is used in ensuring that all parts of the organization work in *harmony*. It involves seven interdependent factors, which are categorized as either "hard" or "soft" elements.

The hard Ss being more easily identified, are namely found in the strategy statements, organization charts, operating manuals, and other documents. The soft Ss are less tangible, more cultural in nature, and highly determined by the people (internal customers) at work in the organization. Although the soft factors are below the surface, they can have a great impact on the hard elements. Most successful companies work hard at these soft Ss.

Source: McKinsey. Enduring Ideas: The 7-S Framework, *McKinsey Quarterly.* http://www.mckinseyquarterly.com

People are behind Every One of these Ss

Frasers Hospitality is a value-based organization that adopts a total approach to learning and deployment of the Mckinsey 7S model. The 7S strategy closely links human-capital efforts with business objectives and provides a comprehensive framework required for Frasers' local and overseas staff to develop shared values and vision. This approach is all the more important because *people* are behind every of these Ss. The 7S strategy closely links human-capital efforts with business objectives and provides a comprehensive framework required for Frasers' local and overseas staff to develop shared values and vision.

The impact of Frasers' organization-wide deployment of this human capital 7S strategy on business performance continues to yield positive business results, with people as the main asset of its business. It continues to register improvement trends in business results through key indicators such as strong occupancy rates of 90 percent for its serviced residences, consistent and high customer-satisfaction levels and staff morale, and overseas expansion and business growth.

Walking the Talk with the Cs

Generally, regardless of the approach or strategy employed by companies in support of internal marketing, an alignment of the various components in the framework has to be achieved.

The key to this successful alignment, thus internal marketing, is good communication. It is about letting everyone on the team know the same information, and moving the right information around the organization at the right time to the right people. These efforts should result in the organization speaking to external customers with a single voice and a harmonized brand promise.

Culture and Central Belief

It is important from day one that the company takes time to contemplate the value of good communication and truly understand the significance of establishing a solid internal marketing practice. Talking is always cheap; an internal marketing exercise needs to be led by someone who understands and is committed to total quality management and the customers. The leader and his team managers must eternally share and adopt a single, common, and central belief in cultivating their environment and its people into its most valued asset through good communication by design.

We are not just talking about a credo here even though it is also a "C." As with any other business objectives, good communication does not exist without a thoughtful design, which is not only an external expression but comes from an internal impetus to want to do things right.

A familiar saying is "practice makes perfect," meaning that if we do the right thing from the outset, we could perfect this right thing along the way, or if we choose to not to practice, we could get confused and end up doing the wrong thing. Thus, it is important that we have a strong foundation in a culture that accords reverence toward our very own people. Only when an organization embraces a people culture, then would its subsequent working mechanism and efforts spin off on the right track, in a holistic manner, cascading to each level of employees throughout the company's people population.

Take for example, the Singapore brand Eu Yan Sang, founded upon its core belief in the Chinese philosophy of health and healing, which is a balanced internal system, a preservation of health over the treating of illnesses. Hence from day one, its culture has dictated a high-level of care and respect for balance and health preservation through the appropriate usage of Chinese herbs. Any staff member, at any level, who exudes faith in the curative power of Chinese herbs, would be actively demonstrating the alignment and strength of Eu Yan Sang's culture. Such an employee would also be a direct outcome of Eu Yan Sang's internal marketing efforts, and thus result in the successful delivery of its brand promise.

Or take Creative Technology as another example. Its brand name already suggests that creativity is a highly prized core value and element in its culture. Whether the company is able to align its internal marketing efforts with its message for creativity calls for every major touchpoint, from the building architecture to the degree of staff empowerment, to be carefully managed and demonstrated. In all instances, this very culture at once pervades and prevails in every internal touchpoint such as e-mail, training manuals, meetings, presentations, the intranet, company business cards, memo pads, T-shirts, office layout, and the staff canteen—and will help align employees' behavior with the marketing or brand strategy of the company.

Furthermore, training courses should aim at making everyone aware that they have internal customers to serve. Every greeting, smile, and intent to be of service will bring us closer to meeting and exceeding customer expectations, internal and external.

Corporate Stature

We all know that first impressions count. But while many companies invest a considerable amount in generating a corporate identity as part of their branding efforts, only a few truly assume their professional corporate image at all times, both internally and externally.

Just as important as the image we project to our external customers, is the image we reveal to our internal customers in the first few weeks, perhaps few days and in some cases, the first few minutes of their employment. New employees are readily able to gather tell-tale signs about the company and determine whether it is dependable, cares about staff welfare, and is a good company to work for or not.

There are many areas that comprise our corporate stature. As far as office mannerisms, office ethics, and social etiquette are concerned, it is unquestionably an internal marketing effort that new recruits believe, agree, and abide by the company's *dos and don'ts* from day one. Otherwise, we shall be breeding a vicious cycle of newer employees tailing the bad examples of the older employees.

A commonly overlooked area of corporate stature is the issue of dress code. Apart from the uniformed departments, most companies do have a code of practice for their administrative staff but very often, they do not emphasize it enough and over time, we see all sorts of fashion come into action in the office. Inappropriate dressing such as the casual resort wear of odd-length pants, flimsy sandals, or revealing clothing, all cause inconvenience and distraction and will not work for the corporate image within the office.

As long as there is no clear and firm message laid down on the dress code in the office, it is almost predictable that staff from the non-customer-facing departments, for example, IT and accounts departments, will turn from business attire to casual wear in a matter of time. The inner message is "it does not matter since I do not face the guests." It goes on and the employees continue to think, "I don't care since it does not concern my department."

Grooming is not an option, it is a necessity. Employee appearance is a part of our brand image. When we care about our brand, regardless of whether we are meeting clients, attending a VIP function, or just working in the office, we should project a reliable and professional image. In doing so, the office will be a better place to work in and employees will be better prepared to perform their daily tasks and activities.

Good internal marketing dictates that internal customers must be treated on par with external customers regarding office etiquette. Staff should be trained to use the desired (according to company standard) telephone etiquette with internal customers. Do they pick up the phone within three rings? Is there a personalized voice mail in place for every extension? For the reservations department, does the reservations staff speak at a comfortable pace when explaining the company's product to internal customers? Do they respond to every internal enquiry within 24 hours like they do with external ones? Other touchpoints where the corporate stature requires a generous amount of consideration for internal customers include the ergonomics in interior design and organization; smooth functioning of an inter-departmental network system; and upkeep of meeting, training, and other office facilities and their related operational systems.

Let our imaginations flow and we should start making sure that every point where first impression counts is carefully aligned with our internal marketing communications.

Consistency

Applying the much-used principle of "Keep it simple and sweet" (or "Keep it simple and short") is almost a play-it-safe technique needed with the good communication design. A simple, single message should be clearly spelt out and remain the same at all times. A simple message ensures that information will not be misunderstood or cause undue confusion. Furthermore, message consistency encourages everyone in the company to move in the same direction, act upon the same information, and see themselves as sharing the same identity. The more consistent the message, the more reliable and powerful employee behavior becomes.

Needless to say, senior managers have to be careful not to be seen as practicing double standards based on their own whims and fancies. When there is flexibility required in a human resource decision, leaders must make it a point to explain the need for exceptional treatment of certain people or the case in question. Should exceptions to a company's policies or rules become too frequent, it could mean that there is a need for review of the policies or rules in issue and a speedy announcement of revisions should immediately follow. Any communication void is likely to invite rumors of favoritism, layoffs, or other undesirable speculation.

Consistency in dissemination of communication is also important. From CEO to receptionist, from permanent position to temporary staff, all should know the same information at the same time. They have to communicate in sync with the brand message in order to be the spokesmen and spokeswomen of the company and its product. Customers will not evaluate contracted employees with any less scrutiny than they evaluate your full-time employees. Talking to customers, internal and external, with a consistent, single voice maximizes the marketing process and increases the retention rate of customers.

Within a relatively short time where consistent, good communication is practiced and applied to all employees, it is almost a guaranteed outcome that the staff will among themselves build better relationships. They will also have a stronger sense of team spirit, enjoy workplace camaraderie, and happily stay where they are, given their trust in the company.

What makes for trust? It is none other than demonstrating consistent and reliable behavior. Trust builds up when the parties are being sincere and honest with each other, and where there is consistency in information delivering and knowledge sharing.

Trust flourishes in an environment where the staff is fairly treated, or where rules and regulations are clearly and properly proclaimed and adhered to. Leaders who trust, recognize that their employees need time to get things done, ask questions in a nonthreatening way, and are willing to listen to the points of view of those who are doing the work.

The culture will take on a new height in a trustful, nonintimidating environment where everyone naturally uses more "us" and "ours" instead of "you" and "your department," by comfortably reckoning that "we are in this together."

Continuity (Ongoing)

Good internal communication is not a one-time affair. It is more than a means to an end for any internal marketing program to work. Good communication is highly prized since communication elements can be found everywhere in a company and effect many aspects of the organization so long as there are more than two people at work. We cannot ignore its prominence nor afford poor communication, which affects human relationships, tears up teamwork, and eventually breaks up our business.

Well-designed communication is really not good enough if it is not done often enough. For any message to produce sustainable change, it has to be repeated continuously. Reinforcements have to work through a number of levels, using a number of mediums. Whether it is to learn, to be informed, to be trained, or to deliver a service while we are assuming our work roles, we have to be immersed in the culture in order to internalize the brand message. Internal communication has to be a continuous effort.

Constant reinforcement set in place for everyone can help us to not only just do it, but do it so often until it is in our blood and we become intimately familiar with our own brand and the message we want others to know about us. It means to be continuously enthusiastic about what is happening around us. From an employee's perspective, say if they belong to a restaurant team, they ought to know by heart the restaurant's address and reservation phone number, specialty food and beverage, and Christmas promotion. From the company's perspective, say if we operate the restaurant, we ought to know each and every one of our employees by their names, understand their strengths and weaknesses, likes and dislikes, be interested in their growth and development as unique individuals, and provide the conditions for them to excel in their position. The process of such two-way understanding and communication requires time and is continuous. This mutual exchange between the company and its staff members is a perpetual force that drives them toward the result of ultimate customer-service excellence.

Continuity also applies, along with consistency, where a company sees its competitive advantage to hire and train staff in advance. As businesses expand globally, the world gets smaller and jobs become freer ranging in nature. This means, firstly, we are reaching out to a wider and more diversified group of customers with increased points for service delivery. Secondly, we have to match increased touchpoints and a growing customer base with consistent service all around, all the time. This effort is more challenging in times of business expansion, staff turnover, and organization restructuring. In such an era, the same job is likely to be handed off to a new person on a regular basis, so a new face may serve the same customers on their very next visit. Hence, there is the importance today of continuity of information and brand message through effective internal communication, allowing no one to be missed in the process.

Hiring more than the required number of employees and training them in advance will prove to be an ingenious way of continually staying ahead in business by narrowing or closing any service-delivery gaps.

Supporting internship programs by working closely with local universities and polytechnics can pave the way for young blood to flow into the organization as needed. Hence, student attachment and management trainee programs should be passionately advocated internally as a platform for attracting and grooming future talent.

Finally, continuous internal reinforcement of customer-service education is particularly appropriate for staff who may not be directly involved in service delivery to our external customers such as the accounting clerk or the IT technician. An incorrectly generated statement or an erroneously assigned e-mail address may still cause a breakdown in the service delivery, and thus, overall customer satisfaction suffers. These back-of-the-house employees can always be trained to perform their tasks in a marketing-like manner when they learn that an ongoing, consistent level of care is required for their internal customers, and that they need to cooperate with them at all times in managing the customer-interface.

Connection (Making Quality Contact)

Another way of applying marketing principles inside an organization is to regard the other departments and individuals as customers and treat them as if they were real customers. As with everybody, we all yearn to be respected and understood, listened to, and connected with others. Making a connection with everyone else in the organization as though they are the most important people can create magic. When we see our working counterparts in this different light, we not only stretch our capacity in the role we play, we experience a greater sense of purpose, enjoy a deeper sense of meaning, and as a result, we increase our productivity and happiness quotient.

Most companies adopt the policy of never allowing the phone to ring more than three times. But when we know that the caller is an internal employee from another department, we tend to regard this call as less important, or we may not answer it in the same bright tone as we would to an external caller. However, just imagine yourself being greeted by a staff member from another department with a bright and cheerful voice, and by the second ring of the phone, would you not appreciate it? A happy mood is contagious and an awareness to simply connect with others with equal respect and sincerity will enhance any relationship without fail.

Companies, which see the value of connecting with their staff and building strong internal relationships, have to emphasize editorial efforts not only in their marketing collaterals, but also in-house employee communication materials. In advertising campaigns, substituting the models in the external campaign with actual employees in the internal campaign can add a further touch of relevance and connection for the internal audience and create a more uplifting message.

From the start, it pays to execute a thorough orientation program that focuses on making connections between the company and individuals with the aim of letting new employees feel at home and welcome. Organizations should budget for premium welcome gifts, similar to our corporate gifts to guests. Employees will be more than happy to receive a quality collar pin or a polo shirt and feel treated like part of the family. Rather than the usual HR policy of reciting or handing down information, which the newcomers can easily read on their own, it can be unbelievably inspiring to have the most energetic speakers talk about what makes them get up and come to work each day and what they love about their respective departments. Subsequent investment in the implementation of educational contact opportunities, for example, company intranet, Internet web cast, and leadership speeches over breakfast meetings, will further engage employees in learning about the brand message.

Regular face-to-face conversation remains a powerful way to connect with people. It does not cost much for senior management to interact with their staff in person, and leaders should involve employees at all levels, not just with those with whom they directly work. Without any change in its content, a message communicated face-to-face versus one that is passed down through an e-mail is more energetic and engaging, leaving employees feeling recognized and, more importantly, enabling the message content to be better retained. Taking the few minutes to say thank you to an employee or check on his or her viewpoint on any matter can, in fact, accomplish more than any group discussion or internal memo.

Whenever possible, one-on-one sessions are most encouraged. There is no need to wait until there is a problem with an employee to meet individually. It always helps to shrink the distance when a leader walks up to the employee at his or her workstation to request for assistance or feedback. Picture your CEO taking time to interact with the receptionist, knowing the employee by name, listening to the employee about his or her job, being interested in the employee's dreams and aspirations—such good information exchange just comes so much more readily. Individual meetings are truly valuable.

Finally, because today there are many hospitality products sold through lifestyle marketing, it would only makes sense for us to promote the same lifestyle message to our employees and provide them the conditions for improved living standards. These improvements could be by way of offering work-life balance activities within the organization, for example, childcare facilities in the office, aerobics classes, dancing lessons, and nutritional health workshops. When our very own employees "get a taste of the pudding," they are more familiar with our products and therefore offer a more compelling message to our customers. In this way, employees are more likely to be retained because they feel involved as an important part of the marketing efforts of the company product. Customers are also likely to stay brand loyal because they can see and feel the integrity of the products through the eyes of the employees.

Customer-conscious

Any viable business has to be a customer-conscious business. When we turn our focus from our external customers to our internal customers, we will find that the same amount of care is always appreciated. If you treat people the way you want to be treated, the quality of internal communication will improve. Internal marketing suggests that organizations should extend the best possible service to each customer, internal and external. Care has therefore to be exercised in all forms of communication—verbal by greeting our colleagues in a warm and cheerful manner, non-verbal by providing accurate and informative updates in our company's e-newsletter, tangibly by issuing salary on time and duly giving increment, and intangible by being considerate to your colleague sitting next to you by not speaking too loudly on the phone.

On a regular basis, audits must be run through all our company's collaterals and information, organization procedures and plans, working environment and facilities, to ensure all management levels are on the same platform of customer-consciousness. It is somewhat disappointing to see examples of a huge contrast between the front-of-the-house and the back-of-the-house of an establishment. One example is the staff restroom in which it is often considered normal to have malfunctioning lockers and toilet flushes; torn and dilapidated furniture; and inadequate air-conditioning and lighting. Ironically, some of the worst staff quarters are found in five-star standard establishments whereby the companies are proudly claiming their state-of-art facilities, exceptional service standards, and top-rated customer-care programs, while they subject their staff to substandard back-end environments.

Customer-consciousness really means having the sensitivity toward customers' needs and wants and our internal customers are no exception. Employers who take a real interest in their employees' lives, problems, and basic needs are taking the first step into their internal marketing exercise. In order to turn our employees into our best marketers, a well-thought through (where all the Cs have been considered) two-way system for internal communication has to be in place. One way to foolproof our internal communication could mean following the customers' footsteps, whereby every part of the internal marketing mechanism is subject to the customers' standard. Explore the typical customer experience and decide what would be considered good marketing to our internal customers at each service touchpoint. It may remind us of role-playing and putting ourselves in the customers' shoes. Is the instruction clear and easy to understand? Is the air-conditioning temperature in the office comfortable? Is the length and pace of the meeting controlled for easy participation? Is the deadline for the report reasonable? Does the canteen food fare good enough so the employees would come back for more?

Internal communication involves scrutinizing just about every aspect of the internal customer relationship in order to align actions that will yield maximum internal customer satisfaction. Without well-functioning internal relationships, external relationships cannot develop successfully.

A solid internal marketing system takes us far in our efforts to get more and better business. Once we align our marketing efforts with our internal communication efforts, everyone gets a share of what is in it for them as customers, employees, and the company as a whole.

Good internal communication is worth every minute of work or our external marketing efforts will eventually go to waste. So take time to have a cuppa with your staff!

Care for the Staff: Generating Goodwill

From mega firms to small companies, caring for staff has always been a debatable topic. Human capital considerations often occupy the minds of goal-driven leaders, "Can I reduce my manpower budget further?" "They are just workers," "We should not pamper the employees or they will climb onto our heads," "We have to be tough to be in control of our staff," and "We must drive them hard—no profit, no job."

Companies that rate staff performance by their commitment and willingness to work extended hours are superficial. Overworked employees do not increase their performance, and this is never the right way to improve the quality of their work.

While many more companies have embarked on improving customer service and instilling better customer-care values into their customer-management programs, it is important at parallel standards of extending kindness and concern toward their very own employees. Unfortunately, there is a common misconception and erroneous belief that showing kindness equals weakness in management decisions on employee care. A "soft approach" in managerial policy and actions means a surrendering of control to some. Very often, many companies stay bureaucratic and regimental only to create a distance between the company and its manpower. Obviously, this is not good for internal communication.

Caring leaders are not weak but strong enough to be gentle. They are patient and speak with their staff with genuine interest and concern all the time. These leaders shift the sight focus of their staff from the work desk to the bigger picture where a clear direction and a massive horizon are to be aimed for.

Management by authority (hard approach) and management by involvement (soft approach) are very different. A successful company must understand that its success does not lie in its size, but in the hands of employees who are united in the pursuit of a common goal. Hence, it helps for us to discover opportunities to work together that serve our mutual best interests.

The care we are emphasizing here is a mutual effort. It means both taking and giving. It involves the deep-seated value of compassion from the start. There must be caring for ourselves, for the others, and for our greater purpose. One major way to care for our employees is to provide direction and lead the way well. We can help employees develop through their work by providing benchmarks where clear, objective, and exacting standards are indicated. This means spelling out goals that are achievable and measurable within the employees' capacities. In this way, they know what is expected of them and feel more engaged with the job at hand. Through effective internal marketing, companies can always seek to raise the bar further and continually, encouraging service excellence.

In the same token, care excellence for the staff implies well-meaning considerations, such as allowing for flexi-hour arrangements, encouraging a healthy work-life balance, providing extra-educational curriculum, and empowering staff at various levels. Caring for the staff is akin to generating goodwill. It is as intangible as it is valuable, and it always shows up in employees walking the extra mile for our business, Frasers Hospitality, in unexpected ways. Employees are our first market and can easily give considerable amounts of business to us. Their word-of-mouth advertising costs us nothing, but is one of the best sources of referral for new business. Think about former staff who left us on good terms, would their continuous excellence not be our success and glory?

It only makes sense to care for staff we hire to be the best possible employees, and it only makes sense to care for them and have them stay with us for as long as our mutual interest exists. Long-term staff increases productivity dramatically by cutting down on both time and resource-consuming orientation and training for every replaced employee. There is no magic pill here—take care of your staff and they will take care of your customers.

Conclusion: Collaborative Approach to Internal Marketing Practice

Internal marketing suggests that in order to take care of the customers, you must first take care of those who take care of your customers. Employees' feelings of satisfaction never fail to *reflect* on the level of service delivery to both internal and external customers.

But more often than not, the internal customers are not recognized, or worse, not identified. Remember, take care of your staff, and they will take care of your customers. A happy and motivated staff person can do wonders in elevating the entire consumer experience. And these staff members are likely to retain the customers, not by hard selling to them but simply by understanding the buyer and being there to look after their unique needs.

It is a pity that not many companies engage their employees with the same voice they use to communicate with their customers. At most, as with many average companies, from time to time, they gather the staff together over standard events such as orientation, monthly staff birthday celebrations, and annual dinners and dances, solely for the purpose of adhering to what is known to them as standard practice. One can hardly find a clue of a single marketing principle applied in the rest of the daily activities, for example, e-mails, memos, training manuals, and intranet, where communication is constantly available as the single most powerful channel for leveraging internal marketing.

There is no better time to take care of your staff than the moment they come into contact with your organization. Those phone calls to inform them of the interviews, the feel of the reception area where they report to work, the acknowledging nod and firm handshake from the department head, the warm smile from a colleague whom they have yet to work with, and a clean and well-furnished work station where business cards have been correctly printed and neatly placed prior to his or her arrival are just the few very basic things and often cost little. However, these efforts form the sure internal touchpoints for our internal marketing efforts to get through, perhaps even quite effortlessly.

Many companies simply leave it to the HR department. It may be both shortsighted and self-limiting to regard HR as just a department, where staff are being recruited, trained, and retained by following through a series of standard procedures, running through bouts of homogeneous trainings, and practicing salary and reward schemes only to be recommended by the government.

The concept of internal marketing as "good human resources management with a view to satisfying external customers" (Cahill 1995, 45) is prompting us further that we have a long way to go before our service management reaches our external customers. It must therefore be a shared objective for every single service-management person of an organization to see our internal customers as the new king.

Marketing excellence cannot be successfully achieved without the help from HR for its training programs on product knowledge and service quality. Operational excellence will remain a far-fetched concept if not for precise performance indicators laid out by HR. As a matter of fact, many so-called HR functions, such as organizational restructuring, recruitment, appraisals, and internship programs, require concurrent efforts where duties are shared by marketing as well as operations.

With the new focus on internal marketing, we are seeing a transformation of HR simultaneously delivering marketing and operational excellence. HR is consequently spreading its roots over marketing and operational initiatives, which are instrumental in striving for profitability and meeting the organization's financial goals.

Understandably, there has to be a collaborative effort in delivering our brand communication from the inside out, from one member to another within the organization. All service deliveries are interrelated and interdependent where HR, marketing, and operations must come together to form "The Service Management Trinity" (Joseph 1996; Lovelock 1996), and play equally substantial roles within our internal marketing program.

The service-management trinity suggests that the three departments shall claim equal ownership for internal marketing and work hand-in-hand to plan and implement the communications program as one. The three functional units are linked and no one function shall overshadow the other, but contribute what it does best from an organization-wide angle. The result will be a highly feasible and cost-effective program that takes into consideration the organization's vision, values, philosophy, culture, style, and goals.

There are no two ways to completing the equation of the product marketing of every organization. The best approach, in my opinion, lies in the optimal cooperation among the HR, marketing, and operational departments.

References

Ahmed, P. K., and M. Rafiq. 2002. *Internal Marketing*. Oxford: Butterworth-Heinemann.

American Strategic Management Institute's 2004 Internal Branding Summit Summary. http://www.asmiweb.com.

Business Development Directives. 2008. Internal marketing: A powerful growth and survival strategy your organization cannot do without. http://www.bddonline.com.

Grönroos, Christian. 2000. *Service Management and Marketing: A Customer Relationship Management Approach*. 2nd ed. Chichester: Wiley.

Guillemette, Melinda. 2002. Making internal marketing work. http://www.aicpa.org/pubs/tpcpa/dec2002/marketing.htm. Kelemen, M. and I. Papasolomou-Doukakis. 2004. Can culture be changed? A study of internal marketing. *The Service Industries Journal* 24 (September):121–135.

Maslow, Abraham. 1954. *Motivation and Personality*. New York: Harper and Row, New York.

McKinsey. 2008. Enduring Ideas: The 7-S Framework. *McKinsey Quarterly* March 2008. http://www.mckinsey.quarterly.com

roi.com.au. 2008. Effective internal marketing for successful external marketing. http://www.roi.com.au.

Ruzek, Paula. 2005. Internal Marketing. http://www.ami.org.au/amimu/0506June/0506_webinar_internalmarketing.htm.

Yang, Jen-Te. 2003. The development and emergence of the internal marketing concept. Unpublished paper, Department of Hotel and Restaurant Management, National Kaohsiung Hospitality College, Kaohsiung City, Taiwan.

10

BEING AN INSPIRING LEADER

By Jennie Chua

Introduction

Leaders are central to organizational success as they provide guidance, direction, and influence, which in turn facilitate achieving institutional goals and objectives.

When it comes to leadership, there are some who are born with a certain something in them—a quality that sets them apart from the rest. However one wishes to label it—a sixth sense or intuition—it is a quality that cannot be defined or learned. It is something a leader is born with and what separates the great from the good.

Having this sixth sense or intuition means not just being able to tell whether it is a good business deal or not for the company, but also being able to read people well. Real leaders intuitively know the values of the people they work with and if they are a right fit for the company and team.

Leaders must couple intuition with a sense of humor, a sense of quirkiness, and playfulness, combined with optimism, without being completely foolish. A slight touch of eccentricity but not overwhelmingly so, creates the lighter quality that makes leaders more humanistic and thus, easier to follow. A sense of humor can be a valuable trait for a leader. Life never goes exactly as planned, so it helps to be able to laugh at oneself and the trials and tribulations that are encountered daily.

Of course, leadership is also about attitude. Not attitude for the sake of being different or showing off but as a way of looking at life and things. For example, one should just get on with it. All of us are born with some form of handicap or other, as we are too short, too fat, or too beautiful. Nobody is perfect. Neither is life, as there are always problems and issues such as prejudices, gender, and race factors. The first thing leaders learn to do is get on with it: work with the cards that life has dealt.

Leaders do not allow life's disadvantages to work against them; otherwise, they will create their own glass ceiling. In life, different things happen, sometimes bad and sometimes good. Leaders just move on.

I had to stop my university education because my family ran out of money. It was devastating at the time because, as a child, every chance I got, I loved to read, study, and learn about the world. But I did not just sit there and think, "Why did this have to happen to me?" I got on with life. Yes, my education was interrupted, but as soon as I could afford it, I resumed my studies.

Take mistakes, it is natural to make them. In fact, some of the greatest leaders in the world have made mistakes and admitted them. But one should not harbor regrets and say: I wish... or I should have... or why didn't I? Real leaders use these experiences as their guiding light, but learn and move on.

Leaders can learn from successes, too. However, leaders should not dwell on past successes and get stuck in that moment, and they should not keep reminding people of what used to be. Instead, leaders inspire others with more of what is to come.

Wallowing in your own sorrow or former glory freezes you. Action moves you.

Lessons Learned

Have a Vision

To be a great leader, one must first have a clear vision and clear objectives of where the organization can go and of what it should be when it gets there. The vision cannot be developed in a vacuum but must meld the vision of the employees with that of the leader, so that the vision becomes a unifying focal point. Leaders stay focused on their vision and their goals. They are achievement-oriented.

For example, there were two key decisions made that were pivotal to the success of the restoration of the Raffles Hotel. Firstly, for it to be sustainable as a heritage project, it had to be true in its restoration. One of the views expressed was "To attempt to restore Raffles Hotel by making additions to increase the density to modern parameters would in itself destroy what is left of the fine old building." (Liu 2005) So the decision was made to include the entire city block in the restoration program. The adjacent land was purchased and a budget of S$160 million was set aside for Raffles' renovation.

Secondly, it had to be financially sustainable and therefore a suitable business model had to be found. As hard-nosed bankers, the owners of Raffles Hotel (1886) Pte. Ltd. knew financial return was important, but they also knew that Raffles Hotel was an important piece of Singapore history that had to be preserved. Much credit goes to the two owner banks for walking that tough line between financial sustainability and heritage conservation.

Another critical decision was to use 1915 as the benchmark for restoration. This was when the hotel was at the height of its fame. It was part of the Grand Hotels of the East, and representative of the fables of the exotic East. "Patronized by nobility, loved by all" was already being used to describe it.

As a leader, I had to stay true to those decisions throughout the restoration and not be distracted by the "noise." Because Raffles Hotel belonged to everyone, everyone had an opinion. And in today's media-intense environment, where everyone is free to write and express his or her opinions, it can be easy to be distracted by the "noise" around you, and allow it to cloud your judgment. When the Raffles Hotel reopened on September 16, 1991, we faced much criticism from the foreign press, mainly the older generation journalists and the foreign correspondent-types who, probably more out of nostalgia than anything else, felt that we had rubbed the soul out of the place. But we won them over with time. Today, the foreign media is one of our biggest fans. In 2003, Raffles Hotel was listed in the travel guide *1,000 Places to See Before You Die: A Traveler's Life* (Schultz 2003).

After the successful restoration and reopening of the Raffles Hotel, we did not just dwell on the success, we used that platform to grow the Raffles brand and build a chain.

No Need for Perfection

Leaders also do not need to be perfectionists. One only needs to be perfect under circumstances that are tied to life and death. If one is in an aerobatic team like the Red Arrows, and every second counts, then yes, one has to be a perfectionist. But whether one's bags arrive in six minutes or eight minutes, and seven minutes is the perfect benchmark, it does not matter, especially if reaching that last bit of perfection costs too much and nobody wants to pay for it.

There is no such thing as perfection in life anyway. For example, what is perfect art? The perfect cut of sushi? How many people are prepared to pay for that? Then there are some who say, "You are not trying hard enough because you don't want to reach perfection." That is not true. One could be trying very hard but the goal is not really perfection. Perfection is subjective, and has no bearing on a person's contribution to the company.

Managing Change or How to Make Arranged Marriages Work

A leader should be capable of managing change that drives the organization forward but does not pull it apart. The ability to manage change is a critical skill and becoming more important given the rapidity of changes occurring in today's micro- and macro-environments.

One of the more difficult tasks to manage is mergers and acquisitions. Mergers and acquisitions are common in today's competitive business environment. However, while the financial due diligence and examination of business compatibilities surrounding mergers and acquisitions are generally thorough, the success rate of effectively integrating two organizations is low. Approximately, half of such ventures fail, (Home 2008) with the blame being placed on sloppy execution of the integration effort (Schuler 2008).

Executives could learn a thing or two about successful integration from arranged marriages. I have a friend whose mother was married off to a stranger when she was 16. The bridegroom was 16 years her senior and she only had one meeting with him prior to their being tied for life. That was the way things were done in those days and continues to be done in some societies today—arranged marriages.

For the bride-to-be, it was a daunting prospect as she was barely a woman herself, and having to live with an old man—at 16, everyone is old—she did not know for the rest of her life. For the bridegroom, one can only assume it was easier for him. He was getting a sweet, child-bride who would bear him healthy sons and look after him for the rest of his life.

She had no choice, he made the choice. She had to submit, he took the lead. She had to learn to live with it; he, if he was a good man, had to make it easy and pleasant for her.

And with time, through constant communication, plenty of compromises, and shared pain and joy, they would learn to live with each other and depend on each other so much so that what God had put together, no man would put asunder.

Mergers and acquisitions can be viewed in the same light as arranged marriages—one company buying into another, and then both having to learn with each other for the greater good of the union while, at the same time, providing a happy and stable environment for family members.

The acquisition is the easy part. That is just an exchange of money or other recognizable forms of currency, a non-emotional transaction.

It is the integration that follows that is the challenge because there are not only systems and processes involved in the entire workings of a company but also the human dimension with all its complexities and complications. That is, people with fears, insecurities, and paranoia, "Will I lose my job?" "Will my boss be fired?" "Will my entire department be closed down?" "Will my best friend lose his job?" "What will I tell my wife, my children?"

It is this human drama that is the most challenging for leaders to navigate and it is the single biggest responsibility of managers to ensure that integration is as easy, pleasant, and dignified as possible.

In 2001, we found this challenge on our hands when Raffles International acquired Swissotel Hotels & Resorts at the cost of S$420.1 million. In one fell swoop, our room count more than doubled to 13,139 rooms, surpassing the original goal of 12,000 rooms by end 2003. At the same time, it diversified the company's earnings base and increased its fee-based income from management contracts by 78 percent from 2000. Buying Swissotel was the right thing to do. It was the right geographic and brand fit, right price, right time.

Due to the acquisition, the brand architecture had to be restructured to comprise two distinct brands—Raffles (mainly owned hotels) and Swissotel (mostly management contracts). With the two brands, the company had a more diversified business portfolio targeted at affluent leisure travelers and savvy business respectively. The geographic diversification also meant it would be less vulnerable to external threats like severe acute respiratory syndrome (SARS) and terrorism.

But we also knew we had to tread carefully because these were two very different companies. One was Singapore-born and bred while the other was Swiss-owned and grown. While you could argue that Singapore and Switzerland are pretty similar in characteristic as both countries are small in size, clean, efficient, organized, surrounded by bigger neighbors, and always punching above their weight, both companies were pretty rooted nationally. The commonality was that both were international in their outlooks.

Integration with Swissotel was a huge challenge. Raffles had a lean team at the corporate office, which had to integrate with a much larger Swissotel team. Further, most of the Raffles corporate staff did not have prior mergers and acquisition experience before this integration effort.

The first thing we did was to set up a small dedicated integration team to coordinate efforts. There was a need to change the "you" versus "me" mentality to an "us" mind-set to steer the company toward a common goal.

Communication was cited as the number one challenge in the integration process as we had to work with a much bigger, global team. We needed to allay fears in job security and uncertainty in staff by ensuring timely communication of integration activities, progress, and results to all employees. Lack of timely communication led to some individuals feeling excluded, and therefore, becoming unmotivated and less productive.

Over-communicate

The first key take-away from this integration experience is that leaders should over-communicate. Over-communication requires that frequent general manager meetings, sales and marketing meetings, and management retreats be conducted in which the vision, strategy, and direction as well as processes, objectives, and results are shared. I quote Diana Ee-Tan, my very able chief marketing officer at the time of Raffles integration with Swissotel and who had to herself manage another integration of the company with Fairmont Hotels & Resorts (Raffles Hotels & Resorts was acquired by Colony Capital, and was later integrated with Fairmont Hotels & Resorts after its new owners purchased the Canadian luxury hotel group in a partnership with Dubai-based Kingdom Hotel Investments) in 2006/2007, "With any integration, there is always uncertainty. Systems change and new paradigms emerged but our employees embraced the changes because they understood the need for a new organizational structure that would enable us to be part of a bigger hotel company and play on the world stage."

What helped the integration process, she said, was the high-level commitment by Fairmont management to be personally involved in explaining the integration and engaging the staff at all levels. "The chief operating officer made it a point to be at all the integration meetings whether in Singapore or Toronto. He chaired biweekly conference calls to employees and explained and encouraged discussion."

The second integration must have been successful. In 2007, Raffles Hotels & Resorts was recognized as the third top employer in Singapore, and ranked among the top 20 in Asia among 700 companies according to Hewitt Associates, a global management consulting firm. The Best Employers in Asia 2007 is a study of people management practices across 750 companies in China, Australia, New Zealand, India, Singapore, Hong Kong, Japan, and Korea.

As Shakespeare said, "Action is eloquence" and "Be great in act, as you have been in thought." These are the two qualities of leadership that will get one through the most challenging of integration exercises.

Cultural Differences

A second key learning point is to be mindful of cultural differences, a very important element when managing the type of change that integration requires. First, it is key to remember an innuendo implies different things in different languages. For example, when our hotel in Osaka developed its launch collaterals for a new Executive Club, we chided our director of marketing for "erroneously" printing "New Open" instead of "Now Open"—for us, a glaring error. We were surprised to learn that such phrases are commonly used in Japan and are generally acceptable. Also, in Japan, a newly renovated hotel is known to have undergone renewal.

Second, incorporate cultural differences into the appropriate settings. For example, we appointed a "son of the soil" as the hotel's general manager at Raffles Hotel, Vier Jahreszeiten; and for the relaunch of Swissotel Sydney in December 2003, we released butterflies, a quintessential Australian culture, signifying a new beginning.

Third, create an alignment of corporate cultures. For instance, it took us one year to explain why business-class travel was no longer the norm under the new ownership of Raffles International. Privilege of business-class travel was more prevalent when Swissotel was owned by Swissair. In addition, our Swissotel colleagues also had to adjust to Raffles' discipline of risk management and review of new management contracts.

Final Lessons

A few final lessons remain. First, leaders must listen and respond to customer and employee concerns, and second, be alert to pre-symptoms of burnout among the employees who are heavily involved in the integration process.

As for my friends' parents, they remained married till her father passed away 13 years ago. Her mother said, "He was the best man I ever knew." Such is the magic that can come from forced unions, if managed correctly.

Moving Forward

Good leaders demonstrate concern for employees. Caring can be expressed through both tangible and intangible means. The leader should ensure that everyone has the appropriate knowledge, skills, and equipment to do their jobs in the most efficient and safest manner possible. In addition, a strong leader publicly and privately recognizes those who have done their jobs well.

A good leader always puts his or her people first in challenging situations. At the time of the Raffles and Swissotel purchase, the media was filled with speculation as to what would happen to the two brands—Raffles and Swissotel—and also, as to what would happen to me as chairman. I told them, "When you do negotiations, your first focus is the best price and whether your staff will have a good future. The last person you think of is yourself, otherwise you will not be a neutral negotiator."

Building a Great Team

Having a good team is critical, is a given, a fundamental. Nobody can do it alone. Leaders are not Superwomen or Supermen, although some might think they are.

More importantly, true leaders know that it is crucial to surround themselves with people who are better, smarter, more beautiful, and have more potential. If managers surround themselves with people who are their clones or who are more inadequate than they, the company will be weakened. Having smarter people around means managers will be constantly challenged. This does not mean that leaders want people who argue all the time as that would be time-consuming and energy-draining but people to spar with; people who are thoughtful, thought-provoking, different; and people who are confident in themselves. Brainstorming with such people is the best way to surface new ideas and different ways of thinking. Besides, having smarter people than the leader around makes the leader look good, so it is the smart thing to do.

In addition, one who is good in a leadership role also encourages leadership development for others. Leaders should not be fearful of others who are potentially strong leaders but should facilitate their development and take pride in their achievements.

Finally, a leader should seek diversity in people and in thinking. Individuals of different races, religions, ethnicity, and experiences bring fresh perspectives and add synergy to the organization. Different ideas and ways of thinking can offer a means for capitalizing on opportunities by utilizing previously unconsidered approaches.

The Importance of Reinvention

Reinvention is important but one has to watch what is reinvented. The basic principles such as qualities like integrity and fairness must remain constant and be the core of the leader. A constant leader commands respect, not someone who wavers from basic principles when it suits him or her. That is, the leader must do what is morally and legally right at all times and treat people in an appropriate and equitable manner. A leader must establish and exhibit the moral and ethical standards for the organization.

But the rest—the way leaders behave, the way they dress, their style of management and leadership—that should change every decade or every five years in today's faster-paced world.

It could be something as simple as dressing. A woman general manager, for instance, needs a style that is her signature yet versatile enough to take her from that morning's briefing to that evening's cocktail with celebrities and dignitaries. For example, I started off with cheongsams (I have 200 of them) and then moved on to pants suits (100, all silk and still counting). Why be concerned about dress? When reporters interview leaders, especially female leaders, they always talk about how we dress first rather than what we have to say.

Customers also come with their own customs, which can be a minefield to navigate, especially for women hoteliers. If VIPs are from countries where it is customary for women to walk behind the men, should the female leader lead the way a male general manager would? Again, one must develop one's own style—a style the leader is comfortable with because it is only when the leader is comfortable that others around that leader can also be comfortable.

Management styles must also evolve. A dictatorial management style, which worked 10 years ago, may not be as appropriate today. The manager may still be a dictator at heart but the style has to change to suit the times. In the 1970s and 1980s, leadership was a bit top down when leaders had to be larger than life. Thing are more subtle now. Today's workers are different from one or two decades ago. They want more time to themselves and they want to climb faster. Leaders have to manage changing expectations.

Teams today also have more color and diversity in backgrounds, education, thinking, and geography. Leaders now need to manage a spectrum of styles and beliefs. Having said that, today's leadership style in the hospitality industry has become "too soft," too politically correct. Managers seem to have gone to the other extreme. There is a lot of "counseling" going on, and almost no "disciplining."

One has to dare to be a leader, make decisions, discipline, and dismiss.

Need for Personal Time

Every job is demanding and yes, the hotel industry has its particular pressures, but no matter how demanding, successful leaders must always take time away from work.

For example, no matter how busy I am, I make it a point to have a family holiday once a year with my sons. And I am delighted that tradition has continued and in fact, expanded to twice a year. Our family holiday has become much bigger because now it includes my grandchildren.

Leaders must strike a good balance between work and personal life. They must know when to have their own quiet time and know when they need to work. In other words, maintain the right proportion of work-life, which should vary according to what is one's stage of career.

Obviously, when managers are aged 20, they need to be more work-focused and work can take up 70 percent of their time but not when they are aged 60. Leaders need to know how to adjust work-life balance as they progress in their career. People who do not make time for family, in the end may diminish their leadership. One way is to find a passion for something besides work and make "me" time an integral part of life.

Technology has made work much more intrusive and makes it more difficult to find "me" time. Everyone has his or her Blackberry on all the time. But, one must control that machine and not the other way around. For example, I read my Blackberry three times a day—in the morning, after lunch, and before I go to bed. I also have two personal assistants. Some people say that you do not need personal assistants today because technology does that for you, but on the contrary, I think, with the amount of communication we get these days, you need even more assistance.

Even when the leader is on holiday, that time should also be managed. While one still needs to be contactable, one must decide when or how.

A good leader need not do everything but probably needs to know everything that is happening.

Women as Leaders

Fundamentally, women have different attributes than men—thank goodness—and their paths thus have to be different. Men tend to be more focused on one thing—their career—while a woman was born to multitask.

Take the picture of a mother. She is cooking, carrying her child on the back, her three other children are playing in the garden, she hears a doorbell, and her husband is coming home. She knows at once everything that is happening.

Perhaps, it is because of this that women are also able to empathize better. Women can put themselves in other people's shoes and see a situation from different perspectives. That is a good leadership quality: empathy.

Something interesting is also happening in today's societies. More girls are availing themselves of tertiary education than boys. So women are entering the workplace better educated than men. And if one believes that a good education is fundamental to a good career, then some changes are ahead in the business world.

Women are also more fortunate because their success is not measured by career alone. Women can play more roles in life because they are much better at multitasking than men. In fact, families can often hone women's leadership skills as managing a home is often much more challenging than managing the workplace.

Leadership in a woman is not only measured by career but also by her life.

Crisis Leadership

There is a Chinese saying, "With high tide, all boats float." Good times are not a good test of leadership. Crises separate the men from the boys, the women from the girls. In a crisis, a good leader will always be able to seek out the opportunities and see the silver lining, as it were, and seize them to move the company forward. Having identified the opportunities, leaders need the courage to make decisions, have the conviction to stand by them, and then, communicate their ideas clearly.

The great leader is a man for all seasons.

A friend of mine once said, you make things look easy. I think that is part of leadership—it should not have to be too hard or difficult. I have never had a sleepless night over work. Over love, yes, but not work. At 11pm, if I cannot resolve a work-related problem, it will not be resolved that night.

Even as a child—I was the first of 12 children—I just naturally took charge. I believe your birth order has something to do with whether you have the natural ability to lead. I do not have scientific evidence, only going by experience.

Measuring Great Leadership

Leadership must also have a legacy; if not, the manager is merely competent. After the manager leaves, people should talk, not about the manager's personality but about what the manager left behind and what he or she did for them and the company.

Legacy is not about thinking the leader is IT, that is, that the company equals the leader. Because what happens when the leader leaves? This is about sustainable leadership—leadership that is sustainable both to oneself personally and the organization that one leads.

The key to ensuring one's leadership lasts and leaves a legacy is to avoid becoming delusional. There are some leaders who genuinely believe that everything that is great has been achieved by them, and that every great idea is theirs. This happens when they become isolated and their feet are no longer on the ground. They create their own hubris.

The concept of sustainable leadership means staying relevant to the company and society. When leaders begin to think they are invincible and that without them, their companies are nowhere, that is the beginning of the leaders' downfall.

It happens quite often. Take Napoleon at Waterloo—he always believed that at every battle, his generals would be there for him. He was still waiting for someone to come to his side at Waterloo up to the end, and he did not understand why no one came.

Conclusion

Leaders are at the core of all organizational success. To be effective leaders, executives must strive for a positive attitude, humanistic approach, and a sense of humor. They must stay focused on their vision, communicate frequently with their staff, incorporate cultural differences into the organization, and place the needs of their employees above their own. They should surround themselves with the most intelligent, competent people they can find and avoid personal stagnation by reinventing themselves every five to 10 years.

Strong leaders must find an appropriate work-life balance. Finally, they must leave a legacy and prepare the organization for sustainable leadership. Following this strategy will allow leaders to always have someone at their side.

References

Home, Mike. 2008. Merger and acquisition aftermath: Seven lessons of successful integration executives. http://www.leadershipacts.com/article7.html.

Liu, Gretchen. 2005. *Raffles Hotel*. Singapore: Editions Didier Millet.

Schuler, A.J. 2008. You bought it, so don't break it: Five best practices in post acquisition integration. http://www.schulersolutions.com/post_acquisition_integration.html.

Schultz, Patricia. 2003. *1,000 Places to See Before You Die: A Traveler's Life*. New York: Workman Publishing Company.

11

DEVELOPING AND IMPLEMENTING BEST PRACTICES

By Judy Siguaw

Introduction

The Asian landscape has increasingly been the focal competitive arena of the hospitality industry over the past decade. Large international chains, regional groups, and independent properties have vied to stake their claim in this territory of burgeoning tourist interest. To survive and prosper, however, these hospitality organizations must develop novel approaches to their service products, processes, and procedures through knowledge development, deployment, and diffusion. Consequently, interest in the constant creation, execution, and dissemination of best practices remains high.

Across a broad range of industries, the implementation of best practices has been linked to decreased operating costs, improved revenues, increased customer satisfaction, superior perceptions of value and quality, and enhanced utilization of scarce resources (Lee and Liu 2008; Sullivan 1995). Furthermore, in accordance with the work of Bellin and Pham, the interweaving of best practices throughout an organization establishes a unifying bond that guides all functional areas and properties toward a common identity and mind-set when recognizing and solving problems. Consequently, a hospitality firm which has an anthology of institutionalized best practices, is better equipped to surmount the challenges of conducting business in distant lands and among disparate cultures (Bellin & Pham 2007).

Defining Best Practices

A multitude of definitions exist for best practices. In general, however, best practices are highly effective and efficient strategies, processes, or practices that allow an organization to outperform competitors. Best practices may be situation-specific, in that the context of events enables certain strategies, processes, or practices to generate outstanding results, but these same practices may not produce equivalent outcomes in different circumstances (O'Dell, Grayson, and Essaides 1998). Moreover, best practices are not everlasting. Successful companies willingly and incrementally evolve and adapt their best practices on a continuous basis. Moreover, they exhibit a willingness to completely discard a current best practice for a radically different means of achieving organizational goals.

Barriers to Best Practices

The development of best practices, however, is not a simple undertaking for hospitality businesses, resulting in a perpetuating industry-wide reputation for unoriginality (Chen 1998; Smith 2000; Berry et al. 2006). The unique characteristics of services industries include intangibility, heterogeneity, perishability, and inseparability (Shostack 1977). These characteristics plus the convoluted relationships within the hospitality industry among owners, brands, management companies, and other key partners, create barriers to the creation and adoption of best practices (Smith 2000; Dubé et al. 1999). Nonetheless, the broad incorporation of best practices into hospitality firms is vital if these organizations are to achieve their optimal potential.

Beyond the general characteristics of the industry, other barriers exist that deter the creation of best practices. Past research has found that highly successful practices are not generated equally across levels, segments, and functional areas of the hospitality industry. Instead, innovative strategies, processes, and activities are more likely to be developed at the corporate versus property level, in the luxury segment rather than other segments, and in human resource over all other functional areas (Dubé et al. 1999). These findings are not unexpected given a large percentage of hotel rooms worldwide are controlled by chain operators, which establish strategies, tactics, processes, and procedures at the corporate level. By job design, corporate executives should be focused on the development of best practices.

General managers, on the other hand, may lack the time to create and adopt best practices at the property level where just managing daily operations and unpredictable events already result in extremely long days. Indeed, the property level is the indisputable epicenter for the guest interface and the focal point is on managing the experience of an inexorable flow of guests. However, these factors may restrict communication and interactions between personnel in various functional areas, as they focus solely on guest relationships and service; hinder the availability of resources or tools for utilization in developing new processes and procedures; and limit job flexibility, span, mobility, and cross-training (Kanter 1983; Rabe 2006).

Finally, the dominance of best practices produced at the corporate level may indicate a "not made here" bias such that the innovations produced at the property level do not receive sufficient cultivation, validation, and support from corporate executives. These barriers to innovation at the property level are problematic because front-line employees are situated to better understand what changes and new practices would positively impact the guest experience, thus increasing loyalty and potentially, profitability.

As noted, more best practices are derived from the luxury segment than any other segment. The luxury segment provides a higher staff to guest ratio, which in turn may allow for more time to brainstorm and contemplate ideas on how to improve services, processes, and procedures. While the luxury segment is to be commended for its efforts, the failure of the far more populous mid-scale and economy hotels to yield a higher percentage of best practices is of concern.

The dominance of best practices focused on human resource is not surprising as the success of the industry rides on the back of its employees. However, this concentration on a single functional area, no matter how critical, signifies that many areas such as design and technology, which are valued by guests, may not be receiving the attention for innovation that is needed. The industry should seek to expand best practices across a broader spectrum of functions.

Lastly, a final barrier to utilization of best practices is the mobility of industry managers. This impermanence means that the best practices the managers develop are often dropped once these managers depart a property or the organization for another.

Generating Best Practices

The creation and adoption of a best practice can nearly always be traced back to the efforts of a single person, who conceived the idea and then championed its implementation, overcoming multiple obstacles and detractors along the way. Teams and committees charged with the development of best practices are rarely able to produce truly innovative ideas, as researchers in this stream have previously noted.

Indeed, groupthink is now viewed as a process that forces conformity and suppresses minority views (Rabe 2006). Instead, it is that *one* person who conceives the idea, passionately believes in it, relentlessly advocates for the practice, fights through the barriers, convincingly argues for approval, and then implements the practice that will truly make the difference for the organization. Given how challenging the process can be, it is not surprising that few practices bubble up from the property level despite the staff's baseline perspective and close proximity to guests.

To rectify this situation, top management at the property and corporate levels must be willing to encourage and support innovative concepts so that they move from idea stage to implementation. Hence, executives must be willing to listen to the communication coming from these advocates of the innovative practices. Top management must demonstrate interest, encouragement, and support to stimulate innovative ideas for others (Arleth 1993; Crespell and Hansen 2008; Freeman 1994; Galán, Monje, Zúñiga-Vicente 2009; Keily 1993; Thamhain and Kamm 1993). This step sounds easier than it may be. Heath and Heath (2007) found that the innovator often has difficulty conveying the idea to others because the innovator has so much knowledge about the practice being proposed that they fail to recognize that the others do not have the same knowledge. Thus, what they hear internally is not what they are explaining to others. As a result, a really good idea could not recognized as such because the champion of the idea fails to be able to communicate it well enough. Top management may have to make a special effort to draw out the information.

In addition, employee involvement in the innovation process is equally critical. Beyond the champion of the idea, other employees must subscribe to the idea or else the concept will fail because in the final analysis, they will be responsible for the success of the implementation. Consequently, some champions of an idea strive to involve and empower employees in the adoption process early on so as to create a contingent of believers over time (Dubé et al. 1999).

Pilot tests can also be used as a mechanism to demonstrate the viability of the idea to employees (Rogers 1995). Unfortunately, neither the involvement of employees or the employment of pilot tests can truly occur as needed without the approval of top management. Thus, top management is a driving force in ensuring that best practices are developed and implemented within their respective organizations. Senior executives must also be accountable for ensuring that a best practice developed and implemented within a functional unit or at a single property is disseminated across departments or other properties. Few systems are in place to facilitate this level of dissemination. Intercontinental Hotel Group and Starwood are notable exceptions, utilizing their intranets to encourage better communication and broader adoption of best practices.

Moreover, a best practice champion may intentionally avoid dissemination of the practice to other units if it helps the champion's own unit to hold a better competitive position within the organization. Again, it is then up to those senior executives who are knowledgeable of the practice, to create awareness and promote integration throughout the organization via the use of multiple means of communication including company newsletters, recognition ceremonies, intranet postings, and e-mails. Furthermore, these communication channels should incorporate a common language and motivational techniques that will steer employees toward desired behaviors and actions. Leadership is key to the development, adoption, and dissemination of best practices.

As previously noted, best practices typically begin with a single individual who establishes and promotes the practice. Unfortunately, these practices also end with the departure of the same individual. That is, when the champion of the practice leaves the property or the organization, the practice will be invariably dropped by new managers. This finding also indicates that the practices were never fully integrated into the overall organization and thus, a better process or procedure is simply lost when the original initiator of the practice moves to a new challenge. As a result, good ideas are not retained nor the effort to generate best practices likely to be modeled. Best practices are fragile and not sustainable if senior managers do not take appropriate actions to ensure broad adoption and dissemination.

In both the United States and in Asia, the bulk of best practices developed within the hospitality industry are first focused on human resource, especially training and development, followed closely by operations. These two functional areas are at the heart of every successful hospitality product and the best practices developed are generally designed to improve employee engagement and satisfaction, and increase guest satisfaction with the longer-term goal of enhancing revenues and profitability. Innovations in the areas of human resource and operations are ones that will have the greatest impact on the corporation's or property's long-term viability.

Nonetheless, while best practices in these two areas are certainly critical, other areas that contribute to customer value and guest satisfaction should not be ignored. Unfortunately though, the development of innovations in food and beverage, design and information technology is largely ignored. Yet, these areas are also instrumental in shaping the guest experience. Moreover, in Asia, in-house restaurants often account for half of revenues, so this is an area that should not be neglected. The few food and beverage practices that surfaced in an Asian study were generally focused on cost savings and food safety, while only one was developed to create a greater bond between the guest and the hotel restaurant (Siguaw and Wee 2008).

General managers and corporate managers should be examining every facet of the business and strongly encouraging the development of best practices within the lower ranks. Although rare, occasionally a best practice is created by a lower-level staff member at the property level. This finding does indicate that property-level staff, who have the greatest customer knowledge and contact, do have the ability to devise innovative processes and procedures. Senior management, however, must establish the supportive and accommodating environment necessary to cultivate these ideas.

The importance of a culture of shared values and norms that promotes innovative thinking and rapid execution of these ideas within the organization cannot be overestimated. Such a culture manifests itself in increased employee creativity (Jaskyte and Dressler 2005; Sethi and Nicholson 2001). This culture incorporates a nonthreatening, trusting climate that welcomes the proposal of new ideas; encourages constructive but disparate opinions across and within all functions and levels; facilitates information sharing and frequent contact across functional areas; and provides verbal and practical support for innovative concepts (Anderson, Hardy, and West 1990; Droge, Calantone, and Harmancioglu 2008). Within such an organizational culture, employees are more likely to propose and implement new ideas or solutions.

To further foster innovative behavior within an organization, management may also want to consider personality type in its hiring decisions. Individuals with proactive personalities have been found to more frequently display innovative behaviors (Siebert, Kraimer, and Crant 2001). According to Siebert, Kraimer, and Crant, a proactive personality is a "stable disposition to take personal initiative in a broad range of activities and situations." Thus, a proactive individual will intuitively seek to improve processes and procedures rather than just accept things as they are. While formalized scales exist to measure proactive personality, potential recruits could simply be asked during interviews to describe what they changed in their last job.

Better Metrics to Link Best Practices to Results

The outcomes of best practices must be empirically measured if the purpose of the practice is to improve the competitive advantage of the business. Thus, precise and objective metrics directly or indirectly connecting the best practice to increased profit should be identified. Often, there is little empirical validation for practices, which have been instituted, with intuition replacing metrics. That is, proponents of a particular practice sometimes believe that the practice has been effective but have no data to support that belief. Rigorous and objective measures of the outcomes yielded by innovations allow the organization to emphasize and disseminate only the most effective practices throughout all properties.

Empirically assessing outcomes, however, is difficult. Given the abundance of data collected at both the property and corporate level, the availability of data is not likely a problem. However, the required data are not always easily collated in a usable form or format, making the assembly of the information a time-consuming process. In addition, managers need time to ponder potential outcomes of the practice and the optimal method for measuring the effectiveness of the practice. Time, unfortunately, is a scarce commodity for most managers in the industry.

The potential outcomes of the innovative practice have to be carefully specified and measured in a multitude of ways, incorporating both direct (for example, guest satisfaction) and indirect (for example, profitability) assessments. Specifically, best-practice champions should ask:

- What needs to be measured?
- How will it be measured?
- Why does it need to be measured?
- What is the starting point for measurement?
- What will be the benchmark or point of comparison for success?
- What extraneous factors that may influence the selected outcome above and beyond that of the best practice must be controlled?

The objective of this process is not to make measurement an onerous burden but instead to ensure that the outcomes of the practices are empirically substantiated to heighten widespread acceptance and dissemination of the practice. While the Siguaw and Wee study in 2008 indicated that the large multinational chains generally have incorporated quantitative validation processes into their assessment of best practices, there is still much room for improvement among regional chains and independent properties. In addition, as Dubé et al. (1999) advocated over a decade ago, metrics must be developed that link the best practice to the subjective experience of the customer. For example, rarely are measures of customer satisfaction with the attributes of a particular practice measured but instead overall customer satisfaction is utilized. This global metric, however, can readily be influenced by a host of other elements and any change may not be a function of the implemented best practice. Guests can verbalize what specific attributes engendered particular subjective feelings regarding their visits. Consequently, hospitality organizations should link practices and their precise assessments to clearly defined guest values.

Previously, I have argued that the most effective practices are those that should be disseminated and integrated throughout the organization. However, determining which are truly the most effective practices can be difficult. In their book, Carlson and Wilmot (2006) describe how SRI International calculates a value factor, which is derived by dividing benefits of the practice by the costs, rather than using the more common method of subtracting costs from benefits. Using the SRI method generates an order of magnitude of the value, which helps differentiate a less impactful improvement of 10 percent for example, from a best practice that may yield a magnitude of 75 percent or more. Carlson and Wilmot also offer a practical method for quantifying benefits and costs. Each benefit of the practice is measured on five-point scales for both the importance of the attribute to the guest and the practice's ability to satisfy the customer's need for that attribute. These scores are multiplied together and then all benefit scores are summed. Nonfinancial costs can be calculated the same way. This allows the benefits:costs ratio to be calculated.

Best Practices and Environmental Turbulence

Superior performance in the hospitality industry continues to be a function of creating exceptional customer value in a manner that offers satisfying returns on the investment. Best practices are often developed as a means of increasing customer value and satisfaction, yet the creation, adoption, implementation, and institutionalization of such innovations are especially difficult during times of environmental turbulence and hyper-competition. When the business environment is in a state of flux, the constant adaptation to change can be so mentally exhausting that the managerial focus is often on simply maintaining the status quo or creating incremental advancement. As volatility is often commonplace in many global markets, managers must understand more effective approaches for developing practices in an unpredictable environment.

One such concept may be the effectual approach, as first advocated by Herbert Simon. Using this method, according to Read et. al. (2009), managers place little reliance on historical data as it is likely an inaccurate predictor for the future. Instead, managerial attention is focused on the cocreation of strategies with other managers, owners, shareholders, and guests through a shared understanding of the business's purpose and the pursuit of achieving excellence in that purpose, as a means of yielding a strong competitive advantage and increased profitability. New practices are determined by starting with current assets, contacts, and knowledge, and progressing from there. Opportunities are pursued based on how much the business can afford to lose if the potential of the opportunity is not realized. Innovations and opportunities are developed with external partners who can share the rewards rather than one organization maintaining its own secret store of processes and procedures. Finally, under the effectual approach, market turbulence is seen as a positive because the change may offer new or transformed opportunities. This method of decision-making may produce better, more innovative practices that offer inimitable competitive advantages. As Dubé et al. proposed, hospitality organizations must "move toward an integrated, action-oriented approach that captures the information of today while creating the knowledge of tomorrow."

Conclusion

The development of best practices continues to be of interest within the hospitality industry as each firm strives to leapfrog the competition and gain a sustainable competitive advantage. While there are many barriers to the creation, implementation, and organizational integration of these practices, a continuous effort to create new processes and procedures is critical for ensuring long-term success. Most importantly, it is the purview of senior management to establish and consistently monitor the organizational environment, so that innovative ideas from all levels of the organization are encouraged, heard, and acted upon in a timely fashion.

Moreover, senior management must accept responsibility for ensuring the most effective practices are disseminated and institutionalized throughout all properties, so that the practices do not disappear when the individual who initially championed the idea through the whole process, changes roles or companies. Senior managers must emphasize the contributions of best practices and ensure that the ideas of champions are sustained. In the long run, the reputation of the overall industry will be enhanced and perceived as more progressive and innovative, as even laggards will eventually adopt better practices.

References

Accenture's Policy and Corporate Affairs. 2006. The rise of the multipolar world. http://www.accenture.com/Global/Research_and_Insights/Policy_And_Corporate_Affairs/Multi-PolarWorld.htm.

Anderson, Neil., Gillian Hardy, and Michael West. 1990. Innovative teams at work. *Personnel Management* 22 (9):48–52.

Arleth, Jens H. 1993. New product development projects and the role of the innovation manager. In *Handbook of Innovation Management*, eds. Anton Cozijnsen and Willem Vrakking, 122–131. Oxford, UK: Blackwell Publishers.

Bellin, J.B., & Pham, C.T. 2007. Global expansion: Balancing a uniform performance culture with local conditions. *Strategy & Leadership* 35(6): 44–50.

Berry, L.L., V. Shankar, J.T. Parish, S. Cadwallader, and T. Dotzel. 2006. Creating new markets through service innovation. *MIT Sloan Management Review* 47 (2):56–63.

Carlson, Curtis R. and William W. Wilmot. 2006. *Innovation: The Five Disciplines for Creating What Customers Want*. New York: Crown Business.

Chen, W-H. 1998. Benchmarking quality goals in service systems. *The Journal of Services Marketing* 12 (2):113–28.

Crespell, Pablo. and Eric Hansen. 2008. Managing for innovation: Insights into a successful company. *Forest Products Journal* 58 (9):6–17.

Droge, Cornelia , Roger Calantone, and Nukhet Harmancioglu. 2008. New product success: Is it really controllable by managers in highly turbulent environments? *Journal of Product Innovation Management* 25 (3):272–286.

Dubé, Laurette, Cathy Enz, Leo M. Renaghan, and Judy A. Siguaw. 1999. *The Key to Best Practices in the U.S. Lodging Industry*. Washington, D.C.: American Hotel Foundation.

Freeman, Chris 1994. Innovation and growth. In the *Handbook of Industrial Innovation*, eds. Mark Dodgson and Roy Rothwell 78–93. Aldershot, England: Edward Elgar Publishing Limited.

Galán, Jose I., Juan Carlos Monje, and Jose Ángel Zúñiga-Vicente. 2009. Implementing change in smaller firms. *Research Technology Management* 52 (1):59–67.

Heath, Chip and Dan Heath. 2007. *Made to Stick: Why Some Ideas Survive and Others Die*. New York: Random House.

Jaskyte, Kristina and William W. Dressler. 2005. Organizational culture and innovation in nonprofit human service organizations. *Administration in Social Work* 29 (2):23–41.

Kanter, Rosabeth Moss 1983. *The Change Masters: Innovation & Entrepreneurship in the American Corporation.* New York: Simon & Schuster, Inc.

Keily, Thomas 1993. The idea makers. *Technology Review.* (January):33–40.

Lee, Yao-Kuei and Tsai-Lung Liu. 2008. The effects of innovation diffusion on customer loyalty. *The Business Review* 10 (1):254–262.

O'Dell, C. and Grayson, C. J. with Essaides, N. 1998. *If Only We Knew What We Know: The Transfer of Internal Knowledge and Best Practices.* New York: The Free Press.

Rabe, Cynthia Barton 2006. *The Innovation Killer: How What We Know Limits What We Can Imagine and What Smart Companies Are Doing about It.* New York: AMACOM.

Read, Stuart, Nicholas Dew, Saras D. Saravathy, Michael Song, and Robert Wiltbank. 2009. Marketing under uncertainty: The logic of an effectual approach. *Journal of Marketing* 73 (May):1–18.

Rogers, Everett M. 1995. *Diffusion of Innovations.* New York, NY: The Free Press. 355–356.

Rogers, P.B. 1997. Raising the bar. *Journal of Property Management.* 62 (November/December):48–51.

Sethi, Rajesh and Carolyn Y. Nicholson. 2001. Structural and contextual correlates of charged behavior in product development teams. *Journal of Product Innovation Management* 18 (3):154–168.

Shostack, G.L. 1977. Breaking free from product marketing. *Journal of Marketing* 41 (2):73–80.

Siebert, Scott E., Maria L. Kraimer, and J. Michael Crant. 2001. What do proactive people do? A longitudinal model linking proactive personality and career success. *Personnel Psychology* 54 (4):845–874.

Siguaw, Judy and Wee Beng Geok. 2008. *Exploring Best Practices in the Hospitality Industry in Asia.* Singapore: The Asian Business Case Centre.

Smith, A.M. 2000. Using consumer benchmarking criteria to improve service sector competitiveness. *Benchmarking* 7 (5):373–88.

Sullivan, D. 1995. Benchmarking: Case studies in success. *National Petroleum News* 87 (February):46–47.

Thamhain, Hans J. and Judith B. Kamm. 1993. Top-level managers and innovative R&D performance. In *Handbook of Innovation Management*, eds. Anton Cozijnsen and Willem Vrakking, 42–53. Oxford, UK: Blackwell Publishers.

12

LOOKING AHEAD AT HOSPITALITY TRENDS IN ASIA

By Russell Arthur Smith

Introduction

The future of the hospitality industry in Asia promises great opportunity for continued growth, and this potential is in line with the projected estimates of tourism arrivals to this region in the next few years. The changes in the Asian hospitality and tourism sector were accelerating before the global economic crisis began. With this region emerging first from the economic crisis, it is highly likely that growth will continue apace as before, although other regions may remain economically subdued. The Asian region will be significantly transformed within five to 10 years.

According to Michael Enright and James Newton (2005), the Asia Pacific will overtake the Americas to become the world's second largest tourism region, as measured by arrivals, after Europe. Among the major destinations in the region, China is the unrivalled market leader, followed by Hong Kong, Malaysia, Thailand, and Singapore. This forecast is supported by the United Nations World Tourism Organization (2009), which sees East Asia, and the Pacific and South Asia growing at annualized rates of 6.5 percent and 6.2 percent over the 25-year period up to 2020. These compare with the forecast rates of 3.8 percent and 3.1 percent for the Americas and Europe, respectively. This growth is despite the impact of the global economic crisis.

The global financial crisis of 2007 to early 2009 had slowed the expansion that the hospitality sector had experienced in preceding years in Asia. The economic downturn had indeed presented unique challenges, which resulted in the delayed launch of new initiatives, slowed implementation of ongoing projects, and, in some organizations, caused major restructuring.

However, despite the economic meltdown over those two and the half years, the tourism and the hospitality industry is expected to bounce back and enjoy continuous growth in the next few years. Economic indicators, such as the analyses by STR Global (2009), a leader for lodging-industry benchmarking and research, support the notion that while other regions continue to be mired with the aftermath of the global financial crisis, the Asian region has bottomed out and is set to expand. The reasons for the region's economic positive performance now are much the same as before the economic crisis. The governments of the Asian region had taken positive steps to encourage economic development, moved to build the necessary infrastructure, and encouraged local and foreign investment in the sector. These reasons still hold true and will continue to propel the region ahead of other regions.

Major Challenges Ahead

Emerging from the crisis in 2009, the tourism and hospitality sector faces major challenges in the next several years. These challenges are related to the quickening pace of change and expansion within the sector in Asia, the ongoing pipeline of projects across Asia, and environmental impacts.

Quickening Pace of Change and Expansion

With the transition of many countries such as China, India, and Vietnam to market economies, there has been significant rapid economic growth in these places. This growth has fueled higher demand and higher requirements for quality standards for travel services. This trend is for both domestic and international across all demand segments—business, leisure, education, and others.

The tourism scene in Asia Pacific is getting very competitive with different countries coming up with new attractions and offerings to attract tourism dollars. For example, a new Disneyland was announced in 2009 that will be located in Pudong in Shanghai, China. In Singapore, the two resorts, Marina Bay Sands and Resorts World Sentosa, opened in 2010 while Macau continues to improve its casinos and tourism-related attractions in order to keep ahead of the competition.

These large-scale projects are integrated projects as they include a range of integrated facilities, which complement one another. A central developmental theme is that each mega-project is a destination unto itself. They also have the capacity to meet the demand for the mass segment as well as the much smaller high-end segment.

Ongoing Pipeline of Hospitality Projects

A consequence of the expansion of the tourism sector is that many hotel chains plan to open new hotel operations in many countries across Asia over the next few years.

According to STR Global (2010), the Asia-Pacific hotel development scene will continue to grow, as the pipeline helps to gauge how much supply is coming onstream in the next few years. The Asia-Pacific pipeline by chain includes an existing supply of 2.15 million rooms, 171,457 rooms in-construction, and a total active pipeline of 976 hotels comprising 248,156 rooms. Among the key markets, Shanghai, China, reported the largest amount of rooms in the total active pipeline (14,378 rooms). Next is New Delhi, India, with 6,731 rooms in the total active pipeline. Third is Beijing, China, with 5,775 rooms in the total active pipeline. All this will contribute to a promising outlook for the hospitality industry in the Asia Pacific.

International hotel chains are making concrete plans for expansion. Marriott has 58 hotels now under development, and will add more than 16,000 rooms to its Asia-Pacific portfolio. Shangri-La will be opening 13 new hotel properties in Asia by 2013. For Accor, it is opening 97 new hotels in the near future, which will add around 20,000 rooms in total—a clear sign of its commitment to growing its business in the Asia-Pacific region.

The continuing expansion of hotel room supply in major tourism hubs, such as Singapore and Macau, continues to add hotels, entertainment, high-end food services, and attractions.

Environmental Impacts

Growth is racing ahead in Asia, but the outcome of this is not always positive, as there are often environmental impacts. The hospitality industry is enthusiastic about environmental sustainability as it feels that if it is responsible today, there will be a better environment tomorrow. However, there is a general public perception that hospitality, leisure, and travel are unnecessary as some people say that these activities are contributing to environmental pollution considerably.

The industry is very aware of this misconception and should be aware, especially in Asia, where environmental protection and regulation are not as strong in many countries as in the more developed economies. There will be considerable interest, not all welcome, on this issue in Asia. Savvy hospitality organizations in Asia will move the environment to the top of the list of actions under their corporate social responsibility charters (Smith 2008a).

Human Resource Challenges

The tourism and hospitality is a people-business, which demands a vast pool of people dedicated to catering to consumers' and customers' needs and wants. Thus, most governments and entrepreneurs will face significant human resource challenges. These key challenges include competing for advantages and human resource, finding managers to drive their businesses, and providing education and training

Competing for Advantages and Human Resource

The consequences of current and future hotel and tourism developments result in the frenetic competition for advantages and human resource. Many countries have revealed plans to stay ahead of the competition in terms of its product offerings and meeting the demands of human resource. According to Joachim Willms (2007), five of the top 10 countries which will have the most jobs in the travel and tourism industry in 2017 are from Asia: China (75.7 million), India (28.3 million), Japan (9.4 million), Indonesia (6.8 million), and Thailand (4.7 million). The consulting firm Accenture (Leung 2008) believes that China alone will need an additional 1.6 million employees in the travel and tourism sector in the 10 years up to 2017.

As part of the Singapore government's commitment to grow the tourism sector, the Singapore Tourism Board (2007) has unveiled plans to boost its tourism product and expand the tourism employment to 250,000 in 2015 from a base of 150,000 in 2004. It has projected bold targets to ensure that tourism remains a key economic pillar by tripling tourism receipts to S$30 billion, doubling visitor arrivals to 17 million, and creating an additional 100,000 jobs in the services sector by 2015. These targets will catapult growth in the tourism industry over the next 10 years, and are supported by the S$2 billion Tourism Development Fund.

The fund has been set up to support initiatives in these four areas: infrastructure development (developing critical infrastructure to support tourism growth); capability development (enhancing the capability of Singapore-based travel and tourism players and attracting world-class travel and tourism businesses and organizations to set up in Singapore); anchoring iconic and major events (attracting iconic or mega events that will highlight Singapore as a premier destination for leisure, business, and services customer segments); and product development (developing strategic tourism products) (Singapore Tourism Board 2007).

The Japan Tourism Agency has also relaunched its previously successful "Visit Japan Campaign" (Karantzavelou 2008) to boost inbound tourism to Japan, a country where outbound tourists have consistently outnumbered inbound.The recent economic crisis has hit many countries worldwide, and Japan's tourism was similarly affected badly too. JTB Sunrise Tours, which has offered tours to English-speaking travelers for 40 years, says for the industry to grow, tour operators would have to expand travel options to areas outside the "Golden Route," which is a five- or six-day tour of Japan. This has traditionally been the most popular inbound tour for first-time visitors arriving at Narita airport. Starting in Tokyo, tourists go to Hakone, Kyoto, and Nara, before departing the country from Osaka. This "Golden Route" reinforces the fact that Tokyo and Osaka have remained the leading destinations for visitors to Japan for a long time.

But as the volume of tourism into Japan has increased, styles of travel, as well as needs and desires of travelers, are diversifying more to include short stays and experience-based tours. Karantzavelou opined that Japan has a lot to improve to meet diversifying needs and highlighted that the Japanese government must improve the nation's infrastructure to make rural areas more accessible for inbound tourists.

Finding Managers to Drive their Businesses

Finding the people who will staff the expansion of the hospitality sector in Asia is proving difficult. Hospitality enterprises have and will generally be able to recruit and train the vast number of people necessary to staff the lower levels of operations. The tough challenge is to find enough mangers, especially senior mangers, to drive their businesses. Mangers require skill sets that typically require years of formal education to acquire. Generic management is of limited use for the hospitality sector with its intense focus on services, thus managerial education has to be hospitality-specific.

With the expansion of hospitality services to second- and third-tier cities across Asia as well as to resort areas, senior managers may not easily be recruited in these locations. Finding managers who can fill these posts and are willing to relocate to these places will be difficult. This problem is compounded by the desire of many Asian organizations to have nationals from their home country head their foreign operations.

According to Berry's (2008) master's dissertation at the University of Nottingham, United Kingdom, it appears that the human resource shortage in the Indian hospitality industry will remain a challenge over the coming years, despite the development of its training and HR programs. Staff turnover remains high and the sector is not the most preferred employer compared with other industries. These problems cannot be ignored.

Providing Education and Training

How is this need for human resource being managed in the hospitality sector by both global and local hotels? Are the increasing number of training courses and professional and degree programs in Asia helping in these areas?

Universities often focus on mid- to senior-level manager education with technical and vocational institutes providing training for sub-managerial positions. Supplementing this supply, hotel chains have established their own in-house training institutes in Asia Pacific. Shangri-La has an institute located in China, with satellite centers in other parts of the region to deliver training locally. Jin Jiang Hotels also has a training institute. Accor, with its training centralized in Evry, France, has a global network of hubs for regional training, including one in Bangkok. Training within these institutes tends to meet in-house demand, mainly for the nonmanagerial levels that constitute the bulk of staff in hotels. Managerial training is usually outsourced, or undertaken jointly with a specialized provider. Given that training for the junior posts entails less time and expense per capita, the industry is generally able to meet its needs.

The major challenge is the supply of senior managers, for whom training often requires years with high cost. Generally, there is a shortage of managers, so recruitment is increasingly from other, nonhospitality sectors. Those with the educational and career records suitable for senior managerial posts in the hospitality sector have been able to demand better positions with branded organizations in desirable locations. To meet demand, educational institutes are expanding their capacity to produce managers for the hospitality and tourism sector. To fast track this, many are entering into joint ventures with established non-Asian institutes so as to produce graduates quicker (Smith 2008b).

In contrast, independent hotel operators located in less desirable, secondary or tertiary cities, for example, have had difficulty in filling their senior posts. Aggravating the problem is the quality of graduates from some Asian hospitality degree programs, whose graduates often fail to obtain suitable employment. The key problem here is the lack of rigor and relevance of the training for the sector, thus employers are reluctant to engage these graduates. A parallel issue is the comparatively low starting salaries offered by some employers for graduates from hospitality-business programs. This, regrettably, encourages fresh graduates to seek jobs in other sectors.

According to Dwyer et al. (2009), there was substantial support by the hospitality sector for the view that education and training can foster a more innovative tourism workforce to achieve destination competitive advantage; but it must be recognized that perceptions of poor conditions, poor career paths, and low pay relative to other industries will not attract committed and productive labor. The authors emphasized that hospitality and tourism education must prepare students to play a leadership role in an industry that is undergoing rapid and continuous change. Managers need to know content and have adaptive capabilities to apply their knowledge in changing contexts.

To these views must be added the necessity for managerial expertise that can span Asia with its diversity of cultures and levels of economic development. In a global era of international hospitality operations, organizations must be able to develop and maintain corporate visions across the region. To do this effectively, their senior executives must be adept at cross-cultural management. They must also have a strong sense of business ethics and be able to deliver their organizations' services in different economic contexts.

Trends in the Hospitality Scene

The key trends in the hospitality sector can be identified as the internationalization of hotel operations, expansion of brands by international hotel organizations, broad-based growth of two- and three-star operations in Asia, and the development of low-cost hotels.

Internationalization of Hotel Operations

The internationalization of hotel operations will increasingly take a central role in all aspects of the hospitality sector. Asian hotel organizations, for example, will intensify their drive to become major global hotel operators. Taj Hotels, Resorts and Palaces of India seeks to take its long and successful domestic operational experience global. In North America, it manages several hotels including Taj Boston and The Pierre, New York. The challenge with this approach lies with the ability of the operator to export and adapt its model of hotel operation to very different cultural and business contexts.

Likewise, Jin Jiang Hotels, which is China's largest hotel operator, will leverage its domestic scale of operations to mount international operations. Rather than go immediately global, Jin Jiang Hotels, in contrast, has entered into arrangements for international operators to manage some of their properties such as the Fairmont Peace Hotel in Shanghai. The benefit is that the domestic operator may learn from the international operator before venturing abroad.

As some forays have demonstrated, domestic competence does not necessarily translate into international success, as operating in different countries with new markets requires reshaping of products and services. To help better understand the global challenges and to better prepare for expansion out of their home countries, large Asian hotel organizations are entering into joint-venture arrangements both domestically and in other countries.

Expansion of Brands by International Hotel Organizations

Long established international hotel organizations are also seeking greater depth to their operations in Asia. Large organizations such as Accor, Hilton, Intercontinental Hotel Group, and Starwood have for some decades operated flagship five- and four-star properties in the primary cities of Asia. Recently, these hotel operators have sought to expand their penetration by rolling out a full range of their brands, particularly at the lower star-rated level. Accor's rollout of its ibis brand is a case in point. In doing so, these operators are demonstrating that they have a good understanding of consumers' demand and operations in Asia.

Broad-based Growth of Two- and Three-star Operations in Asia

The expansion of two- and three-star operations in Asia is broad-based. Asian hotel operators are also expanding at this product level. Jinjiang Inn and Taj's Ginger are two brands in the economy sector. There is also considerable ongoing expansion of budget services in airline operations. Established legacy airlines such as Singapore Airlines and Qantas are aggressively expanding the networks of their respective subsidiaries, Tiger Airways and Jetstar. New startups, which include Air Asia, are proving to be successes too.

Development of Low-cost Hotels

The global financial crisis has proved to be a wonderful opportunity for budget hotel and air service operators as corporations and individuals downgrade their travel budgets. Having expanded their network of budget properties and services to take advantage of the crisis, it is likely that that these operators will have established a solid market share from which they can continue to rapidly expand over the next few years.

Part of the attraction for travelers with low-cost carriers and low-cost hotels is the lower cost, though it would be a mistake to believe that these guests all want to fly cheap and to stay cheap too. Some operators will bundle those services, but there will be others who will want to fly cheap but stay expensive. And then there are others who want to fly expensive because it is long haul, but when they arrive at their destination, they will be prepared to stay in budget accommodation. The prospect is a complex set of different combinations of demand. This will prove to be challenging for marketing and price setting.

The advent of economy products and services does not herald the decline of the luxury category. We have seen the retreat of demand for five-star lodgings, flights, and food services with the global financial crisis, but this is short term. The continued growth of the economic juggernauts, China and India, along with that of many other Asian countries, will ensure that there will be many more people willing to pay more.

The addition of economy services to their other services is expanding the suite of brands that some operators must now manage. Over the next few years, there will be a proliferation of brands. The challenge that operators will be avoiding is brand confusion for their customers and quite possibly, their own marketing and sales staff.

Key Players in the Hospitality Scene

The movers and shakers in the hospitality sector in Asia will continue to be the governments of major regional countries with the business sector playing an increasingly more prominent role. It will be exciting to see Asian operation organizations taking a more significant role not just in Asia, but also worldwide. As for the top Asian tourist destinations, many major countries will strive through various strategies and initiatives to attract the most number of tourists and their tourism dollar. However, it is widely acknowledged that China and India will be the leading players to benefit from the hospitality and tourism business in the foreseeable future.

Governments

The governments of major regional countries that see the hospitality and tourism industry as key to contributing to their economies will continue to be key drivers for the expansion of this sector and will, through regulatory measures, seek to direct that growth.

They are primarily responsible for the essential major infrastructure of airports and seaports, and the important land-transportation networks that link these ports to the tourism destinations, hotels, and attractions. Government policies can encourage private-sector investment through, for example, relaxation of developmental restrictions and outright grants.

Often, in Asia, government agencies, such as the Tourism Authority of Thailand, Korean Tourism Organization, Japan National Tourism Organization, and Singapore Tourism Board (the latter two organizations as mentioned above), have a major role in the promotion of inbound tourism and even in the guiding of development targets. It is fair to state that without the positive intervention of these agencies, their respective tourism sectors would not have developed as rapidly or as successfully in their respective countries.

Business Sector

There will also be a much more prominent role for Asia's business sector. Asian financiers, developers, and owners have been and will continue to have a major role and often decisive role in the sector. Operation of hotels, serviced apartments, theme parks, exhibition centers, and other facilities will continue to be undertaken by Asian and international organizations, though Asian operation organizations will become much more prominent not just in Asia, but globally.

Top Asian Tourist Destinations

The leaders in terms of absolute growth will continue to be China and India. Other strong performers will likely be Vietnam and, to a lesser extent, Indonesia. With the civil war concluded in 2009, Sri Lanka has considerable upside potential. Should Thailand be able to resolve its domestic politic problems, this country will likely perform very well.

Hospitality Trends (2009) reported that the American Express Business Travel's two surveys—Global Business Partnership (GBP) survey and its annual China Business Travel Survey of large China-based clients (The Barometer)—offered separate yet similar predictions on the health and future of business travel heading into 2010. The findings indicate that their clients expect China and India will lead business-travel recovery. The GBP survey, which polls American Express' largest business clients, reported that 89 percent of companies surveyed expect their companies to invest in China in 2010 and 79 percent in India.

Case Studies: China and India

China

According to The Barometer, respondents expect China to be the first country to emerge from the current economic cycle, with 72 percent of firms expecting to invest in China in 2010. Interestingly, 60 percent of Chinese organizations surveyed had already or intended to hire additional staff. Most global companies believe the worst of the economic crisis is over with 79 percent of executives predicting a modest economic expansion.

In an address to the World Travel & Tourism Council International Conference on Human Resources for China's Travel & Tourism Industry, (Shanghai, China, January 2008), Liu Yi, standing vice president of Beijing Tourism Group, said that in China, the tourism industry has become a new engine of economic growth. The gross revenue of the Chinese tourism industry was increasing rapidly by an average rate of more than 12 percent annually, higher than the average growth rate of the nation's gross domestic product (GDP) in the same period. In the past 10 years, the quick growth of the labor-intensive hospitality and tourism industry has directly or indirectly provided jobs to more than 35 million people in China.

According to Liu, China's tourism saw fast development in recent years, which in turn intensified competition among travel and lodging companies. In the future, people majoring in tourism and hotel management will have bright working prospects and opportunities in China; and driven by severe competition, travel and lodging companies will ask for more talent with a sound background in tourism and hotel management in the major tourism companies in China as well as the world.

Citi Investment Research (CIR), a division of Citigroup Global Markets Inc., says six key themes will affect China's travel sector in the near and mid-term (China Daily 2008). These include robust demand, competition, deregulation and consolidation in the sector, infrastructure and operations upgrades, expansion into second-tier cities, and the impact of a continued slowdown in the global economy.

CIR believes that the expected continued strong Chinese economic growth and rising consumer spending will drive rapid growth in a string of travel-related sectors, such as airlines, airports, hotels, travel consolidators, and intermediaries. In addition, China is hosting two world-class events in 2010. The Shanghai World Expo and the Asian Games in Guangzhou will increase travel, both international inbound and domestic. The expo in particular will have a major impact since it will run for six months, unlike the much shorter Beijing Olympics of 2008.

With its entry into the World Trade Organization in 2001, China undertook opening its travel industry to foreign participation. CRI believes that China remains protective of its travel sector. Despite the intended benefit of deregulation, China has to balance its national interest with allowing foreign entry. China is not alone in having to grapple with and strike a balance between these major and often conflicting interests.

Along with many other analysts, CIR forecasts continued expansion by the travel industry into China's second-tier cities. Going further, the large third-tier cities will also have considerable potential for the hospitality and tourism sector. To support this, the Chinese government is developing airports to service these destinations. While this enhanced infrastructure will undoubtedly provide for many business opportunities, the frontier nature of these new markets will heighten the brand, human resource, training, and environmental challenges noted above. Hospitality and tourism businesses may be attracted to these third-tier cities by the hoped-for first-mover advantage but the outcome may not translate into a positive bottom line. Clearly, optimism alone will not suffice. Considerable market analysis and detailed planning will be the key for success, where those organizations with, or working with those that have solid hospitality- or tourism-industry experience in China will command a strong competitive advantage.

India

A Tourism and Hospitality report by the India Brand Equity Foundation (2009) highlights that the tourism industry in India is being utilized as a powerful tool to facilitate international understanding and enable building of broader cultural horizons. The contribution of travel and tourism to GDP is estimated to be at 6 percent (US$ 67.3 billion) in 2009 rising to US$187.3 billion by 2019. The report also states that real GDP growth for the travel and tourism economy is estimated to be 0.2 percent in 2009 and expected to increase to an average 7.7 percent per annum over the 10-year period.

The Tourism Ministry of India is planning to develop three niche products—wellness tourism, caravan tourism, and helipad tourism. The hospitality sector is expected to rise to US$275 billion in the next 10 years with the domestic hospitality sector receiving investments of over US$11 billion in the next two years and 40 international hotel brands making their presence in the country. To strengthen the Indian tourism sector ahead of the Commonwealth Games in 2010 and to double foreign tourist arrivals from 5.37 million in 2008 to 10 million by 2010, the ministry is taking measures such as rationalizing taxes, increasing focus on infrastructure, and facilitating easy visas.

The India government is moving to upgrade and expand airports and major surface-transportation networks, such as highways and inner-city freeways. This key infrastructure is essential for India's tourism sector to develop. As noted in the case of China, its fast-paced infrastructure expansion has greatly facilitated the expansion of its tourism sector. India's tourism sector will also benefit from extensive infrastructure development, but the pace and extent should be increased to maximize the benefits.

According to Knight Frank Research's India Hotel Review (Express Hospitality 2007), there were close to 110,000 hotel rooms across all categories in India in 2007, but this number was abysmally low when compared with other countries of the world; for example, China had 10 times more rooms and the United States 40 times the number. According to Berry (2008), the Indian hospitality industry is maturing with the supply of hotel rooms increasing, but supply will soon match demand. The room rates will then be better aligned with the service provided, and this will remove many market distortions. Long-established Indian hoteliers such as Leela, Oberoi, and Taj have moved to apply their local knowledge in the expanding market while international hoteliers, such as Accor, Hilton, and Marriott are also expanding in the Indian market.

Berry is right to assert that all segments of the hospitality and tourism sector have the potential to flourish as they cater to diverse needs. For example, MICE (meetings, incentives, conventions, and exhibitions) will benefit from improved transportation services, thus enabling operators to convene larger-scale meetings in India. In addition, restaurants that now have traditional food preparation operations can be expected to adopt international practices that will help maximize profits by undertaking less basic activity in their individual kitchens. Increases in productivity will lower labor levels in the high-quality restaurants and hotels. Information technology will also drive innovations in marketing and operations management, thereby forcing changes in the sector. The outcome will be a better and stronger tourism industry. With these changes, the outlook for India looks very positive.

As the Indian economy expands and the government strengthens its transport and other infrastructure, the hospitality and tourism industry can be expected to invest aggressively in new projects. There have been considerable changes in both the public and private sectors, but for hospitality and tourism to continue to grow, more institutional changes will indeed be necessary.

Conclusion

Over the past decade, Asia has been the fastest-growing tourism region in the world. Despite the hiccups experienced with the 2007–early 2009 economic downturn, the outlook is bright for the hospitality and tourism sector. This is due to the fact that many governments in the Asian region have taken concrete and positive steps to stimulate economic development, build the necessary infrastructure, and encourage local and foreign investment in the sector.

Although there are numerous challenges facing the industry, these challenges are not insurmountable. Indeed, they provide an excellent opportunity for national tourism and hospitality organizations, private sector bodies, and entrepreneurs to restrategize and implement new initiatives and developments to gain their market share and economic pie. In the foreseeable future, the hospitality scene in Asia holds much promise for those who are enterprising, innovative, and bold to make and seize the many and vast opportunities available in the region.

References

Berry, Priyaanka. 2008. Trends in the Indian hospitality industry 2007–2008. Master of Science dissertation thesis. University of Nottingham, United Kingdom.

China Daily. 2008. Robust outlook for China's tourism sector. February 4. http://www.chinadaily.com.cn/bizchina/2008-02/04/content_6441031 .htm.

Dwyer, Larry, Deborah Edwards, Nina Mistilis, Carolina Roman, and Noel Scott. 2009. Destination and enterprise management for a tourism future. Tourism Management 30 (1):63–74.

Enright Michael J. and James Newton. 2005. Determinants of tourism destination competitiveness in Asia Pacific: Comprehensiveness and universality. Journal of Travel Research 43 (May): 339–350.

Express Hospitality. 2007. Indian hotel sector on high growth path: Knight Frank study. May. http://www.expresshospitality. com/20070515/market07.shtml.

Hospitality Trends. 2009. American Express clients expect China to lead business trend recovery. October 28. http://www.htrends.com/ trends-detail-sid-41921.html.

India Brand Equity Foundation. 2009. Tourism and hospitality. August. http://www.ibef.org/industry/tourismhospitality.aspx.

Karantzavelou, Vicky 2008. Japan looks beyond tourism's "Golden Route." Travel Daily News. http://www.traveldailynews.com/pages/ show_page/28122-Japan-looks-beyond-tourism's-'Golden-Route'. November 24.

Leung, Patrick. 2008. Economic Sector and Demographic Overview, Speech. At World Travel & Tourism Council International Conference, Human Resources for China's Travel & Tourism Industry, Shanghai, China, January 16.

Liu Yi. 2008. Human Resources for China's Travel & Tourism Industry. Speech. At World Travel & Tourism Council International Conference. Beijing Tourism Group. Shanghai, China. January 16.

Singapore Tourism Board. 2007. Tourism 2015. http://app.stb.gov .sg/asp/abo/abo08.asp.

Smith, Russell Arthur. 2008a. Environmental responsibility in the spa industry: A business perspective In eds. Marc Cohen and Gerard Bodeker *Understanding the Global Spa Indus-try*, 297–302. Oxford, UK: Butterworth-Heinemann.

Smith, Russell Arthur. 2008b. Joint international hospitality management programs: The Cornell-Nanyang Institute of Hospitality Management, Singapore. *Journal of Hospitality and Tourism Education* 20 (1): 38–44.

STR Global. 2010. STR Global reports Asia/Pacific pipeline for March 2010. http://www.hotelresource.com/article45165STR_Global_Reports_Asia_Pacific_Hotel_Pipeline_for_March_.html.

Willms, Joachim. 2007. The future trends in tourism—global perspectives—the future of tourism. Speech. At the Club of Amsterdam Conference. Amsterdam, The Netherlands. May 31.

World Tourism Organization. 2009. Tourism 2020 Vision. http://www.unwto.org/facts/eng/vision.htm.

Index